Storytelling in World Cinemas

Storytelling in World Cinemas

Volume One: Forms

Edited by Lina Khatib

WALLFLOWER PRESS
LONDON & NEW YORK

A Wallflower Book
Published by
Columbia University Press
Publishers Since 1893
New York • Chichester, West Sussex
cup.columbia.edu

A complete CIP record is available from the Library of Congress

ISBN 978-0-231-16204-3 (cloth : alk. paper)
ISBN 978-0-231-16205-0 (pbk. : alk. paper)

Design by Elsa Mathern

Columbia University Press books are printed on permanent
and durable acid-free paper.
This book is printed on paper with recycled content.
Printed in the United States of America

c 10 9 8 7 6 5 4 3 2 1
p 10 9 8 7 6 5 4 3 2 1

Contents

Rethinking Storytelling Forms in African Cinemas

Storytelling and Visual Forms

Refusing to Conform: Forms of Non-narration

Acknowledgements

The idea behind this book was inspired by an essay written by my former student Celia Sommerstein on the influence that traditional storytelling strategies in Korean theatre had on those in Korean cinema. This led to me to organise a symposium entitled 'The Form and Context of Storytelling in World Cinemas' in March 2006, supported by the University of London's Screen Studies Group. I would like to thank Mandy Merck and Laura Mulvey for their encouragement and help with making the symposium happen, and for paving the way for this book to be born. I would also like to thank Yoram Allon for being a wonderful editor and the contributors to the book for their hard work and patience.

I dedicate this book to H. E. Mr. Michel Eddé, for his continuous support, consistent en-couragement and strong belief in my work, and for his tireless dedication to the promotion of knowledge, education and the value of culture.

Notes on Contributors

Savaş Arslan is Associate Professor of Film and Television at Bahçeşehir University in Istanbul, Turkey. He is the author of *Melodrama* (in Turkish, 2005) and *Cinema in Turkey: A New Critical History* (2011) and co-editor of *Media, Culture and Identity in Europe* (2009), and has contributed various articles on cinema, arts and culture to different journals, magazines and edited volumes.

Matthias De Groof is a Fulbright visiting scholar at the Cinema Studies department of the Tisch School of the Arts at New York University and a PhD candidate in Cinema Studies at the University of Antwerp in Belgium. He has contributed to edited anthologies and published articles relating to African studies.

Lindiwe Dovey is Senior Lecturer in African Film and Performance Arts at the School of Oriental and African Studies, University of London. She is the author of *African Film and Literature: Adapting Violence to the Screen* (2009) which won a Choice Outstanding Academic Title award. She is Co-Director and Programming Director of Film Africa 2011, and Founding Director of the Cambridge African Film Festival.

Gesine Drews-Sylla is Assistant Professor of Slavic Literatures and Culture in the Slavic department of Eberhard Karls University, Tübingen. She is the author of *Moskauer Aktionismus. Provokation der Transformationsgesellschaft* (2011). Her research interests include comparative literature, transculturalism, postcolonial studies and gender studies. She is currently working on a project about the entanglements of Russian and African film and literature.

Matthew P. Ferrari is a PhD candidate in the Department of Communication at the University of Massachusetts, Amherst. His research focuses primarily on the social and ideological functions of representations of primitivism and wildness in cinema and television. Most recently he has published in *Flow*, an online journal of television and media studies.

Adam Ganz is Senior Lecturer in Media Arts at Royal Holloway, University of London, as well as a script consultant for a number of companies including the BBC, Complicité and Working Title. He has published widely on various aspects of screenwriting and has written on the screenplay as oral narrative in the *Journal of Screenwriting*. He is founder of the London Screenwriting Research Seminar and has written drama for film, television and radio and directed several short films.

Jennifer L. Gauthier is Associate Professor of Communication Studies at Randolph College in Virginia. Her research on film and cultural policy has been published in the *American Review of Canadian Studies*, the *International Journal of Cultural Studies*, the *Canadian Journal of Film Studies* and *CinéAction* and her chapter on Maori filmmaker Barry Barclay appeared in *Global Indigenous Media: Culture, Poetics, and Politics* (2008).

Lina Khatib heads the Program on Arab Reform and Democracy at Stanford University's Center on Democracy, Development, and the Rule of Law. She is the author of *Filming the Modern Middle East: Politics in the Cinemas of Hollywood and the Arab World* (2006), *Lebanese Cinema: Imagining the Civil War and Beyond* (2008) and *Image Politics in the Middle East: The Role of the Visual in Political Struggle* (2012). She is a founding co-editor of the *Middle East Journal of Culture and Communication*.

Anna Manchin is Aresty Visiting Scholar at Rutgers University. She has contributed to *Cinema, Audiences and Modernity: European Perspectives on Film Cultures and Cinema-going* (2011) and *Rural History* (2010) and is currently working on a book entitled *Jewish Identity, National Culture and Comedy Films in Interwar Hungary.*

Linda Mokdad is a PhD candidate in Film Studies in the Department of Cinema and Comparative Literature at the University of Iowa. She is the co-editor of *The International Film Musical* (with Corey Creekmur, 2012), and is currently teaching film studies and literature courses in the Department of Comparative Cultural Studies at the University of Iceland.

David Murphy is Professor of French and Postcolonial Studies at the University of Stirling, UK. He has published widely on African cinema, and is the author of *Sembene: Imagining Alternatives in Film and Fiction* (2000) and co-author of *Postcolonial African Cinema: Ten Directors* (with Patrick Williams, 2007). He is also co-editor of several collections of essays, including: *Francophone Postcolonial Studies* (2003) and *Postcolonial Thought in the French-speaking World* (2009).

Erik Tängerstad is Assistant Professor in History at Gotland University, Sweden. He has published very widely on various cultural studies subjects. His current research interests include the political and cultural history of the twentieth century, especially in the fields of film and historical represenation.

Claus Tieber is Research Assistant at the University of Salzburg. After years as a commissioning editor for the Austrian Broadcasting Corporation (ORF), he started an academic career in 2001, teaching film history and theory at the Universities of Vienna, Kiel and Salamanca. Recent publications include *Passages to Bollywood: Einführung in den Hindi-Film* (2007), *Schreiben für Hollywood: Das Drehbuch im Studiosystem* (2008), *Fokus Bollywood: Das indische Kino in wissenschaftlichen Diskursen* (2009) and *Stummfilmdramaturgie: Erzählweisen des amerikanischen Feature Films 1917–1927* (2011).

Stefanie Van de Peer is Research Fellow at the Five Colleges Women's Studies Research Center in Massachusetts. She is the co-editor of *Art and Trauma in Africa: Representations of Reconciliation* (with Lizelle Bisschoff, 2012), and has published widely on Tunisian, Egyptian, Moroccan, Syrian and Lebanese cinema. She was Africa in Motion Film Festival's director, and continues to work on women in cinema.

Chris Wood studied World Cinemas at the University of Leeds and has had research published in *The Journal of Chinese Cinemas* and *Post Script*. He is a practicing sound and media artist. Examples of recent work can be found at http://wordthecat.com.

Introduction to Volume One

Lina Khatib

In how many ways can cinema tell a story? Where does this storytelling come from? And what purpose does this storytelling serve? The aim of this two-part project is to locate cinema within a wider cultural and artistic framework: this volume focuses on the theme of storytelling form, on *how* different cinemas in the world tell stories; the second volume, forthcoming, focuses on *what* stories are told, and *why*.

'World cinemas' is used in this collection not to refer to a particular category of film, but to emphasise the global scope of the collection, beyond the classical Hollywood narrative. That is not to say that the classical Hollywood narrative, based on Aristotle's model, is completely unrelated to storytelling forms in other cinemas. On the contrary: as shown in the first three chapters of this volume that discuss 'national' cinematic forms in India, Turkey and Hungary, the classical Hollywood narrative as well as other Hollywood influences form a key component of the (nevertheless distinct) identity of those 'national' cinemas. This synergy destabilises the dichotomy of national versus Hollywood cinemas. It also shows that national cinematic storytelling is a hybrid form, attesting to the inherent global identity of film as a medium.

This idea is demonstrated in David Murphy's chapter on storytelling in West African cinema. Murphy challenges the notion that for films to be popular in West Africa, their storytelling form must emanate from a 'local' source. Instead, he shows that popular West African films have narrative structures that – in addition to sometimes utilising 'local' oral traditions – are influenced not only by Hollywood but also by Bollywood and Hong Kong cinematic storytelling forms. West African cinema sometimes also uses 'Western' forms of storytelling as a form of critique (as demonstrated in Matthias De Groof's chapter on Jean-Pierre Bekolo). Playing with form becomes a method of negotiating between African and Western storytelling techniques, calling for a rethinking of storytelling in African cinemas that frees African films from the clichéd binary of Africa versus the West. But this does not mean that the notion of a storytelling form rooted in local cultures should be completely abandoned. As Claus Tieber shows in his chapter on Indian cinema, and Lindiwe Dovey in her chapter on African cinemas, local influences do exist and create a link between different cinemas from the same locality or region.

The way cinemas use Western narrative forms can also have the aim of producing a distinct identity beyond the 'national'. The films of Aboriginal filmmaker Tracey Moffatt do exactly that, alluding to Hollywood conventions only to challenge them. Moffatt's films also reference (and again destabilise) artistic elements of national Australian cinema, such as featuring the expansive Australian landscape in long and wide shots that showcase the breathtaking nature of this land. Moffatt uses landscape and *mise-en-scène* to send the message that this is a confiscated land, reminding us of the traumatic history of Aboriginals in Australia. Thus, the stories that her films tell as well as the way they are told call for a rethinking of what a 'national' cinema in Australia is, or could be, about. This call for the inclusion of 'others' when considering 'national' cinema is also reflected in Anna Manchin's chapter on Hungarian cinema which focuses on the use of Jewish humour in Hungarian cinema in the 1930s to show that it is an integral part of this cinema, despite the characterisation of Jewish Hungarians at the time as outside the national imagination.

One of the classical ways of examining influences on cinematic storytelling form is to address the role of literary and oral traditions. This volume addresses this issue through three chapters that unearth the complexities of those influences. Often, thinking about cinematic adaptations of literary texts focuses on the canonical nature of texts or on the relationship between written and cinematic content. Chris Wood goes further in his chapter on the adaptation of Haruki Murakami's short story *Tony Takitani* to show that it is not just the text that is being adapted to the screen, it is also the style of the text that is being adapted. Stefanie Van de Peer also writes on the adaptation of style in her chapter on the way oral storytelling techniques and forms in the *1001 Nights* are found in the Tunisian film *Halfaouine*. Adam Ganz wraps up the discussion by taking it to a different level: through taking British ballads, an oral storytelling form, as a case study, he shows how ballads are in fact visual mediums of storytelling that mirror screenplays in their structure and storytelling techniques. This unearthing of the visual component of oral narration, which relies on the audience to fill in the gaps and construct the images for themselves, parallels Savaş Arslan's discussion of Turkish cinema's lack of reliance on 'realistic' sets as the audience is expected to approach the films from a similar perspective to that of watching theatre, and Jennifer L. Gauthier's discussion of the films of Tracey Moffatt that are composed of 'open' cinematic texts.

But film is a visual medium of course. Gesine Drews-Sylla and Erik Tängerstad pay attention in their chapters to storytelling reliant on visual forms. While Drews-Sylla's chapter examines the way paintings are used as metaphors in Georgian film in the Soviet era, Tängerstad's shows how visualisation in film can do the opposite, and how film can subvert visual narrative conventions to deceive the audience and force a rethinking of the way in which we approach images on the screen. This effort to engage the audience actively is shared by several filmmakers, and the final three chapters in this collection deal with the work of filmmakers whose work asks the audience to fill in the gaps, whether through inaction, as in the case of the storytelling forms of the films of Apichatpong Weerasethakul, presenting partial information, as in the case of those of Tracey Moffatt, or through directly challenging the audience's narrative expectations of a 'national' cinema language, as in the case of Elia Suleiman.

Part one of this book deals with the question of whether a 'national' form of storytelling exists. In chapter one, Claus Tieber poses two key questions: what are the frameworks influencing the way popular Indian films tell their stories? And can the specific narrative structure of these films be explained by Indian traditions and specifics? Tieber argues that the way film production is organised, the target audiences of the film industry and Western traditions such the melodrama are the most influential elements of storytelling in Hindi cinema. These factors are discussed in the context of the changes within the production process in India, which have been taking place since the late 1990s. Nevertheless, he argues that even in the 'Westernised' films that were produced during this period, some Indian peculiarities still remain, making Hindi storytelling a hybrid form.

Yeşilçam, the popular film industry of Turkey which persisted from the 1950s to the 1980s, is another hybrid form that presents a variety of visual and oral storytelling conventions. Enmeshed with a melodramatic narration that has a specific history in the West, Yeşilçam's melodramatic modality is inscribed not only with traditional forms of oral narration but also with a combination of a two-dimensional way of seeing with a perspectival one. While production quality was often low, Yeşilçam included many types of film, ranging from mainstream star productions to auteur films, as well as many genres, ranging from family melodrama and action to horror and sex comedies. Though many of these films rely upon the 'Turkification' (i.e. remakes or free adaptations) of Western films, they also present a melodramatic modality that enmeshes elements of a melodramatic narration with an authentic practice of realism. A poor *mise-en-scène* or poor quality shooting and editing did not present a direct problem because the traditional performing arts in Turkey, such as theatre-in-the-round, did not rely upon the sets but on the explanation of the situation and the start of the play through a series of descriptive instructions. Similarly, Yeşilçam's presentation of its stories was based on oral more than visual narration. Savaş Arslan's chapter on Turkish cinema in the 1960s and 1970s shows how such

a homegrown melodramatic narration and visual vocabulary is articulated in relation to and as different from Hollywood, which served as the prime and unreachable
example for Yeşilçam.

In Hungarian cinema of the 1930s, the classical Hollywood narrative style was
also referenced, but this time constantly challenged and undermined by another
style of storytelling: the urban central-European Jewish joke. The tradition of the
urban Jewish joke – self-deprecating, pessimistic, self-ironic – appears in comedies to
question and parody the main narrative, augmenting its message of optimistic wish-
fulfillment with self-reflexive commentary on the realities of everyday life. Jewish
minor characters representing the 'unheroic' in everyone question and mock the easy
happy ending and fate of the glamourous protagonist(s). Although this alternative
storytelling appears as a sideline, it is ultimately central to the message and worldview of the films, leading to a hybrid storytelling form. Anna Manchin argues here that
this is a result of the peculiar historical (cultural and political) context in which these
films were created. The films were made by and for a modern urban middle class and
mainly Jewish segment of the Hungarian public (and public culture) that was increasingly coming under attack from exclusionist, Christian-Hungarian nationalism in the
1930s. The films' narratives, punctured by a Jewish tradition of 'distrustful' humour,
represent the tension between the two coexisting cultural worlds – conservative
Christian nationalism and modern urban Jewish cosmopolitanism.

Part two of the book deals with the link between cinematic storytelling and literary and oral forms. One key element under this umbrella is adaptation, and Chris
Wood offers an examination of Haruki Murakami's short story *Tony Takitani* as
adapted for the screen by Jun Ichikawa. The process of adaptation is considered
to be mutually constructive, altering the means by which both the short story and
film of *Tony Takitani* are approached and understood. In film, the mode of telling is
key and pre-empts what is told. In this way a variety of apparatuses come into play
and can be deployed to create an impression which complements the literary original. Through a textual analysis of the film, the chapter argues that disruption of the
narrative voice in the film conveys a sense of unreality associated with Murakami's
writing style. Indeed it is argued that it is Murakami's style which is being adapted to
screen as much as it is a particular text.

The influence of oral storytelling traditions is explored in Stefanie Van de Peer's
study of the Tunisian film *Halfaouine*. Van de Peer offers a complex understanding
of the film that focuses on its structure and form while taking into consideration the
cultural context in which the film was produced. She shows how the film's storytelling devices such as fragmentation, narrative interruptions and embedded cycles,
assisted by visualisations, parallel those in the *1001 Nights*.

Adam Ganz takes a different angle when approaching the influence of oral storytelling traditions on film. His chapter on British preliterate ballads, particularly
Lamkin (Child 93), looks at how storytelling techniques in time-based oral narratives foreshadow techniques used in screenwriting, in particular the use of editing

techniques, crosscutting, contractions and extensions of time, multiple points of view and implicit camera positions. This leads to comparisons between oral and film storytelling, where in both mediums the story is retold in collaboration with the audience, and the aim of both storyteller and filmmaker is not to tell a story but to give the audience the tools to tell themselves a story.

Part three of the book calls for rethinking storytelling forms in African cinemas. The section begins with a chapter by Lindiwe Dovey that responds to the impasse in African film criticism over the imagined 'incommensurability' of celluloid film production (primarily in 'Francophone' West African contexts) and video/digital film production (in 'Anglophone' West African countries such as Nigeria and Ghana). Dovey argues that, on closer analysis, West African films and videos are not as conflicting in their forms and functions as it would initially appear. Indeed, Nollywood is an integral part of 'African Cinema' whose storytelling strategies are a hybrid of 'traditional' and Western forms.

Although it is a critical commonplace that African filmmaking is deeply influenced by the oral narrative tradition, there is no consensus on the precise nature of the (supposed) influence of the oral tradition, for example, whether it results in linear or non-linear storytelling structures. At the heart of these conflicting arguments about narrative structure lie (often unspoken) assumptions about the popularity of African cinema: the argument runs that, for an African film to reach, make sense to, and for some critics, 'teach', a wide African audience, it must utilise narrative structures with which its local audience is familiar. However, in this process, what significance, if any, should be accorded to African audiences' familiarity with the narrative codes of Bollywood musicals or Kung-Fu movies? For well over fifty years, there has existed a vibrant cinema-going culture in Africa, which has shaped popular African expectations and understanding of how film narratives operate. Consequently, David Murphy argues that a more productive critical approach to African cinematic narratives must attempt to explore the confluence between Western (modernist) artistic practices and 'popular', African oral narrative devices.

An example of this confluence is exemplified in the work of Cameroonian filmmaker Jean-Pierre Bekolo. Matthias De Groof takes Bekolo's film *Aristotle's Plot* as a case study to show how Bekolo fundamentally questions the classical (Aristotelian) scenario structure. This illustrates how he embraces, examines and explores Aristotle's ideal scenario formula to redefine what cinema is, and to create a subversive way of storytelling. Bekolo is shown to operate within a universal cinematic language while managing to show that cinematic codes are relative. As such, Bekolo emancipates himself from the African storytelling in cinema which expresses itself in particular languages, but at the same time he stands closer to African storytelling strategies to deal with the continent's history and contemporary reality. Bekolo, as a representative of the new African storytelling, positions his 'countercinema' *vis-à-vis* Western as well as African traditions of storytelling, creating a storytelling form that is based on negotiation of those two traditions.

Part four looks at the use of visuals as a storytelling form. Gesine Drews-Sylla examines the use of paintings in Georgian films about Niko Pirosmanashvili, a painter whose work is considered one of the primary national symbols in Georgia. Focusing on Giorgi Shengelaya's film *Pirosmani*, she shows how the film's language closely follows the visual elements of Pirosmanashvili's paintings which, form the main elements of a quasi-biography based on myths about the artist's fate. Drews-Sylla argues that Pirosmanashvili's life, his works and film narration in *Pirosmani* form an inseparable unit that must be contextualised within Soviet-Georgian (film) history. As the Soviet-Georgian cinema developed a unique narrative film language which was told in parables and myths – partially in order to avoid Soviet censorship when dealing with contemporary problems – *Pirosmani* is approached as part of this tradition. In the style of the so-called 'archaic' or 'poetic' school of Soviet cinema, the film uses the mythological layers of Pirosmanashvili's biography in order to rephrase it as an allegorical Christian passion. Using this allegory, at the threshold of the Soviet thaw and stagnation periods, the film deals with questions of Georgian nationalism, an artist's individual moral integrity and the legacy of the historic Russian avant-garde.

Erik Tängerstad's chapter that follows illustrates a radically different way of using visuals in filmic storytelling. It takes as a case study Milcho Manchevski's second feature film *Dust* and analyses its narrative principles as an example of what Manchevski calls 'Cubist storytelling'. Tängerstad argues that instead of being a film that tells a story conventionally, *Dust* sets out to provoke spectators to critically reflect on established film conventions. The narrative of *Dust* circles around a narrative told in the film. But instead of being a narrative within a narrative, Manchevski has placed the story told in the film on the same narrative level as the film's story, thereby short-circuiting established film conventions. Images, particularly photographs, form a key part in which the film challenges conventions. Instead of using images in a 'what you see is what you get' way, what we 'see' in the film is certainly not what we get, allowing the film to raise questions about how to narrate traumatic events (in this case, the atrocities that took place during the 1903 Ilinden Uprising in Macedonia) that never have been recorded in history, and of which no visual evidence exists.

The final part of this book deals with the works of filmmakers who refuse to conform to conventional narrative forms. One of the most renowned filmmakers in this context is Apichatpong Weerasethakul. Through examining his two films *Tropical Malady* and *Blissfully Yours*, Matthew P. Ferrari illustrates how the films' non-narration privileges characters and the symbolic environments they exist in over an unfolding story. In this sense, their storytelling creates a sensual cinema of inaction.

Jennifer L. Gauthier examines another example of refusal to conform through the work of Tracey Moffatt. She shows how non-conforming to film narrative conventions allows Moffatt to speak back to the dominant language of Australian national cinema, and in turn, the notion of national identity in Australia that has historically excluded Aboriginal people. At the same time, Moffatt appropriates dominant film discourses of otherness to subvert them. Her use of soundtracks, *mise-en-scène*, Aborginal cultural icons, mixed genres and avant-garde aesthetics make her films an exercise in audience participation, where the viewers have to work through the many layers of the films not just to find out what the story is, but also to engage in a dialogue about the cultural politics underlying the films' messages about Aboriginal people, historically and in the present. As such, storytelling form becomes a political statement speaking against colonial discourse.

A similar strategy is taken by Elia Suleiman in his two feature films *Chronicle of a Disappearance* and *Divine Intervention*. In those films, the director's work strategically moves away from the conventions and techniques of Palestinian film narrative. Suleiman's films, with their reliance on stasis, distantiation and ambiguity, dramatically depart from most contemporary Palestinian films which instead emphasise action, pathos and causality in constructing narratives of Palestinian dispossession and trauma. While Suleiman has most commonly been assessed in relation to the traditions and techniques of art cinema, Linda Mokdad recontextualises his films in order to highlight his citation of, and engagement with, the broader tendencies of Palestinian cinema. By addressing how both *Chronicle of a Disappearance* and *Divine Intervention* comment on other Palestinian films, she argues that Suleiman's work poses a critical challenge to the forms that narration and narrative take in Palestinian cinema at large. With the dominant discourse of Palestinian cinema being consumed with representing trauma, and with that of film audiences being consumed with the content of those films rather than their style, Mokdad powerfully illustrates how 'Suleiman's work asks us to consider how our own expectations and biases have confined Palestinian film narratives to a self-fulfilling melancholia'.

The aim of this collection is to approach storytelling from a cultural/historical multidisciplinary perspective, which goes beyond the scope of merely examining storytelling though theories of narratology. The contributions here illustrate the diversity of storytelling forms in world cinemas, but also bring to the surface the various synergies that exist between them. This volume will be followed by a second focusing on storytelling contexts, where questions of *what* stories are told and *why* will be addressed. Ultimately, the aim of the entire two-volume project is to arrive at a well-rounded examination of the cultural context in which storytelling in cinema exists and by which it is shaped.

'National' Forms of Storytelling

Aristotle Did Not Make It to India: Narrative Modes in Hindi Cinema

Claus Tieber

The way Bollywood 'tells its stories' is usually considered as being quite different from Western modes of narration. Storytelling in Hindi cinema (a more accurate term than the popular 'Bollywood') is often associated with three-hour films, many musical numbers only loosely connected to the rest of the film, conventional love stories and happy endings. This view is a common cliché of Bollywood, especially outside of India. This cliché also regards storytelling in Bollywood as a distinctively Indian peculiarity. The purpose of this chapter is not only to outline a view of storytelling in Hindi cinema, but also to answer the question of how much of this specific narrative mode can be seen as specifically Indian.

Mode of narration/ways of reception

In Indian fiction film two modes of narration can be found: one is commercial film-making, mostly in Hindi, Tamil, Telugu and other Indian languages; the other is called Middle or New Indian Cinema. These two modes differ significantly in the way film production is organised, stories are told and the way the audience is addressed. Both modes are characterised by a set of conventions and can be identified quite easily. Hindi cinema (and commercial cinema in other Indian languages) mostly targets a domestic and diasporian audience, whereas Middle cinema finds its audiences at international film festivals outside of India.

Those two modes of narration have their own history and are constantly shaped by economic, sociological and political developments in India. In the films of the so-called Golden Age from 1947 until the early 1960s, elements of both modes can be found. The only films that differ completely in style and narration are those made by Satyajit Ray, who directed his first film *Pather Panchali* in 1955. But the division into those two modes can be observed since 1969, when the first films financed by the official Film Finance Corporation (FFC) were released. *Buhuvan Shome* (Mirnal Sen) and *Uski Roti* (Mani Kaul) are regarded as the beginning of the Indian 'new wave', the 'New Indian Cinema' (see Prasad 1998: 122–3).

In the years since 1998, when the Indian government finally granted Bollywood cinema official industry status, a shift in the mode of production of Hindi films can be observed – often termed 'corporisation' – that is heavily influencing their way of storytelling (see Dudrah 2006: 148). But before examining this recent shift, I want to sketch out how 'classical Bollywood cinema' – as I would like to term Hindi cinema from 1947 to the mid-1990s – tells its stories.

Heterogeneous manufactory

In a nod to Karl Marx, M. Madhava Prasad calls the mode of production of Hindi cinema a 'heterogeneous manufactory' (as opposed to the serial manufactory of Hollywood). This mode is defined as follows:

> The whole is assembled from parts produced separately by specialists, rather than being centralized around the processing of a given material, as in serial or organic manufacture. This is of significance to the status of the 'story' in the Hindi film. (1998: 32)

The most significant trait of Hindi cinema is not the way it tells its stories, but the status of the story itself in the film. Whereas in classical Hollywood cinema everything is submitted to the narrative (at least in the account of its most prominent scholar, David Bordwell; see Bordwell 1985: 53), in Hindi cinema the story is only one of many elements of the film.

Prasad continues to define the status of the screenplay and therefore the story in Hindi cinema:

> The written script, which enabled 'disjunctive shooting schedules' and other measures aimed at economy and efficiency and necessitating the division of the task of writing into several stages is one factor of extreme importance to the Hollywood production process, whereas everyone who writes on Bombay cinema notes that this is conspicuous by its absence there. (1998: 44)

The elements of a Hindi film therefore are not integrated as tightly as in classical Hollywood cinema, because they are developed more or less separately and are not organised and coordinated by the screenplay.

How Indian are Hindi films?

Some of these elements therefore may be considered as isolated from or – with regard to the development of the plot – as 'interrupting' the flow of narrative information. Lalitha Gopalan calls Indian popular cinema a 'cinema of interruption' and she mostly refers to the musical numbers and the intermission in every Hindi film (2002: 16). The intermission is a significant dramaturgical device for almost every Hindi film and is one of the characteristics of Indian cinema culture. People are used to leaving the projection room to eat, drink and talk and then return to a more plot-driven second half. In classical Bollywood cinema the first half is lavishly used for exposition and music, and later in the second half the plot has to come to its closure. So as a rule there are more musical numbers in the first half than in the second (see Tieber 2007: 61).

But musical numbers do not necessarily stop or interrupt the plot the way the interval does; 'They provide commentary on the story, and regularly contribute plot developments', Gregory Booth writes (2000: 126). Even if musical numbers are considered an interruption of the plot, they cannot be regarded as an Indian particularity *per se*. In structural as well as in narratological terms, these musical numbers are equivalent to those in Hollywood film musicals and are therefore not necessarily indigenous.

Another approach to emphasise the specific 'Indianness' of these films comes from Vijay Mishra (1985) who argues that the narrative structure of the *Mahabharata* is the model for the narrative structure of Hindi films; the epic should therefore be further examined in these terms. The problem with this approach is that the *Mahabharata* consists of not one single story, but of a whole collection of stories, an epic told in episodes. I would suggest that the way these episodes tell their stories is not significantly different from Western narratives. The plotlines themselves do not differ very much from Western ones. The influence of Western melodramatic theatre and literature of the nineteenth century should be added to the counter arguments (see Vasudevan 1995); this influence can be considered as strong as that of the great epics, at least in narratological terms.

Unity of action versus 'convolutions of plot'

But Mishra's argument mostly hints at the specific way in which Hindi cinema combines plotlines. Hindi films are often seen as a chaos of multiple plots without any unity of action. One of Bollywood's most famous opponents, Satyajit Ray, once called it a 'penchant for convolutions of plot and counter-plot rather than simple unidirectional narrative' (1994: 23).

The three classical unities that Aristotle demanded from every tragedy are rarely found in films, wherever they are made. The unity of time and place is a demand which Bollywood often ignores; the unity of action is also challenged. Screenwriting manuals are full of advice to keep the plot simple, not to use too many plotlines and to end every one of them satisfactorily. But such manuals as well as screenwriting courses arrived in India only recently. In most Bollywood films a unity of action cannot be found. This can be partially explained by the above-mentioned dramaturgy of the interval. In this way of storytelling, a completely new plotline in the second half of the film is not unusual at all. The beginning of such a second plotline usually takes place at the end of the first half, to ensure that the audience will want to come back to the cinema after the interval. Whereas in Hollywood cinema plotlines are usually told in parallel and are interwoven in the end, in Bollywood it is a common practice to tell one story after the other and connect them only loosely. But to call the narrative form of Hindi films 'a convolution of plots' is massively exaggerating. The storytelling can be described far more accurately as a mode of Hindi films in terms of interruption and continuity, as Gopalan does. Even if the elements that Gopalan defines as interrupting can in fact be considered as contributing to the plot much more than is noticed in general, these elements are only 'attractions' or spectacular, highly emotional situations – be it a music number or a comic interlude. They cannot be regarded as plotlines in their own right. In fact there are seldom more than two plotlines in a Hindi film, so there is not much difference to a Hollywood film. The difference lies in the chronology of plotlines, not in their quantity.

My objective here is to take a closer look at some specifics of storytelling in Hindi cinema, to analyse these aspects of classical Bollywood cinema and finally to ask if, how and why they were changed by developments that have taken place in the last ten years. These aspects are:

- the relation of story and plot; the effectiveness of storytelling
- Indian heroes or the question of protagonists with or without a goal
- intertextuality as a storytelling device and the question of religion
- the influence of nineteenth-century Western melodrama

The effectiveness of storytelling

One of the main distinctions in narratology is the one between story and plot (or *syuzhet* and *fabula*, if one prefers the Russian formalist version, made popular by David Bordwell). Story is defined as 'the set of all the events in a narrative, both the ones explicitly presented and those the viewer infers' (Bordwell & Thompson 2003: 70). On the other hand plot 'is used to describe everything visibly and audibly present in the film before us' (2003: 71). That means that much of the story is not shown. The temporal gaps between two parts of the plot are usually called ellipses. Every relationship between story and plot is possible – at least in theory.

A narrative mode can also be regarded as a distinct relationship between story and plot. In classical Hollywood cinema this relationship is a very efficient one, where as little plot as possible is used to tell a big story. Screenwriting manuals constantly advise screenwriters to avoid scenes that are not essential for the development of the plot. This is just another way to describe the very economic ratio between story and plot.

In classical Bollywood cinema, less story information is left out. Much more plot is used to tell the story. This is not only a question of length: there is a tradition in Hindi cinema of telling the whole backstory of the protagonists, mostly their childhood and youth. This backstory is not necessarily told at the beginning of a film; it may be shown as a flashback somewhere in the middle of the film. In a Hollywood film this scene would last only a couple of minutes; in classical Bollywood cinema such backstories usually last for half an hour or even longer. These parts became such a convention that Sudhanva Deshpande noticed that the 'new hero' of Hindi cinema 'is someone without a past and consequently without memory' (2005: 187).

Classical Bollywood cinema tells a story from the very beginning until the very end. Not necessarily in that order, but almost nothing is left out. This is one of the reasons why sequels are very rare. Bollywood started to make economically successful sequels only in the last five to ten years. These films were made possible by a shift in the narrative mode of classical Bollywood cinema and therefore can be considered a defining element of post-classical Bollywood, as I would like to call it. Storytelling in classical Bollywood cinema can therefore be described as baroque (see Thomas 1985: 117) or endlessly meandering. Screenwriter and lyricist Javed Akthar addresses exactly that matter with the following definition: 'The difference between Bollywood and a Western film is that between a novel and a short story' (cited in Thomas 1985: 123).

Heroes, anti-heroes, goals and desires

According to David Bordwell and most screenwriting manuals, the goal-oriented hero is one of the trademarks of Hollywood cinema. A Hollywood plot is driven by the actions of a (usually male) hero to achieve his goal. The relation of this type of character to a genuine bourgeois and American ideology is obvious (see Bordwell, Staiger & Thompson 1997). Looking at classical Bollywood cinema, the issue of the goal-oriented protagonist raises a lot of questions. First of all: can such an active agent be found in most of the films?

One of the most popular characters in Hindi cinema is Devdas. Sarat Chandra Chatterjee's novel (1917) has been adapted many times; the film directed by Bimal Roy in 1955 is probably the best-known version. Devdas is in love with Paru, but he is not allowed to marry her because of caste differences. For most of the film Devdas is shown as an unhappy lover who tries to forget his sorrow with the help of alcohol. He is a rather passive agent of his fortune; the only thing he achieves in the end is his return to his home village, where he dies. The character was so popular that 'being a Devdas' became a popular phrase for being a passive alcoholic without much will to live. Of course there are a number of Hollywood films that deal with alcoholism

– from the 1950s on, when the power of the Production Code waned and the discussion of issues like that became possible without risking box office failure. But there is no similar passive character in Hollywood cinema with comparable popularity.

In classical Bollywood cinema, Devdas is not the exception, but the rule. Guru Dutt is passive and suffering in most of his films, Raj Kapoor is the object of a social experiment in *Awara* (Raj Kapoor, 1951), and a tramp who became the (more or less passive) victim of a gang of con artists in *Shree 420* (Kapoor, 1955). The case of *Mother India* (Mehboob Khan, 1957) is more complex because in its second half, Birju, in his raid for his mother's wedding ornaments, may be seen as a goal-oriented hero. Radha herself, the character that gives the film its title, has no goal whatsoever.

All these characters are mostly passive and do not have any recognisable goal, at least not one that would structure the plot. All occurrences just happen to them, they do not strive towards any defined goal. Even after this short overview of some of classical Bollywood's best known films, it can be stated that the goal-oriented hero we know from Hollywood was rather hard to find in Indian cinema until the early 1960s – at least not in most parts of a film. As Ravi Vasudevan writes 'the capable, goal-centred hero of American mainstream cinema ... is often stated in the Hindi film – with local inflections – but at a later point in the narrative' (1989: 31).

In terms of class, the goal-oriented hero in Hollywood cinema and in Western cinema in general is fuelled by the ideology of the bourgeois subject, who is master of their own fate. The character therefore is mostly embedded in a bourgeois environment. In classical Bollywood cinema, bourgeois characters are almost completely absent from the screen. The above-mentioned characters are either aristocrats like Devdas, or tramps, outcasts of society (but not 'untouchables', *dalits*, who are absent from popular Indian cinema) like the Raj Kapoor character, or peasants like the ones in *Mother India*. Mehboob Khan's *Andaz* (1949) is one of the few films from the Golden Age that deal with bourgeois characters – but in this film the characters stay passive as in an Anton Chekhov play.

The first characters in Hindi cinema that had a clearly defined goal to be achieved by any means were those played by Amitabh Bachchan in the 1970s. Bachchan's 'angry young man' persona successfully mixed elements of gangster film, social critique and personal charisma. Most of the characters Bachchan played were proletarians: coolies, mine workers and so on. Although public morals forbade that the Bachchan character wins at the end, he was the perfect active agent of the plot. His actions propelled the narration forward – he was the driving force. The action-packed type of film that Bachchan made famous in India went on until the 1980s, when it slowly lost its audience. The action genre, if one wants to call it that, petered out.

In the 1990s the Indian middle class became an internationally registered phenomenon. The middle class grew to a size that made it interesting for foreign economic investors as well as for the Indian film industry (see Dwyer 2000: 58–95). The initial films of the renaissance of the so-called 'feudal family romance' (Prasad 1998: 64) either presented protagonists who were completely passive, like the ones in *Hum*

Aapke Hain Koun (Sooraj R. Barjatya, 1994) or showed heroes that needed the whole first half of the film to find their goal, such as Raj in *Dilwale Dulhania Le Jayenge* (Aditya Chopra, 1995). But from this moment onward, the Indian middle class began to dominate Hindi cinema in every way. The characters on the screen were middle class, or more precisely, a fantasy of a middle class that was shared by most of its real members. The protagonists of these films as well as the films themselves were modelled more and more on Hollywood formulas and with an international audience in mind. This means that they reached their goal and achieved it with a happy ending. (Before the 1990s happy endings in Hindi films were not as endemic as in Hollywood.)

Before analysing this shift into a post-classical Bollywood, I want to reflect on the changing type of protagonist in Hindi cinema. As much as the goal-oriented protagonist of most classical Hollywood films represents the dominant ideology of the bourgeois subject who is the master of his own fate, the Indian equivalent can only represent an Indian ideology. In the decades after independence, individualism was not very popular in a state that was officially called secular, but where religion played an important part in many ways. Secularism means something different in the Indian context: it is not the absence of religion, but a proposed 'peace treaty' between religions.

So it will not come as a surprise that in this ideological environment there was no room and no need for a goal-oriented protagonist to propagate individual initiative and self-responsibility. This is made quite clear by scenes in which religion directly influences the plot. In Hindi cinema religion is not a special character trait as it is in Hollywood, but something that actually works, with little or great wonders, from making blind people see as in *Amar Akbhar Anthony* (Manmohan Desai, 1977) to bringing back the strength of the protagonist by simple religious signs as in *Mother India* (see Chatterjee 2002: 56). In a setting where turning points can be induced by religion (which would be regarded as mere coincidences in Western cinema and therefore as bad filmmaking) there just is not a need for an active agent.

It is interesting to observe that the arrival of the active agent in Hindi cinema happens in the shape of a proletarian hero, instead of a bourgeois protagonist. This can be explained by India's social development of the 1970s. The industrialisation plans of Jawaharlal Nehru produced a growing working class (see Guha 2007), whereas the Indian middle class achieved an economically relevant size only in the 1990s. Classical Hindi cinema always tried to find the biggest possible audience for its films. Therefore it had an integrating function in Indian society. The Bachchan films of the 1970s were clearly aimed at a male urban proletarian audience, but they also reached other classes. People who believed in Indian independence were frustrated when the government got itself involved in corruption scandals and their former hopes faded away. In this situation – especially during the Emergency of 1975–77, when political activities like strikes or rallies were forbidden – an active protagonist on the screen could fulfil at least a few hopes and dreams for this kind of audience.

The final shift of the hero in Hindi cinema came with the rise of the new middle class. The possibility to combine West and East, represented usually by the character of a Non-Resident Indian (NRI), is the dominant ideological subtext of the 'feudal family romance' films since the mid-1990s. In these films individualistic ideology and personal success are no longer regarded as contradicting traditional 'Indian' values, such as arranged marriage or Hindi rituals. In short, the sociological and political developments in India since independence have heavily influenced Hindi cinema, its characters and its ways of storytelling.

Intertextuality

One of the main characteristics of Hindi cinema is the heavy use of intertextuality in its storytelling. Intertextuality of course is a narrative device found in films around the world, but the specific way it is used, as well as the amount and visibility of this use, can be regarded as an Indian particularity.

Intertextuality in Indian cinema is mostly connected with the use of the two big epics for storytelling purposes. The *Mahabharata* and the *Ramayana*, with their legions of characters and stories, are used in different ways and for different purposes. Here I focus on the verbal references to the epics: the naming of characters, dialogue references and visual signs, both pictures and statues. I do not refer to undisguised representation of gods or other characters from the epics, or to adaptations of stories taken from one of the big epics (for this topic see Dwyer 2006).

The names of characters in Hindi cinema bear great significance; in most cases they directly refer to a character from the *Mahabharata* or the *Ramayana*. The name itself can inform the audience about the type of character they are confronted with for the next three hours. An Arjun will seldom be a villain; a Sita will always be a good loving wife, and so on. Hindi cinema is able to reveal a lot more about its characters with these mythological and religious names than Hollywood is.

Another way of addressing the epics is even more direct. Their characters and/ or scenes are explicitly referred to in dialogue. For example let's take *Deewaar* (Yash Chopra, 1975): when Ravi, the good brother who is now a police officer, is about to pursue his gangster brother, knowing that in the end he will have to kill him, his girlfriend reminds him of what God told Arjun. In the *Mahabharata* Arjun has doubts about going to war against a part of his own family, but God tells him to go and fight for justice and *dharma*. In the plot the short dialogue of this scene not only has the task of destroying Ravi's doubts and present him as a believing Hindu, while showing his brother as an unbeliever – it also tells the audience how to comprehend the whole situation and so bestows it with a greater significance. This direct commentary is a common device in Hindi cinema. The audience is told how to read a scene, how to interpret the situation with the help of the two big epics.

The connection to the epics can also be pointed out by pictures or statues. For instance in the famous scene from *Mother India*, where Radha walks to the house of the money-lender, the statue of Lakhsmi, the Hindu goddess of wealth, is treated in the scene as if she were a real person. Parts of the scene are edited in classic shot/reverse-shot tradition, as if Lakshmi is indeed talking to Radha.

Targeting a Western audience, as Hindi films of the early twenty-first century aim to do, renders this specific type of intertextuality useless. Most people of the Western hemisphere cannot be expected to be familiar with the Indian epics. Nevertheless the use of intertextuality as a narrative device can also be found in a 'secularised' way. This starts with the above-mentioned *Deewaar*, where pictures of Ghandi and Nehru comment on the events that are happening in front of them. 'Secular' intertextuality in Hindi films can also be found in other ways. In *Life in a Metro* (Anurag Basu, 2007), a character makes his first appearance in front of a poster of *Brokeback Mountain* (Ang Lee, 2005) and later on has homosexual intercourse (again with the poster in the background). In this case the intertextual reference to a popular Hollywood film is used to foreshadow the character's real self.

But in the Indian context, intertextuality is not a tricky sophisticated game, just a way to tell a story, to comment on the characters and events, and most of all an attempt to provide the whole film with a deeper meaning. Gregory Booth sums up the intertextual functions of the epics in Hindi cinema, stating that the epic content 'usually forms a secondary or allusory subtext rather than primary text' (1995: 173). In another essay Booth writes that the connection to the epics is not necessarily understood in religious terms: 'such reference does not automatically consign ... to a category that most Indians would identify as religious' (2000: 129). Reference to the epics therefore can be regarded as a storytelling device.

Melodrama

It is a commonplace that Hindi cinema tells its stories in a very melodramatic way, that is, heavily influenced by Western melodrama from the nineteenth century. The criteria of this melodramatic mode of storytelling can be summed up as follows: 'The system of dramaturgy is a melodramatic one, displaying the characteristic ensemble of manichaeism, bipolarity, the privileging of the moral over the psychological, and the deployment of coincidence' (Vasudevan 1995: 307). That way Hindi cinema could also be described as the last remaining outpost of Western melodramatic narration, which is hard to find anywhere else (except in 'dead' art forms like the opera).

The melodramatic side of Hindi cinema was always under critical attack by advocates of a more realistic and socially conscious cinema. In India this discussion commenced most prominently between Nargis, the star of *Mother India* and Satyajit Ray, India's best-known film director. As Rosie Thomas (1985) demonstrates, the arguments in this debate were created in India and then transported to Europe and the USA, where they still constitute the core of anti-Bollywood clichés.

As much as Hindi cinema is loved specifically for its melodramatic aspects, films that want to reach a Western audience and middle to higher class audiences in

India turn towards a more realistic way of filmmaking – a development that can be observed since the late 1990s. But before we have a look at these shifts, I want to sum up the characteristics of classical Bollywood cinema.

According to Rosie Thomas, Hindi cinema is a genre 'in which narrative is comparably loose and fragmented, realism irrelevant, psychological characterization disregarded, elaborate dialogue prized, music essential, and both the emotional involvement of the audience and the pleasure of sheer spectacle privileged throughout the three-hour duration of the entertainment' (1995: 162). Most scholars agree on these specifics that distinguish classical Bollywood from its American counterpart. Their discussions focus on the reasons for these differences and on the assessment of them as either being escapist, shallow fare or an alternative form of commercial cinema that should be taken seriously.

Before presenting economic and organisational issues as the main reason for these differences, I have to state that the view of classical Hollywood cinema that Bollywood is constantly compared to can verge on superficial. In this comparison, an idealised vision of Hollywood filmmaking is often implied that never really existed. One of the 'collateral' results of research in the field of Indian cinema is the possibility of looking at Hollywood cinema in a new de-familiarised way. With a Bollywood-trained view you can detect many elements of classical Hollywood cinema that were missed for quite a while, for example, overstating the tight structures and norms and conventions that classical Hollywood cinema is supposed to adhere to.

I have already argued that the political and ideological circumstances in India made it difficult and rather useless for a goal-driven protagonist to become an essential factor in Hindi cinema. This also has formative consequences for the narrative structure of Hindi cinema. The most important reasons for the specific form of narration in Hindi films are the position of narration itself in the production process and the expectations of the audience.

Filmmaking, especially commercial filmmaking, is always a collaborative process. In Hollywood this process is controlled and organised by the screenplay. It does not matter if the screenplay is written by just one or by many screenwriters. Filmmakers discuss a screenplay before the shooting of a film begins. They not only argue about certain plot twists or lines of dialogue; they also discuss the whole film, and they want their version to be written down in the screenplay in order to ensure that the film is made the way they want it. The screenplay is more or less the blueprint of the film.

In classical Bollywood cinema the production process differs significantly from the practice in Hollywood. In most cases a written screenplay does not even exist. The story of the film is told in many so-called 'narrations' (see Tieber 2007: 45) to the director, composer and the stars. The composer does not necessarily know the accurate plot when he writes the music scenes. The lyricist may not know the exact situation in which his song is heard. A music number may be inserted into the film after general shooting just to have enough songs for the CD, the music rights having been sold in advance to finance the film. The integration of the different elements during the production process of a film is clearly visible in the finished product. This is not necessarily an indication of bad filmmaking: in Indian film culture the narrative is just another part of the film. Its less important status – as compared to Hollywood films – is one of the preconditions for multiple viewings of a film, which is a common habit in India.

The influence of this specific organisation of production on the narrative structure of films becomes even more visible when this mode changes. After the 1998 government recognition of the film business as an 'official industry', production firms could become corporations allowed to borrow money from banks. This decision signified a shift of official politics towards the film industry. This development occurred due to the economic success and international recognition of popular Indian films. The government also wanted to eliminate the influence of black market money on the Indian film industry. One result of this 'corporisation' of the Indian film industry, as it soon would be called (see Tieber 2009: 7–11), is the greater importance of the written script. Banks do expect detailed information about projects that they are asked to finance; the whole process of financing a film has become less dependent on oral communication and more and more on written details.

Screenwriting was never a big issue in the Indian film industry, although it has produced popular screenwriters such as K. A. Abbas or Javed Akthar. This is about to change: screenwriting schools and contests are popping up like mushrooms from Indian soil. Screenwriting 'gurus' such as Syd Field are being hired by production companies like UTV to transform Indian screenplays to Hollywood standards (see Sen 2007). In addition to this change in the mode of production, Hindi films have begun to target new audiences: the New Middle Class, NRIs and Western audiences in general. The results of this shift in production and the change of target audiences can be noticed in the content of recent Hindi films, where representatives of anything but middle class members are vanishing, as well as in their narrative form.

Post-classical Bollywood

The three most obvious changes from classical to post-classical Bollywood can be described as follows:

- the films get shorter: ninety-minute films are no longer an exception
- there are more and more films without musical numbers
- the use of the English language is increasing; more and more films are being produced completely in English

A good example which combines all three aspects is *Being Cyrus* (Homi Adajania, 2005, 90 minutes). Examples of shorter films are *Kabul Express* (Kabir Khan, 2006, 104 minutes), *Eklavya* (Vidhu Vinod Chopra, 2007, 105 minutes) and *Life in a Metro*

(132 minutes) – to mention just a few. There are no musical numbers in *Kabul Express*, *Black* (Sanjay Leela Bhansali, 2005), *Sarkar* (Ram Gopal Varma, 2005), *Khosla Ka Ghosla* (Dibakar Banerjee, 2006), *Bheja Fry* (Sagar Ballary, 2007) and *Sarkar Raj* (Ram Gopal Varma, 2008). The increase of English dialogue can be noticed in most Hindi films; there also are more films that have got an English title. Classical Bollywood films of course are still being produced, but the above-mentioned changes start to build a series of films that may be called post-classical.

The main differences between classical and post-classical Bollywood have their origin in the shifting of the mode of production and the accompanying change of the target audience. Whereas classical Bollywood cinema integrated cinematic and narrative means and forms from early Hindi cinema, from classical Hollywood as well as from Indian traditions in order to integrate their audience (see Vasudevan 1995), post-classical Bollywood is heavily influenced by contemporary Hollywood films and targets almost exclusively a middle class and/or Western audience. Indian film producers expect this audience to relate better to a more realistic way of storytelling. So the first result of this shift is a more integrated way of filmmaking, where most of the content considered indigenous to Hindi cinema is almost erased now. Musical numbers are more tightly integrated in the films, they no longer must be sung by the characters (as for example in *Rang de Basanti* [Rakesh Omprakash Mehra, 2006], a film with an abridged version especially produced for a Western audience). The songs mostly illustrate montage sequences; there is no longer any difference between comparable sequences in Hollywood films. Another important factor influencing the development of Indian cinema is the financial investment of American film studios in the Indian film industry. They do not produce Hollywood films there, but Hindi films with a Western approach. The screenplay becomes more important, and the integration of cinematic elements is almost complete.

But is there anything specifically Indian left in post-classical Bollywood films? Yes indeed, there is: even in films quite obviously made in this new context, like *Life in a Metro*, attributes of classical Bollywood cinema can hardly be ignored. *Life in a Metro* is what David Bordwell calls a 'network narrative' (see 2008: 189–252), a form of narration used in Hollywood since the days of *Grand Hotel* (Edmund Goulding, 1932), but which has really become popular since the 1990s, especially after Robert Altman's *Short Cuts* (1993). A network narrative consists of many different plotlines; the characters and their stories are loosely connected by time and/or space or through more or less coincidental circumstances. *Life in a Metro* is structured by the songs of a pop band, pictured in the rainy streets of Mumbai. These musical numbers can be called meta-diegetic, because the musicians can be seen performing, but the characters in the film are not able to see the musicians. Their songs comment on the narrative. This way the musical numbers structure the narrative rather than interrupt it. The musical commentary by a band that is visible to the audience has a long tradition in Hindi cinema. Mostly *qawwali* parties, as these specific musical ensembles are called, take this part. The best-known example is *Awaara*, where a *qawwali* party is seen in rainy streets commenting on the abandoning of Leela, a Sita-like character, and therefore explicitly connecting the narrative to the *Ramayana*. Another characteristic of classical Bollywood cinema is intervals, even in short films. This tradition has its origins in the habits of the audience and the economic needs of the cinema owners, but not in dramaturgical conventions. It is rather interesting to notice that even when these conventions are being changed, the interval still resists any 'Westernisation'.

The narrative form of Hindi cinema is heavily influenced by the way film production is organised in India. Recent shifts in this organisation have led to changes in the narrative structure of the films. But even films made for a Western audience do not completely abandon narrative devices that are considered specifically Indian. Hindi cinema always was and still remains a hybrid form of cinema and storytelling; this is its main characteristic.

Bibliography

Aristotle (1968) *Poetics*. Trans. L. Goldon; Comm. O. B. Hardison. New Jersey: Prentice-Hall.

Booth, G. (1995) 'Traditional Content and Narrative Structure in the Hindi Commercial Cinema', *Asian Folklore Studies*, 54, 169–90.

_____ (2000) 'Religion, Gossip, Narrative Conventions and the Construction of Meaning in Hindi Film Songs', *Popular Music*, 19, 2, 125–45.

Bordwell, D. (1985) *Narration in the Fiction Film*. Madison: University of Wisconsin Press.

_____ (2008) *Poetics of Cinema*. London: Routledge.

Bordwell, D. and K. Thompson (2003) *Film Art: An Introduction*. Boston: McGraw Hill.

Bordwell, D., J. Staiger and K. Thompson (1997) *The Classical Hollywood Cinema: Film Style and Mode of Production to 1960*. London: Routledge.

Chatterjee, G. (2002) *Mother India*. London: British Film Institute.

Deshpande, S. (2005) 'The Consumable Hero of Globalised India', in R. Kaur and A. J. Sinha (ed.) *Bollywood: Popular Indian Cinema Through a Transnational Lens*. New Dehli: Sage, 186–203.

Dudrah, R. K. (2006) *Bollywood: Sociology Goes to the Movies*. New Dehli: Sage.

Dwyer, R. (2000) *All You Want Is Money, All you Need Is Love: Sex And Romance in Modern India*. London: Cassell.

_____ (2006) *Filming the Gods: Religion and Indian Cinema*. London: Routledge.

Gopalan, L. (2002) *Cinema of Interruptions: Action Genres in Contemporary Indian Cinema*. London: British Film Institute.

Guha, R. (2007) *India After Gandhi: The History of the World's Greatest Democracy*. London: Pan Macmillan.

Mishra, V. (1985) 'Towards a Theoretical Critique of Bombay Cinema', *Screen*, 26, 3/4, 133–46.

Prasad, M. M. (1998) *Ideology of the Hindi Film: A Historical Construction*. New Delhi: Oxford University Press.

Ray, S. (1994) *Our Films Their Films*. New York: Hyperion Books.

Sen, R. (2007) *When the Field Played Bollywood*. On-line. Available: http://specials.rediff.com/movies/2007/jan/08slide1.htm (accessed on 23 July 2009).

Thomas, R. (1985) 'Indian Cinema: Pleasures and Popularity', *Screen*, 26, 3/4, 116–31.

_____ (1995) 'Melodrama and the Negotiation of Morality in Mainstream Hindi Film', in C. Breckenridge (ed.) *Consuming Modernity: Public Culture in a South Asian World*. Minneapolis: University of Minnesota Press, 157–82.

Tieber, C. (2007) *Passages to Bollywood: Einführung in den Hindi-Film*. Münster: Lit Verlag.

_____ (ed.) (2009) *Fokus Bollywood: Das indische Kino in wissenschaftlichen Diskursen*. Münster: Lit Verlag.

Vasudevan, R. (1989) 'The Melodramatic Mode and the Commercial Hindi Cinema: Notes on Film History, Narrative and Performance in the 1950s', *Screen*, 30, 3, 29–50.

_____ (1995) 'Addressing the Spectator of a "Third World" National Cinema: The Bombay "Social" Film of the 1940s and 1950s', *Screen* 36(4): 305-324.

Tootsie Meets Yeşilçam: Narration in Popular Turkish Cinema

Savaş Arslan

A three-scene sequence in *Şabaniye* (Kartal Tibet, 1984) begins with a beach scene in which the main character of the film, Şabaniye (Kemal Sunal) is seen at a film shoot after having become a famous cross-dressing singer. *Şabaniye*'s director, Kartal Tibet, has a cameo as the lead actor of the film within a film, which stars Şabaniye as the lead actress. When Şabaniye sees him sitting in a monogrammed chair, s/he says 'Ah, I remember this guy … Kartal Tibet,' recognising the popular actor who starred in over a hundred films between 1965 and 1973, before he started direct-ing films in 1976. Then, the director of the film within a film, Orhan Aksoy, who is a famous director of many melodramas in the Turkish film industry, asks Kartal Tibet 'Are you ready?' (*Hazır mısınız?*). Tibet answers, 'I am heady' (*Nazırım*). Then Şabaniye says, 'I am also heady' (*Ben de nazırım*). Aksoy calls out 'Action' (*Motör*), and Tibet and Şabaniye, lovers in the film within a film, run across the beach and embrace each other. Then Bayram (Kemal Sunal) appears as himself (rather than as a cross-dresser) with Nazlı (Çiğdem Tunç) in various locations as we hear the clas-sical Turkish music song *Bir Sevgi İstiyorum* ('I Want a Love'), sung by Zeki Müren, who starred in several movies as the lead singer-actor and whose sexual preferences are still unclear in the minds of many Turks. A sequence follows in which Bayram and Nazlı are seen in a café at the 'lovers' hill' of Turkish films, fishing together on the Bosporus, playing with the kids at a park, swinging each other on a boat-shaped swing, ice skating with friends and running hand-in-hand through a forest. Nazlı tells Bayram that he taught her how to smile because she had been blinded by the desire for revenge against Şaban (Kemal Sunal) and his family for killing Nazlı's father. As the song comes to an end, there is a transition to a music hall where Şabaniye performs the last line of the same song to an applauding audience.

This long preamble can be understood as a précis for Yeşilçam, the popular film industry of Turkey, characterised by a variety of visual and oral storytelling conventions.[1] Though films from this era rely upon the 'Turkification' (i.e. remakes or free adaptations) of Western films, they also present a melodramatic modality that enmeshes elements of a melodramatic narration with an authentic practice of realism. This chapter will use the example of *Şabaniye* to examine how poor *mise-en-scène*, shooting, editing and post-production which highlighted plot over visual, situational and aural realism borrowed tropes of the Turkish narrative tradition to produce a home-grown mode of melodramatic narration and visual vocabulary that was articulated in response to the example set by Hollywood.

The plot of *Şabaniye*

A late Yeşilçam film, *Şabaniye* is a loose remake of the comedy *Tootsie* (Sydney Pollack, 1982) featuring Şaban (Kemal Sunal). Şaban is a recurring character in Turkish cinema who initially appeared in a comedy film, *Hababam Sınıfı* (Ertem Eğilmez, 1975), and its three sequels made between 1975 and 1977. After Kemal Sunal's character, İnek Şaban (Cow Şaban) became successful as a dim-witted character lovingly and ironically nicknamed Nerdy Şaban, he featured in seventeen films between 1977 and 1985 and two television series in 1993–94 and 1996–97. *Şabaniye* is unique because of the suffix –iye, which indicates a change in Şaban's gender, from male to female. However, in *Şabaniye*, Sunal performs as three different Şabans: Şaban proper; Bayram, Şaban disguised as a male escaping from a family feud; and Şabaniye, Şaban disguised as a woman who becomes a famous singer.

The film is a parody of the high and late Yeşilçam genre of singer melodrama, which featured loosely written melodramatic texts specially constructed as a vehicle for a famous singer who played one of the lead roles. This film recounts the discovery of a talented character from poor, rural roots who becomes a famous, wealthy singer. *Şabaniye* opens with a typical migration story from a rural Anatolian setting to Istanbul. Migration is often fuelled by a search for a better life and, in the case of singer melodramas, for fame. *Şabaniye*'s story adds an extra variation borrowed from the plotlines of rural dramas because Şaban's mother Hatice (Adile Naşit) takes her little boy, a young Şaban, with her to escape a family feud in their village. The adult Şaban displays the typical traits of Şaban from other films – clumsiness, dim-wittedness and thoroughness. He lives with his mother in a squatter settlement. A self-taught musician, Şaban composes songs at home and tries to replace the lead singers at the music hall where Hatice works. When the feuding family, led by Şeyhmus (Erdal Özyağcılar) and his gun-toting, horse-riding tomboy sister Nazlı tracks down Şaban and Hatice, Şaban is able to escape by posing as his female alter-ego, Şabaniye.

Introduced as Hatice's daughter, Şabaniye starts selling flowers at the music hall where nobody recognises her. When Şeyhmus arrives at the music hall, he is similarly fooled. Şabaniye asks Şeyhmus to kill her in place of 'her brother' Şaban while the lead singer at the music hall sings a song titled, 'If I Die, Don't Come to My Grave' (*Ölürsem Kabrime Gelme*). Şabaniye also starts singing. Because the lead singer has a cold, everyone in the hall gathers around Şabaniye, whose performance makes Şeyhmus cry while everyone else applauds. When Şeyhmus tells his family that he has fallen in love with Şabaniye, his sister Nazlı decides to befriend her and find Şaban. Şabaniye's rise to fame is so quick that as she becomes the lead singer, she also starts recording long-playing records at a music studio. The owner of the music hall Dursun (Turgut Boralı) buys her an apartment and wants to marry her. However, Şeyhmus also persuades his family to ask for Şabaniye's hand in marriage. As Şeyhmus tries to win over his beloved, Şabaniye tries to befriend Nazlı.

Şaban decides to frame Nazlı and hires a couple of guys to attempt to rob her. As they stop Nazlı Şaban appears, beats them and introduces himself as Bayram. After they agree to meet up later, Şaban goes to shoot the aforementioned film within the film. As Nazlı and Bayram start to fall in love, both Dursun and Şeyhmus compete to win over Şabaniye. However, Şeyhmus gambles with Dursun and loses all of his family's property. Şabaniye promises to support Nazlı and her family and promises Dursun she will marry him in exchange for Şeyhmus's debts. Bayram asks Nazlı to marry but Nazlı refuses by telling him that she needs to avenge her family. To solve everything, Şabaniye calls Nazlı and tells her that Şaban is back and will be attending her concert. When everyone gathers at the music hall, Şabaniye tells a story on stage about a guy disguised as a woman to escape a family feud and then takes off his wig. Nazlı points a gun toward him but cannot pull the trigger. Then, Şaban leaves the stage and starts walking down on the hallway backstage. Nazlı stops and hugs him and the two walk down the hallway as the film ends.

Turkification and unprompted realism

In the film within a film, the director says '*Motör!*' to start the action. *Motör* is the Turkish spelling of the French word *moteur*, one of many other words borrowed from French in Turkish cinema vocabulary. As a Western medium, cinema, like perspectival painting, was imported to Turkey, which has a unique history of Westernisation and modernisation which often involved the Turkification of imported forms. This practice of re-rendering Western forms into Turkish ones denotes a mechanism or protocol of transformation, conversion, translation and transition (see Arslan 2011), protocols and mechanisms which have shaped the history of cinema in Turkey. Yeşilçam is marked by the Turkification of Hollywood. *Şabaniye*, as a remake of *Tootsie*, plays around the popularity of the Hollywood film, boldly offering itself as its substitute, attempting to be like it, but also staying away from it. Through the Hollywood vocabulary of high concept, *Şabaniye*'s premise is 'Tootsie goes Turkish' or 'Tootsie meets Yeşilçam'. In other words, *Şabaniye* is not just a word-by-word rendering of the original. Instead, like many other Yeşilçam films pirated from popular Hollywood films, it presents a free adaptation incorporating home-grown cultural and moral elements such as the family feud and the singer melodrama's familiar rags-to-riches plotline. Unlike Michael Dorsey's (Dustin Hoffman) perfectionism as an actor, which prevents him from acting in mediocre roles and his turning into Dorothy Michaels, Şaban's case is marked by a typical melodramatic plotline which starts with a poor rural character's rise to fame and the ensuing heterosexual romance similar to that in screwball comedies. However unlikely and unrealistic the story may be, *Şabaniye*, a popular film even today, fulfils its promise as a comedy.

Yeşilçam's relation to Hollywood or other Western cinematic forms is complicated, for it does not present a thorough illusionistic language but an unruly mix of illusion and reality. If the practice of Turkification imbricates a translation and transformation, Yeşilçam's practice of filmmaking also involves a redefinition and authentication of Western realism by tying cinema to already existing forms of entertainment and arts. Two-dimensional shadow plays, theatre-in-the-round and early Westernised forms of theatre have played a role in the development of Yeşilçam. Specifically, Yeşilçam films often include direct address or introduce non-diegetic elements, such as the actor's presentation of the film at the beginning and the direct address of spectators with the characters' gaze directed at the camera. While these may be tied to existing forms of entertainment and art, some of the non-realistic and non-illusionistic effects are due to the fact that low budgets have often required Yeşilçam's filmmakers to make do with insufficient personnel and equipment.

One of the most notable deficiencies results from the prevalent practice of dubbing. To cut costs, films were shot without sound and post-synchronised, initially by professional dubbing artists and later by the actors themselves. *Şabaniye* puns on a frequent flaw in this practice, in which an extra sound is added at the beginning of various words or the first letter of some words changes. One dubbing artist, Abdurrahman Palay, famously pronounced 'evet' (yes) as 'nevet' and 'hayır' (no) as 'nayır.' In the film within a film scene in *Şabaniye*, the play between the words 'hazır' (ready) and 'nazır' (heady/ lit. 'minister') denotes this practice. However, as a Yeşilçam film, *Şabaniye* is also dubbed. Dubbing is not only used to cut costs, but also to make up for various continuity mistakes. This is why Yeşilçam relies more on an aural vocabulary than a visual vocabulary. While we hear Sunal voicing himself in *Şabaniye*, whenever he starts singing as Şabaniye, he takes on multiple personalities. The first song he sings is sung by a female voice, whereas the other ones are sung by male voices, mostly by Zeki Müren. Thus while *Şabaniye* pokes fun at Yeşilçam, it is also itself a product of Yeşilçam as it makes Şabaniye sing and speak with different voices.

Beyond posing a simple problem of dubbing and realistic illusion, *Şabaniye*'s use of Müren's voice for Şabaniye leads to another practice of Yeşilçam which is about extra textuality and a different sense of realism that is inevitably tied to reality. For instance, the border between the filmic and the real is at times blurry for some of the spectators. Several Yeşilçam actors recounted being attacked or beaten on the street because they played villains in films. In *Şabaniye*, the use of Zeki Müren songs invites discussion of his stage and star persona and his real life. In his live shows at music halls or other venues, Müren performed as a drag queen or a cross-dresser. The reputation he earned through his performances, and the fact that he never married, raised a great deal of speculation regarding his sexual preferences. Thus the use of Müren's voice in *Şabaniye* is neither coincidental nor unexpected. Müren was a closeted homosexual, but *Şabaniye* also brings to mind another singer, Bülent Ersoy, who underwent a sex change operation in 1981 and was thus banned from performing on stage, forcing her to live in exile until 1988. Thus, both *Şabaniye*'s use of Müren's songs and its realistic portrayal of a cross-dressing Şaban tie the film to themes of gender that were at stake in popular culture during the early 1980s.

Yeşilçam's genres and stars

In the so-called dark years of Turkish cinema, which spanned the second half of the 1970s when the majority of films produced were sex comedies and other sex films, and during the early 1980s when film production went down from roughly 150 films per year to sixty or seventy films due to the junta rule, Yeşilçam produced some of its classical comedies. The most popular ones included those directed by Orhan Aksoy and others, and Ertem Eğilmez's *Hababam Sınıfı* series, which introduced the İnek Şaban character that later had a life of its own in a number of Şaban films. Perhaps as an antidote to sex comedies, these comedies often showed the bittersweet life of a large family in Istanbul, featuring stock types, such as the good-hearted father and/or mother, the tyrannical businessman, the servant, the cook, the gardener and the dim-witted son. These stock types can be traced to the late Ottoman *tuluat* theatre, which combined traditional performances with Western-style plays and stage organisation. Family comedies follow a melodramatic plotline revolving around the highs and lows of a large, lower-class, honourable family. The young son and/or daughter of the family generally falls in love with an upper-class boy/girl, leading to melodramatic obstacles such as class difference, before the traditional and expected happy ending.

Şaban films are different in that they rely primarily on the foolish but wise, clumsy but virtuous Şaban character who stays honest and true to his lower-class and often rural background. Related to the fairytale character Keloğlan (The Bald Boy) or other comic characters of traditional theatre, the Şaban character provides a nostalgic connection to what has been lost in the process of modernisation and Westernisation. Often Şaban fights against greedy businessmen, landlords or merchants who want to change the environment of the countryside, small towns or lower-class neighbourhoods. In this respect, he is also tied to a modern rendering of the bandit hero, but in the borders of the comedy genre. Şaban becomes a bandit hero only by accident, not because he wants to be one, but because the conditions force him to be one. Although he may be a part of a melodramatic plot involving the love between a lower-class Şaban and an upper-class female, he does not look for a relationship, but instead the relationship happens through funny and unlikely coincidences or because of the female character's actions.

Alternatively, Şaban may be related to Charlie Chaplin and the Marx Brothers. For Sunal himself, Şaban is an outsider like Chaplin's characters; Şaban does not reside in a utopian or unearthly space, but instead he belongs to a rural background (2001: 44). However, in line with the modernisation of the country, Şaban is forced to migrate. Because he does not belong to the urban setting, he terrorises it in a Chaplinesque way and at times turns anarchic like the characters in Marx Brothers films. For him, this anarchic potential inscribes a move away from melodrama, a foregrounding of class conflicts and an instigation of anarchy and chaos (see Sunal 2001: 45–7). In contrast to this potential anarchism, Yeşilçam's melodramatic line of resolution with the overcoming of villainous acts of the upper-classes or tyrants is often a defining trait of the Şaban films. After noting that Sunal's characters invited a connection to Keloğlan, Engin Ayça notes that Sunal continues the culture of fairytales (2001: 181). For him, Sunal belongs to Yeşilçam as much as Yeşilçam belongs to Turkey's cultural structure, and in turn, Sunal's characters were types, reproducing Yeşilçam's culture (2001: 183). By staying within the limits of comedy or perhaps without bringing much social criticism at the end, Şaban films restore the status quo by making every-one happy through the realisation of heterosexual relationships within a patriarchal order. As a dissertation on Sunal's characters by Nazlı Kırmızı notes, Şaban always is an outsider, he always falls in love with a woman and he always overcomes evil (see Özsoy 2002: 109). In contrast to the family comedies of the late 1970s or his Şaban films, Sunal sees his comedies of the late 1980s as more dramatic than come-dic. Despite this shift toward more dramatic characters, as Ayça notes, Sunal was not successful at this for he stayed as a type in the eyes of the spectators (2001: 182). In other words, Şaban is a cliché, an epitome of goodness and purity that fits precisely into Yeşilçam's melodramatic modality that presents a straightforward Manichean conflict between pure good and pure evil.

As a comedy film, *Şabaniye* primarily uses, while also parodying, singer melo-dramas and, to some extent, rural dramas, while it is an example of the cycle of home-grown comedies produced at the time. Its nod to Hollywood-style comedy through the use of *Tootsie*, and the rags to riches and courtship themes of screwball comedies, seems to place *Şabaniye* a little off the track. However, it is still a film fitting snugly into the mould of high and late Yeşilçam comedies. Additionally, in *Şabaniye*, the obstacle to love is spiced up with a dramatic social issue – a family feud – which is also overcome by the love between Şaban and Nazlı. However, the family feud is also represented by a stock character, Nazlı's mother, played by Aliye Rona. While Rona plays the stock tough and unforgiving villainous mother character of rural dramas, Hatice, as played by Adile Naşit, presents the permanently smiling and giving mother character. While there are no fathers in the film except at the start when the reason for the feud is revealed as their murder, father figures are represented by Şeyhmus and Dursun. Yet at the heart of the story is not only a message about the elimination of father figures, but also Şaban's melodramatic love. However, Şaban's struggle against the family feud and his escape from it by posing as a woman denies the film the status of a drama, realigning it within the limits of comedy. On the other hand, in the film within a film, when Kartal Tibet and Orhan Aksoy appear as themselves, the first as the male lead of the singer melodrama and the other as the director of the same film, the element of play goes above board and present us with a late Yeşilçam theme of self-reflexivity.

Late Yeşilçam, reflecting back

Şabaniye's self-reflexive elements and its parodic and playful look at Yeşilçam are also related to the spatiotemporal characteristics of Turkey and Turkish cinema in the early 1980s. After the wave of sex films in the late 1970s and the trauma of the military intervention of 1980, the early 1980s were also marked by the rapid increase of television spectatorship, the introduction of VCR technology, a decrease in film ticket sales and changes in Yeşilçam's genres, and permeated by a restrained and pessimistic view of Turkey and its future. These developments led to the end of Yeşilçam's melodramas and romantic comedies with highly-paid star actors. Instead, melodramas were often low-budget films or singer melodramas, often starring singers of *arabesk* music. In the early Yeşilçam era, a series of singer melodramas starring Zeki Müren not only reflected the influence of Egyptian and Indian melodramas with extended song and dance sequences, but also fastened Yeşilçam's vocabulary of typecasting through the star system, as well as with other *tuluat* theatre-based stock types. In this manner, both Şabaniye's recollection of Bülent Ersoy or other transsexual singers and its use of Zeki Müren songs and performance style on a thrust stage with an elongated 'T' shaped apron extending into the auditorium not only invites a discussion of gender issues, but also reflects on and reproduces the singer melodrama genre. Indeed, while there is an ongoing parody, Sunal's star persona as Şaban is also at stake in this manner. Throughout its lifetime, Yeşilçam's mainstream productions relied upon stars who have often been typecast as in the case of Sunal/Şaban. Whenever Sunal tried to dismantle Şaban, his star persona overshadowed his attempts. Thus Şabaniye is not an anarchic act that dislocates the Şaban figure, but instead a response or reference to Yeşilçam. However, this play or parody is not able to move away from a gendered discourse which restores the patriarchy.

While *arabesk* music's ties to rural or folk Turkish, Kurdish and Arabic music and its hopeless mood was often criticised by urban intellectual circles and some Yeşilçam filmmakers, the supposedly high quality productions of late Yeşilçam were often social issue films focusing either on the situation of women or rural dramas exposing the need to modernise the Turkish East. In the 1980s, as various political groups who were violently punished or oppressed by the military regime started to reflect on what had gone wrong and enabled the intervention, some late Yeşilçam filmmakers also reflected on what went wrong with Yeşilçam. At a time when overt political themes stayed away from the vocabulary of filmmaking, these issue films about gender and rural society tried to fill that gap. In late Yeşilçam women's films, strong female characters are often portrayed as educated and urban who make decisions through their own trajectories by staying free from social and patriarchal pressures. In *Şabaniye*, both Nazlı and Şabaniye are such strong figures. When Nazlı meets Şabaniye, she also begins as a dominant character. However, Şabaniye and Bayram teach her how to become a 'domestic' woman. Thus both of Şaban's alternate personae prepare Nazlı for Şaban. Despite such incursions into issues related to transsexuality and gender, *Şabaniye* only uses these themes to create anarchic comedy. While the tripartite identity of Sunal in this film presents a chaotic confusion of identities, it still falls under the star persona of Kemal Sunal as the foolish but good-hearted, pure and simple traditional male. As such, it was Yeşilçam's patriarchal discourse which was incessantly reproduced by way of Şaban. Like *Şabaniye*, women's films, which were predominantly written and directed by males, were a forum for the filmmakers who were voicing the concerns and problems of women as though they were harbingers of the feminist movement. When, in the film within a film, *Şabaniye* reflects back on Yeşilçam's melodramas, it does not just make fun of them, but also underlines the fact that it reproduces them in the late Yeşilçam era at a time when only a nostalgic look at the popular film industry of the past was possible.

Coda: Yeşilçam as storyteller

With its dubbing practice, unprompted realism, diverse sources and direct address, Yeşilçam was like a storyteller allowing its audiences to share his/her experience. In this respect, *Şabaniye*'s parody and reproduction of Yeşilçam is not surprising for it was a product of Yeşilçam, which created an ambiguity in terms of the border between the real and the fictional, at times by confusing the two and at other times by playing around with the two. As noted above, this is tied to forms of traditional storytelling and performance which persisted in Yeşilçam. On the other hand, when one looks at post-Yeşilçam films or examples of the new cinema of Turkey, 'a concomitant symptom of the secular productive forces of history' and a removal of 'narrative from the realm of living speech' are visible (Benjamin 1968: 87). For Walter Benjamin, the storyteller tells from his/her own or others' experience and makes the audience a part of this experience, but a novelist is 'isolated', a 'solitary individual' who is 'uncounseled' and who 'cannot counsel others' and thus carries 'the incommensurable to extremes in the representation of human life' (ibid.). This is why post-Yeşilçam films such as those of Nuri Bilge Ceylan do not force anything, but leave it to the spectator to interpret things. Contemporary cinema in Turkey does not continuously reproduce Yeşilçam's simple and typical melodramatic modality with tedious and routine storylines. However, with its unprompted realism which led its audience to respond in their daily lives even through the simple act of beating the actors who portrayed evil characters, Yeşilçam offered its audience the opportunity to partake in its repetitive stories. 'For storytelling is always the art of repeating stories and this art is lost when the stories are no longer retained' (Benjamin 1968: 91). Perhaps this is why Yeşilçam gave way to the post-Yeşilçam, or the new cinema of Turkey.

Note

1   The history of cinema in Turkey can be divided into three broad periods: pre-Yeşilçam before the 1950s; Yeşilçam between the 1950s and 1980s; and post-Yeşilçam after the 1980s. Yeşilçam may be further divided into the early Yeşilçam of 1950s, the high Yeşilçam of 1960s and 1970s; and the late Yeşilçam of 1980s (see Arslan 2011). Enmeshed with a melodramatic narration that has a specific history in the West, Yeşilçam's melodramatic modality is inscribed both with traditional forms of oral narration and a combination of a two-dimensional and perspectival way of seeing. While production quality was often poor, Yeşilçam included many types of film, such as mainstream films with or without stars, low-budget productions and some auteur films. This diversity includes a variety of filmic genres, such as family melodrama, action, adventure, comedy and fantasy, as well as spaghetti (or 'kebab') westerns, sex and horror films.

Bibliography

Arslan, S. (2011) *Cinema in Turkey: A New Critical History*. Oxford and New York: Oxford University Press.

Ayça, E. (2001) '*Propaganda*'da da Değiştiremedi Çizgisini, Değiştiremezdi' (He was not able to Change his Line in *Propaganda*, He Could not), in F. Karasu Gürses (ed.) *Kemal Sunal: Film Başka Yaşam Başka* (Kemal Sunal: Film and Life Are Different). Istanbul: Sel Yayıncılık, 181–3.

Benjamin, W. (1968) *Illuminations: Essays and Reflections*. Trans. H. Zohn. New York: Schocken.

Özsoy, O. (2002) *Kemal Sunal Fenomeni* (The Kemal Sunal Phenomenon). Istanbul: İyiadam Yayınları.

Sunal, A. K. (2001) *TV ve Sinemada Kemal Sunal Güldürüsü* (Kemal Sunal Comedy in TV and Cinema). Istanbul: Om Yayınevi.

Jewish Humour and the Cabaret Tradition in Interwar Hungarian Entertainment Films

Anna Manchin

Hungary, a relatively small nation isolated by its unique language and suffering from various economic, social and political crises, created a considerable film industry that produced over 140 films in the 1930s. This industry was dominated by fairly low-budget films of the romantic comedy genre. What is the relationship of these films to the by-then dominant Hollywood model that came into being under vastly different circumstances? Are they merely derivative, low-quality versions of Hollywood? Or do they represent a uniquely Hungarian cinematic style? At first glance, 1930s Hungarian romantic comedies seem to fairly closely resemble Hollywood films, with which they competed for audiences. They are glamorous romances featuring beautiful, emancipated young women and dashing young men eager to succeed on their own merits in the modern capitalist context. Set against the backdrop of stylish Budapest apartments, nightclubs and offices, the films celebrated all that commercial urban modernity had to offer, including consumer goods and leisure activities: new fashions, cars, sports, weekends, nightlife and vacations.

The film industry developed in this tense context. From the start, it was targeted as an influential and highly visible site of 'Jewish' influence. For conservative cultural critics worried about the decline of authentic national culture, developing a uniquely Hungarian film culture seemed necessary for national survival. But they saw Hungarian films made by the commercial film industry as completely lacking in both national character and national sentiment. As the right-wing nationalist film director István György put it in 1934, 'Hungarian films ... lack "personality" ... They do not have a quality like the film products of every other film producing nation.

What is missing from Hungarian films is "Hungarianness".[1]

Contemporaries recognised complaints about films 'lacking in Hungarian sentiment' to be thinly veiled attacks on the films' Jewish creators and the cosmopolitan, capitalist (and therefore Jewish and un-Hungarian) worldview the films represented. For anti-semitic nationalists in 1930s Hungary, 'Hungarian' and 'Jewish' appeared to be incompatible categories. Paradoxically, what distinguishes these films as 'Hungarian' is precisely their constant comic references to Hungarian Jewish identity.

In 1930s Hungarian cinema, the classical Hollywood narrative style was constantly challenged by another style of storytelling that I will call Jewish comedy. Its sources were the Budapest cabaret tradition and a parodic Jewish stereotype that played a crucial role in both cabaret and film. Immediately striking to viewers today is the ubiquitous presence of a self-deprecating, pessimistic and ironic character augmenting the main plot's glamorous dream-world with self-reflexive commentary on the realities of everyday life.[2] Although apparently inconsequential to the main narrative, this comic character was in fact central to the films' storytelling style and transformed the films' messages. Through ongoing yet subtle critical remarks delivered by this seemingly insignificant character, entertainment films (much like the cabaret) gave a voice to an increasingly marginalised perspective in Hungarian public life.

The Budapest cabaret tradition and social satire

In combining humorous entertainment with subtle but irreverent social commentary, the films built on a tradition of urban commercial entertainment exemplified by the Budapest cabaret. Critics in the first decades of the twentieth century proudly proclaimed this genre of popular theatre one of the city's unique attractions. Writing in the most influential modernist literary journal *Nyugat* in 1915, the celebrated writer Dezső Kosztolányi described the cabaret's style and content as both inseparable from and originating in a specifically 'Budapest' identity and attitude.

> Was it 10, 25, or a hundred years ago? I remember the nights in Pest when the first couplets were heard, and there was cabaret everywhere, not only in the 4 or 5 spaces created for this purpose, but in coffee houses, private homes, and even between two individuals who ran into one another on the street … The Budapest cabaret is satire. It incarnates the sugared bile, incredulity and fine acrimony that live in all Budapesters. It is the product of a certain shrewdness that is one of this city's important character traits… (1915)

The cabaret first appeared as an independent theatrical genre around the turn of the century and soon became one of the defining features of Budapest nightlife and entertainment, mainly catering to and representing the perspective of the liberal Jewish bourgeoisie. The cabaret addressed issues of serious public concern from a comic angle, interpreting them though biting cultural and political commentary. Cabaret programmes consisted of short theatrical sketches, scenes with humorous commentary, monologues, 'couplets' (humorous poems), readings from avant-garde poetry and prose and *chansons* and other musical numbers. But perhaps most important was the figure of the *conferencier*, a kind of master of ceremonies who addressed the audience directly and provided running commentary on daily politics and culture. As I will show, this MC tradition was transformed in comedy films through the figure of the Jewish comedian. Although this Jewish theme and the satirical social commentary were relegated to the margins in the films, they were, paradoxically, central to their meaning.

For the purposes of tracing the influence of the cabaret on comedy films, I want to focus on two aspects of the cabaret: its perceived public role and its comic style.[3] With witty social satire couched in humorous entertainment, the cabaret was recognised as a significant outlet for cultural criticism that could not be expressed in 'serious' public discourse.

Since the late nineteenth century, critics saw the cabaret as the only public forum that allowed for true freedom of expression in an underdeveloped public sphere dominated by illiberal politics. They argued that in the early twentieth century Hungarian public context, truths about society could be articulated only through distortion, humour and satire.[4] This sentiment persisted even in the late 1930s. As a critic of the liberal cultural magazine *Színházi Élet* put it in 1937, the cabaret remained the only medium capable of presenting a 'faithful mirror image of the present day' reflecting 'unaltered reality' through 'humorous distortion'.[5]

As the above quote from Kosztolányi also makes clear, satire was one of the defining features of the cabaret. The cabaret's social critique was oblique and ironic; it relied on allusions and on the audiences' imagination to complete the messages. Often, the comedy amounted to a confused look, a loaded gesture or a few satirical words. Audiences were expected to read between the lines, to recognise and interpret subtle hints. Although difficult to censor, this type of satire was easy for audiences (and critics) to recognise.

As a right-wing critic pointed out about one of the most successful Jewish cabarets, László Békeffi's *Pódium*, in 1937, 'What this artist Békeffi (with a reassuring, Hungarian-sounding name) does not explicitly state in his conferrals but implies through his gestures and between the lines offends everything that is tasteful, Christian and Hungarian'.[6]

Cabaret and film comedy

In one sense, the continuity between cabaret and film is obvious: many of the cabaret's writers, screenwriters and actors were active in the film industry as well as in cabaret theatres until well into the 1930s. Despite the constantly changing constellation of Budapest's cabaret theatres – over seventy distinct companies appeared over the course of the first half of the twentieth century – these enterprises actually represented a relatively small and stable group of writers, directors and actors. Although critics had already lamented the demise of the cabaret in the early 1920s, a handful of cabaret theatres did continue to run shows until the anti-semitic laws of 1938–39. Many of the most successful cabaret writers (including László Vadnay, László Békeffi, Andor Kolozsvári, Andor Gábor, Tamás Emőd, Rezső Török, Károly Nóti, Miklós Lőrincz, Adorján Stella, István Mihály, Lajos Bíró, István Békeffy and István Zágon) wrote for film while continuing to work in cabarets as writers, MCs and even owners throughout the 1930s. The most successful comic film stars Gyula Gózon and Gyula Kabos both performed in a number of different cabarets throughout the period.

Neither the films nor the cabarets openly addressed political issues, but the cabaret was much more likely to allow for direct political allusions. Some cabaret artists continued to make political remarks on stage well into the late 1930s. In 1936, a right-wing newspaper critic censured the Pódium cabaret (run by Békeffi) for its 'Jewish' liberal politics, expressing the belief that the cabaret catered to a Jewish audience, insisting that this perspective had no place in Hungarian public life and was politically dangerous. This critic claimed that the audiences and creators of this kind of political comedy were all Jewish (if not ethnically, then culturally).

> We don't know why a certain Budapest cabaret owner thinks that, protected by the freedom of the stage and the theatre, he has the right to constantly … hold political speeches – going far beyond political jokes – in accordance with the tastes of the Lipótváros [a wealthy Jewish district of Pest]. Perhaps Békeffi, being a good businessman, wants thus to serve the audience that provides him a living. […] But this is no excuse, and for our part, we very sharply dissent against the operation of this minor parliament called the Pódium Cabaret. […] If the owner of the Pódium Cabaret has political ambitions, he should become a representative. But he ought to immediately discontinue performing the green pig story, which is neither witty nor piquant, but rather an uncouth and lowly reference to a nation with which we have friendly relations. (Quoted in Bános 2008: 125)

Film, however, with its recognised national significance, propaganda potential, wide cultural reach and international prestige, was quite different. Films had a much larger and more diverse public. While the audience for cabaret was fairly exclusive, movie theatres were accessible to the working class and to rural audiences as well. Films had to speak to a broader public from more diverse backgrounds and experiences, and they were much more closely scrutinised because of their recognised political significance.

Although the films were not political, they were connected to the institution and tradition of the cabaret in comic style and content and also in their reliance on

'Jewish humour'. Both the cabaret and comedy films employed a parodic Jewish ste-reotype to deliver their messages, and subtle innuendo, comments and gestures that made up their social satire.

On the surface, film comedies were entirely apolitical: they were love stories about the meeting and eventual marriage of a young couple. The cabaret (and with it, social critique) entered the films through the minor and seemingly marginal, comic character. As I will show, this Jewish character brought to the films 'Jewish humour' and subtle, between-the-lines social commentary that had been associated with the cabaret.

Jewish comedy in entertainment films

The idea that these films would be centred on jokes about Jewishness seems odd, considering the loaded significance and public preoccupation with the 'Jewish ques-tion' in interwar Hungary.[7] Hungary's succession of authoritarian and conservative governments veering increasingly towards fascism saw Jews as representatives of foreign, cosmopolitan commercial culture in Hungary and blamed Jewish assimila-tion for all of modern Hungary's failures and shortcomings. Following World War I, the image of Hungarian national identity that came to dominate official politics was rural, Christian and based on the culture of the land-owning noble elite.

Despite these warning signs, the political direction that Hungary would eventually take and its tragic consequences could not be foreseen in the 1930s. Films, although recognised by government officials as crucial for nation-building and coveted as pro-paganda tools by some right-wing pressure groups as well, continued to be created largely on a commercial basis. In spite of the publicly expressed intent of some right-wing filmmakers and government officials to create a film industry reflecting the conservative-traditional national identity, until the late 1930s the Hungarian film industry continued to be dominated by a group of liberal, internationally trained writers and directors, most of whom came from Jewish backgrounds. In effect, the influential popular form described as Hungary's 'national' film industry was the product of a group whose national status and cultural identity were regularly called into question by the radical right. At a time when political and intellectual discourses were concerned with the creation of a new national culture and the so-called 'Jewish question', films seemed to be a crucial forum for imagining and creating a new form of national identity.

In fact, Jewish film directors increasingly came under attack from right-wing cul-tural critics. As a pamphlet by a fascist student organisation (Turul) claimed, Jewish Hungarians could not be trusted with creating Hungarian national culture. As the authors of the pamphlet perhaps correctly sensed, the type of Hungarian identity that they demanded was being parodied in the films: 'Hungarian film production is in foreign hands. It serves foreign goals, spreads immorality and filth, and turns Hungarian ideals inside out, disgracing them. [...] Székely [one of the most prominent directors of the 1930s] has no connection to the Hungarian race, and therefore is incapable of directing a film about the Hungarian people!' (quoted in Zsolnai 1937).

Anti-semitic attacks notwithstanding, most comedy films continued to include Jewish comedy at their centre. The problems of Jewish identity and anti-semitism were, with a single notable exception,[8] not raised explicitly in the films. Yet jokes about a distinct Jewish culture coexisting with the dominant culture of the Christian nobility were ubiquitous and formed the core of the films' comedy. The romantic story gained political meaning because the protagonists, the young couple, were coded as representatives of Hungarian traditional elite culture (usually the groom) and modern bourgeois culture (often through the addition of a Jewish father character who marks the bride-to-be as a member of the modern urban bourgeoisie). Because the social critique was delivered by a caricatured Jewish character, a figure with which contemporary audiences were quite familiar, the brief exchanges, comments and gestures were connected to a larger interpretive framework and could make statements about values, culture and community.[9]

The Jewish stereotype in the films – and to a large extent the Jewish comedy itself – was the creation of the brilliant Jewish comedian Gyula Kabos. A short, stodgy and bald middle-aged man, Kabos became a household name in the early 1930s and was widely believed capable of selling movies just by his presence. Besides his main career in the classical theatre, he appeared in various cabarets and over forty entertainment films before he emigrated to the United States in 1939. Kabos was often called the 'Hungarian Chaplin' in reference not only to his local influence but also to his character's relationship to authority and oppressive social structures. His hallmark slapstick style of physical comedy was very different from Chaplin's: Kabos gave a slapstick performance of 'Jewishness'.

Kabos's roles ranged from lower middle class office clerks to doctors, lawyers and bank presidents, but they were almost without exception minor and comic roles. Kabos united all the characters he played in a more or less uniform stereotype through his interpretation of his characters as bumbling Jewish assimilants. Whether as wealthy capitalists or petit-bourgeois office workers, they shared a lack of familiarity with the traditional culture of the Hungarian nobility and their adherence to an entirely different system of values.

None were explicitly described as Jewish, or marked recognisable through dress, language, religious activity or physical characteristics. 'Jewishness' could not be immediately discerned from appearance but was implied by cultural attitudes and social positions. Rather, Jewish identity, in the films as elsewhere, was imagined as a complex matrix of class and culture (and gender). It was precisely this intangible, merely implicit cultural difference that was the main source of comedy in the films.

Kabos's characters were eager to participate in elite society but never quite successful at assimilation into it. They were awkward, anxious and ill at ease in the face of the culture of the traditional nobility. Even if they followed the outside forms, their rational, frugal and pessimistic worldview prevented them from understanding the logic of traditional noble culture. Kabos performed this cultural difference through body language, speech and mannerisms that were slightly off-kilter in the context of mainstream society. His characters were unfamiliar with the correct usage of words related to traditional culture and rural life, uncertain about social conventions and confused by mundane social formalities.

The Jewish jokes in the films were not simply about Jewish identity, but rather about Jewish identity as it related to larger questions of Hungarian national identity in the context of European modernity. They were really about the struggle to define Hungarian culture, its common values and shared beliefs and whether Jews could be part of it. Who was a 'real' Hungarian, and what did that entail? At the centre of these romantic tales and jokes is the conflict between the traditional culture of the noble elite and the bourgeois culture of the (Jewish) urban middle class. Jewish comedy proposed an alternative understanding of the Jewish stereotype and gently mocked the mainstream vision of national identity.

Cabaret on film

One of the most intriguing examples of the cabaret's influence on film is a short sketch (from a trio of sketches) entitled *Szenzáció* (*Sensation*, István Székely and Ladislao Vajda, 1936). What sets it apart from other cabaret films is that here the comedy is not a sideline contained in a larger romantic plot, but appears on its own, and is also much more blatant and outrageous than in the majority of the cabaret films. At the same time, the style of humour, the stereotyped Jewish character and the actor are the same. It features Kabos as an unemployed middle-class man, Szálka, who is in such dire straits that he is willing to take any job. Szálka is offered a seemingly well-paying position by a circus director; he is to be the assistant of Gordon, an 'Indian' knife thrower whose partner has suddenly fallen ill. Leaving aside the fascinating question of the significance of North American Indians in the East European Jewish imagination, I will concentrate on the way that Jewish identity is revealed and parodied in the film. Two scenes are of particular interest here.

In the first scene, in an elliptical attempt to introduce Szálka to the terms of his employment, the circus director asks him if he likes movies. His intention is to turn to the question of movies featuring Indians, and then to Indians who throw knives at white people. Szálka responds that he would not know about those because they terrify him so much that he leaves the theatre immediately. But before answering properly, Kabos interjects a brief parody of himself and as a filmmaker as well. Asked about whether or not he likes the movies, Kabos goes into a confused rant:

> I love the movies … I love the ones where the wealthy company director marries the poor secretary. Or this one is great: I just saw it recently. A wealthy girl is courting a poor young man … no no no: a wealthy young man is courting a poor girl, and later it turns out that he's actually not a wealthy young man but a poor girl! Or no, it turns out that

the poor secretary is actually … or … well it's so rare that I see these things that it's now slipped my mind.

This aside has little narrative function, except perhaps in depicting Szálka as a ball of nerves. The reason it functions as comedy is because it addresses audiences directly, giving sarcastic, self-reflective commentary on the film they are watching. Kabos is making fun of precisely the types of comedies that the directors and screenwriters of this short film (István Székely, Ladislao Vajda, Ferenc Herczeg, László Vadnay, Jenő Szatmári and Márton Keleti) usually make in great numbers and in rapid succession, and the characters that Kabos as an actor also often depicts. He mocks the interchangeable, hackneyed storylines that are revealed as confusing and improbable as soon as someone tries to actually describe them.

The second scene follows Szálka's final agreement to perform with Gordon, and in a ballerina outfit. Alone with Szálka in the dressing room, it is now Gordon's turn to panic. He kneels down in front of Szálka and begs him to leave. As explanation, he offers a somewhat cryptic confession: 'My name is Gottlieb.' Ironically, the information that Gordon is not who he claimed he is, instead of increasing Kabos's anxiety, comes as a huge relief to him. Addressing the camera and the film audience directly again, he mumbles, 'then it can't be too bad'. In other words, recognising that Gottlieb is (also) a Jew (Austrian emperor Joseph II issued a decree in 1787 compelling all Jews in the former Austro-Hungarian Empire to adopt German surnames) and not an Indian at all, Szálka is overjoyed.

Gottlieb tells Szálka that he is incapable of throwing knives and that in fact he has not thrown one in the past ten years. The way he makes his money is by collecting the advance from circus directors and claiming that his partner has fallen ill. 'It's worked splendidly thus far because there was never a single soul willing to stand there while I threw knives. But here I've been busted; in Pest one can even find a man for that.' Again, Szálka's reaction is telling. Instead of being outraged, he is impressed and inspired: 'Gottlieb, that's pure genius. You're an even greater villain than the circus director.' In other words, it is not an actual skill but rather the talent to partake in a somewhat shady form of commercial success (or simply the talent of surviving in hard times) that Szálka finds commendable. Although the ploy threatened his own life, Szálka still recognises genius when he sees it. What this exchange represents is an alternative cultural and moral world in which cunning, disguise and self-transformation are crucial for survival in a hostile world.

The situation is also a parodic comment on the hard times early 1930s cinema audiences, not only Jews, were experiencing due to economic depression and unemployment, and ridicules the absurd lengths people are willing to go to and the jobs they are willing to take to survive; Kabos actually wears a tutu in this scene. Furthermore, it is also a comment on Jewish identity in so far as Kabos is extremely enthusiastic when he finds out who Gottlieb is (previously he claimed he had nothing against the 'Indian nation' but he did not like knife-throwing Indians). Finally, the self-reflexive strategy is further strengthened by Kabos's jokes, clearly intended to amuse only the audience; he makes remarks that no diegetic characters can hear or understand. In the scene mentioned above, he turns to look into the camera and whispers to the audience, as if he were on a stage. The narrative underscores its own function as a performance aimed at the entertainment of a specific audience.

Romance and comedy

In the following, through two brief examples of how the cabaret tradition was integrated into the more mainstream medium of film, I discuss how Jewish comedy added critical commentary to the main, romantic narrative.

In *Pesti Mese* (*A Tale of Pest*, directed by Béla Gaál, screenplay by László Vadnay, 1937), Kabos plays an anxious newcomer to the Hungarian upper-middle class, a highly successful bank director named Lehel Vadász. Despite his accomplishments, Vadász remains insecure and anxious; he tries to amass everything both tangible and intangible that will enhance his social position. Vadász, eager to make up for a missed high school education, secretly attends night school to earn a diploma. But instead of studying, he tries to earn points with the teacher by claiming that he knows the answer when he does not, and in lieu of giving a substantive response he gives his 'gentleman's word' that he does know the answer. The joke is not just that Vadász, as a nouveau-riche Jew without a high-school diploma, is not, in the contemporary accepted definition of the term, a 'gentleman', someone who was a military officer and as such, permitted to duel. This was a title the traditional nobility wished to hold on to, often at the exclusion of Jews. It is also a parody of the very concept of a 'gentleman's word' as he is clearly lying. At the same time, using physical comedy, Vadász imitates the traditional nobility's pretensions of superiority by using this genteel expression with a fake upper-class accent and bearing in a wildly inappropriate context (night school) and for ridiculous purposes. Finally, Vadász parodies the idea that in this conservative and hierarchical society, a 'gentleman's word', however bogus a concept, continues to trump all else; he uses it with outrageous irreverence.

Lehel's name itself functions as a subtle joke on his identity, marking him as an overeager assimilant. Lehel, a very unusual first name, is the name of a Hun tribal chief (one of the mythical founders of the nation), while Vadász (Hunter) is a reference to a favourite pastime of the traditional aristocracy (newcomers' lack of skill was a common source of levity).

Vadász's glaring 'misuse' of the markers of genteel identity are perhaps most explicit in the following scene. Vadász's bank handles the deposit of a formerly penniless young woman's inheritance from abroad. Vadász, as the head of the bank, offers the young woman advice on the kinds of prestige purchases necessary for a brand new millionaire: a little chateau in the countryside, an elegant residence in the city, a weekend house in the Buda hills and a car. He tells her that he can help her with these purchases, moreover that he happens to have all of these items to hand

and can offer them to her at a discounted price.

The joke here is not only that Vadász is *nouveau riche* as well and that he also recently made exactly the same investments. Nor is it simply that there are so many *nouveaux riches* in Hungarian society trying desperately to fit into traditional society that there is an existing code, a list of items that one must buy. More significantly, the parody relates to Vadász's reinterpretation of the meaning of these purchases. Although he goes along with the outward signs of elite culture, the content he gives them radically alters their significance. While he supposedly bought these properties to fit in and become like the noble elite, he is eager to sell them at the first opportunity if he can make a profit. Despite his alleged purchasing of real estate to enhance his social status, he has not changed the way he thinks about his properties. He has no emotional attachment to them and does not pretend that they are his ancestral heritage, but rather treats them as liquid assets and opportunities for further profit making. He is willing to give them up any time he is able to get a good price for them – and this seems to completely contradict the reason for wanting to purchase them in the first place. In other words, eager as he is to fit in, his values remain very different. Although the Jewish *nouveaux riches* may imitate the traditional land-owning nobility on some level, they do not adopt their worldview but continue to live according to their own moral and cultural norms.

Kabos subverts audience expectations of romance by saying all the wrong things in his effort to woo the woman he desires. It becomes obvious that Vadász has a very different idea of how a gentleman would behave from what viewers might expect. His lack of familiarity with romantic etiquette is obvious in his failed attempt to woo the young and beautiful Annie whose hat salon had gone bankrupt. Vadász, the director of Annie's bank, calls her about the impending auctioning of her store, taking this entirely inappropriate moment to flirt with her. She is completely uninterested, but, desperate to save her business, for a minute feigns interest. What makes this humorous is that contrary to expectations, Vadász does not take advantage of her moment of weakness or use his power to get what he wants from her – but this is not because he is above such a manoeuvre or because he considers romance or feminine virtue to be sacred. Rather, the possibilities of this situation do not even cross his mind. Although he is interested in Annie, money and business matters are even more important to him. He remains a 'gentleman' because he takes money very seriously, not because he is necessarily against indecent proposals. He tells her that postponing the auction would be impossible, because business is business, and in the next sentence starts cooing again. He is not completely ruthless, however, and gives her another week to find the money.

In *Pesti Mese* the romance and the comedy are combined so that Kabos gives a parody of Jewish identity partly through his failed attempt at romance. In the larger context of the story, however, it is not his failure to conform to elite society that is ridiculed; elite society in portrayed as corrupt, dysfunctional and venal. Rather, it is the side-by-side existence of two incompatible worlds – the culture of the Jewish bourgeoisie on the one hand, and that of the traditional elite on the other – their interactions and ensuing misunderstandings that create comedy. Specifically, Kabos employs many of the markers of traditional elite identity, but completely subverts them in the way he uses them.

Another prime example of a romantic plot turned into social satire through Jewish comedy is *Emmy* (directed by István Székely, screenplay by István Mihály based on József Lengyel's play and Viktor Rákosi's novel, 1934). *Emmy* is a love story between a handsome but irresponsible hussar, Korponai, and a general's modern daughter, Emmy, visiting the military base. Korponai, an infamous womaniser, has amassed gambling and other debts, and has an actress lover whom, as his father fears, he might decide to marry. The film rehearses many elements of popular national identity, promising great popular success: the nostalgic setting in the Hungarian countryside; a military base; strapping young scions of the nobility; horses and traditional uniforms.

The comedy is introduced by the Jewish character, Jakab (played by Gyula Kabos), who arrives at the military base at the behest of Korponai's father. Jakab a lawyer and family friend, is entrusted with the job of delivering money to pay the younger Korponai's gambling debts and to steer him away from a disadvantageous marriage. Being an urban, middle-class professional, Jakab is completely unfamiliar with the supposedly glamorous lifestyle of military officers defined by affairs, gambling and drunken revelry. Although curious about these newly discovered possibilities, Jakab does not know what to make of them. Jakab's rational bourgeois Jewish world, revolving around frugality and self-restraint, is contrasted with that of the army base, where wasting money and displaying passion are crucial forms of self-expression. It is Jakab's parody of these genteel exploits and pastimes that introduces social commentary into the film.

Jakab is scared of horses, he has no idea how to court women, he has a frighteningly low tolerance for alcohol, and instead of participating in 'serious' physical exercise he spends his free time in the fields chasing butterflies with a net. The joke is that Jakab's own cultural universe is so radically different from the dominant one. Part of the film's comic appeal is the suggestion that a Jewish 'outsider' could be so oblivious to – and irreverent about – the values and ideals of mainstream society. Lacking practice disarming aggressive *demimondaine* actresses, Jakab bungles the task of removing Korponai's lover from the scene. He takes her out to a restaurant, but she is too much for Jakab to handle. He fails to steer her away from Korponai, and Emmy gets engaged to another officer.

Deeply disappointed, Jakab decides to try the gentry cure for unhappiness: drunken revelry. But his pragmatism prevents him from enjoying this traditional gentry pastime. Imitating others at the pub, Jakab lifts his glass and considers throwing it behind his back. On second thought, he decides to substitute it with a metal toothpick holder, but even then only after carefully removing the toothpicks lest they scatter all over the floor. The joke of course is that Jakab misses the essence of the gesture, which is less the actual throwing and more the dramatic performance of a deep unhappiness in which nothing matters. Prosaic considerations about the impracticality of broken glass or wastefulness render Jakab's performance wholly unconvincing. Jakab's perspective makes these gentry customs appear frivolous, cliched and unbefitting a modern individual. In the cultural context of 1930s Hungary, having an expressly unglamorous Jewish character parodying traditional Hungarian customs, to show that they are rather over the top and ripe for modernisation, seems like a highly irreverent move.

Conclusion

In conclusion, the comic subplot of the films involving a Jewish character influenced the film narrative of romantic comedies in three key ways. First, through the introduction of this stereotype, with its wide resonance and immediate relevance in public culture, the narrative connected the innocuous romantic plot to the specific concerns of 1930s Hungarian culture, turning the romance into an occasion for social satire. The films told their most important stories not through the romantic plot or the actual narrative but through allusions, comments and gestures delivered by a minor comic character. Although the comic sub-theme did not create a coherent narrative on its own, it did change the meaning of the story as it was understood by audiences able to read the character as Jewish.

Secondly, the inclusion of this Jewish comedy allowed the films to introduce into public discussion a concept that was largely taboo in Hungarian public discourse: the existence within Hungarian society of a separate Jewish culture that was nevertheless Hungarian. Part of the joke in the films was that the Jewish character could not follow the logic and customs of mainstream elite culture. But this exaggerated, parodic stereotype of the Jewish assimilant did not of course describe the real cultural identity of assimilated Hungarian Jews and/or Jewish cinema audiences. The humour in the films could only work if audiences (unlike the comic Jewish characters in the film) were perfectly familiar with elite culture, otherwise they would not know what the bumbling Jewish character was misunderstanding and how he was mistaken.

The Jewish stereotype functioned in different ways for different groups and even different individual members of the audience. It functioned as an inside joke about Jewish identity for those who had encountered multiple cultures and identities themselves. It was perhaps also possible to read the Jewish stereotype uncritically, as representing actually inferior Jewish culture. I should stress, however, that this was not a reading favoured or even discussed by anti-semitic detractors of the films. The latter saw the films as promoting a Jewish urban culture that they considered dangerous to the Hungarian nation.

In narrative terms, the presence of a quasi-outsider to the romantic narrative who commented on the romantic plot and offered a secondary, critical perspective established that several simultaneous readings of the same situation were possible, and that conservative, anti-semitic nationalism was perhaps not universally dominant throughout the Hungarian public sphere. The Jewish comedy created a community that 'got' the jokes. In the films, the 'Jewish' character gets the last laugh, and has a privileged relationship to the audiences by laughing at the main plot with them. Audiences, by laughing at traditional society's cultural demands and conventions with the Jewish character, affirmed that a different, more critical way of imagining Hungarian national identity was also possible.

Notes

1 According to his analysis, the commercial, urban, thoroughly un-Hungarian films were generally just as successful in the countryside as elsewhere due to a 'total absence of a consciousness of Hungarian feeling' in audiences. This is the national identity that György believed authentic Hungarian film culture would foster (see György 1934).

2 The Jewish character appeared as the antitheses of the romantic protagonist; it questioned and mocked the beliefs and customs that everyone else seems to accept.

3 By the cabaret's comic style I mean the style that was most often noted and discussed in reviews and debates. Further research on the history of the cabaret will be extremely useful for a more nuanced understanding of how the cabaret functioned in public life. Despite their contemporary popularity with intellectuals and artists as well as the Jewish Budapest public, the cabarets have until now received relatively little critical attention from historians. Although there was, during the socialist 1970s, an effort to rehabilitate the cabaret as a form of 'progressive' politics, much of this effort was focused on the pre-World War I period.

4 See Gluck (2004: 10). The Jewish journalist Adolf Ágai, writing about the historical significance of *Borsszem Jankó*, a humour magazine he edited, stated that the magazine would prove an invaluable tool to historians writing about the age, because 'even if distorted, as in a curved mirror, reality is reflected on [its pages] with the exaggeration of its true qualities' ('Adolf Ágai: A Borsszem Jankó Története' in *Borsszem Jankó* April 10, 1887, p. 11).

5 Imre Farkas, in reference to László Békeffi's performance on the Pódium Cabaret's show, in *Szinházi Élet* March 25th, 1937. Quoted in T. Bános (2008) *A Pesti Kabaré 100 Éve*. Budapest: Vince Kiadó, p. 127.

6 The allusion was to Békeffi's 'Hungarianised' surname (Peaceson, literally) and his Jewishness, which by the mid-1930s was seen as being in conflict with (or even incompatible with) Hungarian identity.

7 After two failed leftist revolutions and in the wake of World War I, Hungary lost two thirds of its territory and forty percent of its population in the Paris Peace Treaty and was profoundly shaken. Conservatives and radical nationalists, dominating public life since World War I, believed that Hungarian national culture could only survive through the restoration of Hungary's geo-political integrity as well as of authentic, Christian national culture and values.

8 This film is *Toroczkó Bride* (Márton Keleti, 1937) which deals with (mistaken) Jewish identity and Hungarian authenticity.

9 These films had great popular success in Hungary in the 1930s and beyond – this brief period is actually known the golden age of film cabaret. Despite being banned under communism, the films and their stars remained cult classics, and they came to form part of national public memory after 1989.

Bibliography

Ágai, A. (1887) A Borsszem Jankó Története'. *Borsszem Jankó* April 10: 11.

Bános, T. (2008) *A Pesti Kabaré 100 Éve*. Budapest: Vince Kiadó.

Gluck, M. (2004) 'The Budapest Flaneur: Urban Modernity, Popular Culture, and the "Jewish Question" in Fin-De-Siecle Hungary', *Jewish Social Studies*, 10, 3, 1–22.

György, I. (1934) 'Magyar Film' *Nyugat*, no. 21. On-line. Available: http://epa.oszk.hu/00000/00022/nyugat.htm (accessed on 5 November 2009).

Kosztolányi, D. (1915) 'Magyar kabaré' Figyelõ *Nyugat*, no 17. On-line. Available: http://epa.oszk.hu/00000/00022/nyugat.htm (accessed on 5 November 2009).

Kovács M. (2006) 'The Case of the Teleki Statue: New Debates on the History of the Numerus Clausus in Hungary' in A. Kovács and M. Miller (eds) *Jewish Studies at the Central European University IV (2003–2005)*. Budapest: Central European University, 191–208.

Zsolnai, L. (1937) 'Sürgősen Állitsák Be a Filmgyártásba a Keresztény Erőket: Hozzászólás a Turul Szövetség Gettófilm Memorandumához', *Filmújság* (17 July).

Storytelling and
Literary and Oral Forms

Third Person Interrupted: Form, Adaptation and Narration in *Tony Takitani*

Chris Wood

Haruki Murakami is a towering literary figure both in Japan and internationally. Critic Yoshio Iwamoto calls him the 'most popular and widely read, if not the most highly respected among the current crop of the more "serious" Japanese writers' (quoted in Kawakami 2002: 309). Internationally, translations of his novels are numerous and his short stories have appeared in high-profile anglophone publications including *The New Yorker* and *Granta*. Aside from a recent adaptation of *Noruwei no mori* (*Norwegian Wood*, 2010), film adaptations of Murakami's work remain relatively obscure. One of the first full-length adaptations was *Tony Takitani* (2004), an adaptation of a Murakami short story of the same name directed by Jun Ichikawa (1948–2008), who alternated between working on feature films and commercials and had won several awards for his previous work including best director at the 1997 Montreal World Film Festival for *Tokyo Yakyoku* (*Tokyo Lullaby*, 1997) and best director at the 1991 Mainichi Film Concours for *Tugumi* (1990).

This chapter is an examination of the process of adapting *Tony Takitani* from text to film. Adaptation is here understood as a mutually constructive process rather than an act of representation. In adapting a text, the film will re-conceptualise the means by which the text is read just as the text more obviously informs the adaptation. This process rests on the difference in medium between text and film and the relationship of the two mediums to the film-as-adaptation and text-as-that-which-has-been-adapted. In this film, Ichikawa plays with narrative positions, interrupting and personalising the extra-diegetic narrator who leads the text. This structural adjustment coaxes out the subjectivity of the characters, giving them space to perform rather than simply be described. Beyond the extra-diegetic narrator, rich use is made of sound in the film to convey internal mental events narrated in the third person in the text. The film also adjusts the temporal character of the narrative. Through the repetition of images and characterisation, the narrative is rendered as less a series of linear events and more the occurrence of one event (the performance of loneliness) from a number of different angles.

Storytelling and adaptation

In his influential study of storytelling, Seymour Chatman describes two distinct levels of what is told: 'story is the content of the narrative expression, while discourse is the form of that expression' (1978: 23). This distinction is certainly useful, but we may wonder to what extent the two remain separate. If the story must necessarily be told through the discourse then it becomes something of a chimera. Access to the story level must come through a discourse and no matter what particular form of realism or proclamations about representation a discourse may claim to carry, it remains a contingent mode of telling. Nothing in it is essential, not even the representative relationship to the story posited above. Interestingly, Chatman has a fairly traditional view of the representative powers of cinema. He writes: 'the cinema cannot *describe* in the strict sense of the word, that is, arrest the action. It can only "let be seen"' (1978: 106, emphasis in original). Cinema, I would argue, describes and arrests at every turn. The filmmaker has control of the visual, sonic and temporal extension of narrative events. In cinema, what is proposed is the means by which what is seen is seen. There is no clear path of representation from the act of recording images to their playback; shot framing, scene length, camera filters, sound design and a host of other apparatuses serve to create a far more immersive environment than either textual or oral storytelling. In this environment, the action is constantly arrested and described over a host of different levels.

In many ways the role of the narrator is similar to the role of filmmaker. The role of narrator can be performed cinematically by the arrangement and timing of shots and cuts. Both the narrator and filmmaker weave a particular impression of a story. By virtue of the indexical nature of cinema, where actors stand in for characters and settings are represented more directly than in text, we can understand the impression created as an impression of reality, even when that reality is the reality of a story. In this way, upon viewing a film adaptation of a story, the cinematic images may come to supersede images derived from the text. Equally it is not uncommon to hear that the cinematic images of a story are not how the viewer imagined them in the text. However, the act of experiencing a visual representation of a story changes not so much the visual images of the characters, but rather exactly *how* the reader imagines the story, in other words, altering the mental channels through which the reader comes to experience the text. At the very basic level a cinematic adaptation gives the viewer a new visual mirror against which to hold the text. It allows the reader options, which they accept, reject or hybridise, and through which they may experience or re-experience what is told. At a more peripheral level, the material paratext is frequently altered. French theorist Girard Genette identifies the paratext as 'what enables a text to become a book and to be offered as such to its readers' (1997: 1). He describes features of the text's physical presentation such as binding, page size, foreword and cover as elements of the paratext. Successful film adaptation can result in a re-printing of the text, perhaps in a paperback edition aimed at the mass-market or introduce further peripheral elements such as a new cover with images taken from the film (or the paratext of the film) or the legend 'now a successful motion picture'. What is relevant, however, is not so much the external changes themselves, but how they alter the cultural conditions the reader negotiates in accessing the text – what makes it into a book or short story. In this way we can understand adaptation as something more than representation; the adaptation of a text into a film is a mutually constructive act which has the potential to fundamentally alter the process by which the original text is read and re-read. What becomes important when studying an adaptation is not so much what is included and what is left out (although that remains relevant), but rather how the space between the author (or the narrator, if used as a proxy) and the filmmaker on one hand and the reader or viewer on the other hand is re-drawn and re-negotiated.

Narrative, narrator and subjectivity in *Tony Takitani*

Tony Takitani depicts the life of a man named Tony Takitani. He is isolated and picked on in childhood because of his foreign-sounding name and thus spends a lot of time on his own, a situation we are told suits his character. From a young age he is proficient at technical drawing and goes on to study art at university, where he finds little in common with the concerns of his politically active classmates and the art they produce. After college he finds work as a technical illustrator and with his modest habits acquires a good sum of money. Through his work he meets a woman with whom he falls in love. In the book she is unnamed, but in the film she is given the name Eiko. She leaves her boyfriend and marries Tony. All goes well in their marriage, apart from the fact that she spends an absurd amount of money on clothes, describing it as something like an addiction or poison (*chuudoku*). She tries to overcome it, but while returning an item of clothing to a shop she is involved in a car accident and dies. Distraught, Tony hires a woman to act as his assistant with the added condition that she must wear his wife's clothes. In the book this woman is again unnamed, but in the film she is given the name Hisako and played by the same actress who plays Eiko (Rie Miyazawa). After Tony shows her the clothes, the woman breaks down in tears. Tony has second thoughts, calls off the employment and has the clothes sold. A year later Tony's father Shozaburo dies. He was a jazz musician who, we are told, spent the war years playing music in Shanghai. Following the war he was imprisoned by the Chinese army before eventually being repatriated. He and Tony had not spent much time together during their lives, but remained on good terms. After Shozaburo's death, Tony stores his father's jazz records and trombone in the house for a while but they begin to weigh on his mind and he has them sold. The book ends here, but the film adds a coda of Tony meeting his wife's former boyfriend by chance and exchanging sharp words with him. The film's final scene shows Tony attempting to re-contact Hisako.

In the text of *Tony Takitani*, the narrator occupies a God-like position, pre-figuring and sustaining narrative events. In the film of *Tony Takitani*, however, this role is re-configured by allowing the characters access to the narrational voice – which, through its externality in the text, renders them into the third person. At numerous points in the film the voice of the external narrator is interrupted by characters who finish his words for him, often accompanied by a change in camera angle from long- or medium-shot to close-up. The medium of film is quite suited to achieving this interruption by virtue of a sonic level of storytelling. The narrator's voice can be clearly and audibly interrupted. A cut to close-up also displays cinema's ability to manipulate the viewer's position in relation to the characters. In text, the change from third to first person lacks the same level of performance.

The French linguist Émile Benveniste identified two orders of language, relevant to this break in narrational position. The first is the *histoire*, a removed, third-person account with no intervention by the speaker. The second is the *discours*, which takes place in the present tense and assumes 'a speaker and hearer, and in the speaker, the intention of influencing the hearer in some way' (1971: 209). Furthermore, as Paul Cobley notes, it is possible to apply this dichotomy to cinematic narration through an analysis of sequence shots in relation to the viewer (2001: 175–8). The overwhelming majority of the shots in *Tony Takitani* fit into the *histoire* category. The viewer is removed from the action by mid- or long-range shots, thus rendering the characters distant and firmly in the third person. In fact this impression is emphasised by the frequent use of highly stylised slow horizontal blended wipes between scenes. This technique places the viewer outside the action, watching events being slowly shifted into one another. One could see this in itself as a kind of paratext analogous to the action of turning the pages of a book (Bowman 2007). Just as the reader becomes aware of their position as a reader every time they have to turn a page, by drawing attention to the apparatus of scene shifting in this way, the viewer is externalised, held outside the action, watching the story being told. With this level of viewer removal, the effect is all the more striking when the *histoire* is broken. As the characters interrupt the narrator and speak directly to the audience and narrator, a shift to *discours* takes place; the speaker has 'the intention of influencing the hearer in some way' (Benveniste 1971: 209). This is a strong break from the text, in which all the narration of action takes place in the third person, described by a voice external to the action. I would argue that this shift takes place because the film seeks to place emphasis on subjectivity by allowing the characters direct access to the audience.

When the characters move to interrupt the narrator it is in an expression of themselves. They feel moved to interject to establish their own presence by speaking as opposed to being established by the narration of another. Kenneth Gergen argues: 'Here I want to propose a relational view of self-conception, one that views self-conception not as an individual's personal and private cognitive structure but as *discourse* about the self – the performance of languages available in the public sphere' (2001: 247).

The characters in *Tony Takitani* are likewise moved to annunciate publicly (to the narrator, to the viewer) something about themselves, a description, a self-conception. The screen is an excellent area within the public sphere in which to perform self-awareness. The focus of an audience's attention is drawn to the screen – the characters are guaranteed an audience for their performance of first-person subjectivity. In his analysis of storytelling, Chatman points to this feature of the screen's existence as a public space:

> Thus, discourse-space as a general property can be defined as *focus of spatial attention*. It is the framed area to which the implied audience's attention is directed by the discourse, that portion of the total story-space that is 'remarked' or closed in upon, according to the requirements of the medium, through a narrator or through the camera eye – literally, as in film, or figuratively, as in verbal narrative (Chatman 1978: 102, emphasis in original).

The use of the screen as a public site of self-performance fundamentally alters the spatial structure of the film. Rather than being removed from the action (as someone hearing and watching the *histoire* as narrated external to the action in both sound and image construction), the viewer is invited to view the characters from a closer camera angle and to hear them annunciate their own self-narration. As Gilles Deleuze notes, the close-up can be used as a means to isolate the face from the space-time of the film (2005: 111), withdrawing the character from the film's temporal flow, or in Chatman's terms 'arrest[ing] the action' (1978: 106). The breaks described above, however, are only ever temporary. The narrator's voice always returns intact for the next piece of extra-diegetic speech. The characters may well intervene at the end of each narration, but this remains a circular process, just as Tony is drawn back to his original position of isolation and loneliness by the end of both the film and the book.

The filmic impression of (un)reality and the use of sound

The characters' narratorial interjections achieve another effect relevant to the process of adaptation. They achieve a disruption of third person, narrated, historical realism, a process recognised as common in Murakami's writing: 'In virtually all of his fiction, with the one notable exception of *Noruwei no mori* (*Norwegian Wood*), a realistic narrative setting is created, then disrupted, sometimes mildly, sometimes violently, by the bizarre or the magical' (Strecher 1999: 267).

Elsewhere, Chiyoko Kawakami cites critic Fukami Haruka as interpreting Murakami's style as the presentation of 'a world that emerges after the 'destruction of meaning' (*imi no hōkai*)' (quoted in Kawakami 2002: 320). It is worth noting that Murakami's writing is also frequently realised from the first-person informal (*boku*), a turn of phrase particularly unusual in Japanese where person is usually understood by the context. As it happens, Murakami's *Tony Takitani* does fit into a realist and third-person-narrated mode. The story is straightforward and is at no point disrupted by strange or inexplicable events. Thus Ichikawa's disruption of the third-person narrator is a strong break from the text. I would argue that, in addition to being an attempt to introduce elements of the characters' subjectivity, this effect can be read as a reference to Murakami's work in general. Murakami is an enormous literary figure in Japan. Many bookstores carry their own sections devoted to his books and books about his books and his work are the subject of vociferous literary debate (see Kawakami 2002). With such an important figure, certain expectations come with making an adaptation, especially in this case where the film is one of the first attempts to translate Murakami's work to the screen. The film does not have to refer only to the specific story being adapted, but also to Murakami as a wider cultural marker. The filmmaker is not just re-telling one story, but also referencing Murakami the brand, with all the assumptions about his writing that that involves. Ichikawa's film comes accompanied by a very powerful paratext. In this way, some disruption of the realist mode is to be expected even if that mode is strong in the specific story which is being adapted, indeed it would surprising if Ichikawa did not nod his directorial head to the wider 'Murakami style'. In turn we can understand the film as an act of contextualising *Tony Takitani* the text back within Murakami's body of work, moving it away from a more realist, narrator-driven mode to a more personal, subjective mode.

Various techniques above and beyond disruption of the narrative voice further work towards conveying Murakami's impression of (un)reality. The impression of reality in a film often rests on spatial and temporal aspects such as the length of a shot, the use of particular cuts between scenes and extra-diagetic sound. Techniques such as these create a sense of space both between the images and between the viewer and the images on-screen. The means of adapting this impression of reality is key to analysing the co-constructive relationship between the text and the film of *Tony Takitani*. Also relevant is the use of sound in the film. Sound and music are constant themes in Murakami's work, references to jazz, classical and pop music appear frequently in his writing to create a particular emotional impression or give depth to a specific character. Likewise in the film of *Tony Takitani* sound plays an important role for the presentation of the story, the film medium allows sounds mentioned in the text to be realised and the relationship between sound, narration and character to be made explicit.

Sound is a key piece of apparatus in the film's treatment of Shozaburo Takitani's time in Shanghai. The establishment of his time there is created on-screen through narration of selected parts of the text. The narration is accompanied by old sepia photographs of street scenes in war-time Shanghai intercut with footage of an old gramophone playing a record. We also hear jazz moving intra-dialectically from the record to soundtrack the photographs. While in the book the Shanghai element of the narrative is treated in the same tone and tense as the rest of the story (third-person past tense), the still photographs give a stark contrast with the full colour moving images of the rest of the film. By locating these events so clearly in the past, the film emphasises memory as a narrational position/strategy. A play is made between the medium of photography and Shozaburo's personal experience of Shanghai. The photographs propose a strong realist/indexical position, giving a space of reference outside the character's personal experience. As the photographic images change into pictures of the war, we see Shozaburo lying in prison. Here the film moves from the external and historical to the highly personal depiction of Shozaburo's war-time experience. In the brief prison scene we see Shozaburo emerge from the shadows of his cell and lie on his side as the narration gives us selected excerpts from the text. The complete text here, although narrated in the third person and external to the character, is very emotionally rich:

> This was the greatest crisis that Shozaburo Takitani had ever faced. A literal hair's breadth separated him from life and death. He assumed he would be dying in this place. But the prospect of death did not greatly frighten him. They'd put a bullet through his brain, and it would all be over. A split second of pain. I've lived the way I wanted to all these years, he thought, and I've slept with tons of women. I've eaten a lot of good food, and had a lot of good times. There's not that much of life I'm sorry I missed. Besides, I'm not in any position to complain about being killed. It's just the way it goes. What more could I ask? Millions of Japanese have died in this war, and lots of them in far more terrible ways than what is going to happen to me. He resigned himself to his fate and whistled away the hours in his cell (Murakami 2007: 227).

In the film no attempt is made to capture every one of these feelings as they run through Shozaburo's head, instead an attempt is made to convey the overall impression of his time in prison. Two photos are used to give the context of Japanese people dying in war (one of a troop of soldiers, the other of an explosion). However, Shozaburo's feelings here are largely conveyed through sound. This mode of narration is more evocative than explicit. We hear Shozaburo whistling before we see him emerge from the background of a shot. A counterpoint to his whistling is given by the shouts of prison guards and the crack of a pistol. The narrator says: 'In that place the boundary between life and death...' before Shozaburo interjects to complete the sentence by saying: '...was as slim as a single strand of hair.' This interjection renders both the effects created by the sound and the third-person narration personal, something at once both internal to Shozaburo and available to us through his annunciation. Conveying thought processes internal to a character is notoriously difficult for film, a medium whose effects often rely on visual recognition of characters' actions. The action here, however, is very minimal. We see Shozaburo emerge from the shadows in the background of a shot and lie down on a blanket. We cut to a closer shot of him lying on his side, he turns to lie on his back, exhales heavily, completes the narrator's sentence and rolls over before starting to whistle again. The use of sound and narrational interjection here creates an impression of Shozaburo's psychology far richer than the visual elements of the scene would allow on their own. The emphasis on the whistling conveys his resignation to his fate as well as giving us a sense of the space of the cell when used as a counterpoint to the distant crack of a pistol. The narrational interjection personalises both the impression created by the sound and the otherwise distant third-person narration.

The performance of loneliness

The film of *Tony Takitani* seeks to alter the narratorial position of the story. While the text is about the trajectory of one man's life which begins and ends in loneliness, the film is more of a meditation on loneliness itself. Loneliness becomes a single event performed by various different characters. This impression is achieved by repetition of characterisation and *mise-en-scène* across various times and circumstances. For example, the scene described above where Shozaburo lies in his Shanghai cell is echoed near the end of the film when Tony, completely alone after the death of his wife and father, is lying in the room of his house that contained first his wife's clothes and then his father's records. In a short sequence of cuts we see first Tony lying on his side in the room, then Shozaburo lying on his side in the cell, then Tony again in the same type of close-up shot as in the earlier sequence. Sound is also important here; we hear the sound of Hisako crying at the sight of Eiko's clothes, meanwhile the narration tells us that this sound is the one thing that sticks in Tony's memory and resurrects the feeling of those events. Once more sound is used to provide a bridge between the internal emotional states of the characters and the external communication of those feelings to the viewer. In fact, this sequence, which revolves around the expressive use of sound and the role of memory does not occur in the book, a fact that is quite telling for the specificity of the technique to both the medium of film and the emphasis Ichikawa places on subjectivity.

A visual setting which is repeated several times is the cityscape outside Tony's office. It is first used as a background to introduce Eiko, later we see Tony, now married, jogging in the same place. Thirdly, in an echo of Eiko's entrance, we see Hisako arriving at the interview against the same background, a repetition emphasised by the fact the same actress plays both characters. All these repetitive devices create a circular impression of time in the film. Time is almost flat; sounds, themes and characterisation are all repeated. In the book we follow the arc of Tony's character from establishment to complete loneliness. The first sentence of the story is "Tony

Takitani's real name was really that: Tony Takitani' (Murakami 2007: 225) and the last sentence reads 'Once the mountain of records had disappeared from his house, Tony Takitani was really alone' (2007: 248). Apart from an initial paragraph describing Tony as a boy, the book does not put events out of sequence. It describes Shozaburo's escape from Tokyo to Shanghai, his return, Tony's birth, adolescence, marriage and the events subsequent to his wife's death. Superficially, the film follows the same narrative trajectory, however repetition in the arrangement of images and sounds, as well as an emphasis on memory conveyed in the extra scenes, fundamentally alter the film's depiction of temporal space.

A repetitive device, played up in the film but absent in the text, is the similarity between Tony and his father. In the book we are told a great deal about Shozaburo's charm, especially his success with women:

> He slept with more women than he could count. Japanese, Chinese, White Russians, whores, married women, gorgeous girls and girls who were not so gorgeous: he did it with anyone he could get his hands on (Murakami 2007: 226).

Elsewhere we are told that despite the passage of time Shozaburo 'had all the tasty treats he wanted, and he always had a woman' (2007: 233). Surprisingly, this aspect of Shozaburo's life, important for his characterisation in the text, is given no space in the film. The only woman mentioned in relation to him is Tony's mother, who, like Eiko, died a short time after their marriage. The repetition of this characterisation and the similarities in composition of scenes featuring the two characters (both Eiko and Tony's mother have their appearances rendered in slow motion) creates a sense of repetition across the two characters and by implication, repetition of the time and space in which the characters are extended. Likewise, despite Shozaburo's being in a cell in Shanghai and Tony being in a room in a suburban house, they are both prisoners, contained by their removal from other people and the weight of their loneliness. In this way time (and narrative as an aspect of time) does not move from A to B, but rather remains fixed in a loop. The settings may shift, but images, sounds and characters remain the same, the only difference being what contextual angle they are viewed from. This in turn feeds back into the subjective, dreamlike feel of the film. This is also relevant for the mode of telling; rather than having the power to drive events, the external narrator's position of authority is reduced to context. Rather than a series of events, we are presented with one event (loneliness) viewed from a variety of different angles and described by both the characters and the narrator, rather than driven by the narrator alone. The event of loneliness is conveyed most strongly through the joint characterisation of Tony and Shozaburo (both played in the film by Issei Ogata), but even Eiko's character alludes to it when she mentions that the act of buying clothes is an attempt to fill a gap inside her. Hisako subsequently realises and performs this sense of loneliness through her tears as she sits surrounded by the shadows her *doppelganger* left behind.

Conclusion

The process of adapting *Tony Takitani* provides rich material for the study of narrative form across mediums. At the most basic level what becomes clear is that film is able to utilise a wide array of sensory tools not available to the writer who must work more conceptually to achieve similar effects. However, the process of adaptation is mutually constructive in that the discourses (the modes of telling) of cinema and text alter and enliven the way in which both are told. In *Tony Takitani* the film narrates events from a different angle, allowing characters access to their own subjectivity, which they perform for those listening and watching (the narrator and an assumed viewer). An adjustment in the linearity of the narrative focuses our attention less on the causal dynamics of who did what to whom at what time, and more on the description and performance of loneliness as told through sound, editing and interruption of the narrator, a process which feeds back into the reader's experience when they return to the text. In this way we can understand the film as a commentary on and therefore an aspect of Murakami's wider work, not merely as a representative mirror held up against it. *Tony Takitani* the film shows the ability of cinema to re-present subject matter, not merely rendering it into a new medium, but allowing the specificity of the medium itself to cast new light and shadow on the comparative modes of telling.

Bibliography

Benveniste, É. (1971) *Problems in General Linguistics*, Trans. M. E. Meek and C. Gable. Miami: University of Miami Press.

Bowman, D. (2007) *Tony Takitani*. On-line. Available: http://www.midnighteye.com/reviews/tony-takitani.shtml (accessed on 17 August 2008).

Chatman, S. (1978) *Story and Discourse: Narrative Structure in Fiction and Film*. London: Cornell University Press.

Cobley, P. (2001) *Narrative*. London; New York: Routledge.

Deleuze, G. (2005) *Cinema 1: The Movement-Image*. London: Continuum.

Genette, G. (1997) *Paratexts: Thresholds of Interpretation*, Trans. J. E. Lewin. Cambridge: Cambridge University Press.

Gergen, K. (2001) 'Self-narration in Social Life', in M. Wetherell, S. Taylor and S. Yates (eds.) *Discourse, Theory and Practice: A Reader*. London: Sage, 247–60.

Kawakami, C. (2002) 'The Unfinished Cartography: Murakami Haruki and the Postmodern Cognitive Map', *Monumenta Nipponica*, 57, 309–37.

Murakami, H. (2007) 'Tony Takitani', in *Blind Willow Sleeping Woman*, Trans. P. Gabriel and J. Rubin, London: Vintage, 225–48.

Strecher, M. (1999) 'Magical Realism and the Search for Identity in the Fiction of Murakami Haruki', *Journal of Japanese Studies*, 25, 263–98.

The Labyrinth of *Halfaouine*: Storytelling and the *1001 Nights*

Stefanie Van de Peer

Férid Boughedir's *Halfaouine* (1990) is one of Tunisia's most famous and favourite films. Although often defined as a simplistic coming-of-age comedy, it defies genre classifications and has been praised and criticised precisely for its deceptive simplicity. In this chapter a more complex understanding of the film will be suggested with a focus on structure and form instead of plot and setting. Taking into consideration the cultural context in which the film was produced and more specifically its oral storytelling devices reveals the intricacies of the narrative development assisted by the power of details and visuals. Storytelling devices used in embedded cycles such as in the *1001 Nights* have become ingrained in North African popular culture; yet their influence on Arab filmmaking is underexplored. An analysis of the oral quality of both storytelling and filmmaking unveils the deceptive quality of simplicity and a more innovative understanding of the structure and form of *Halfaouine*.

The *1001 Nights*, a cycle of centuries' old orally disseminated interconnected stories, written down by numerous scribes worldwide, features Sheherazade, who marries the vengeful Shahriyar in a brave bid to save womankind from extinction. She postpones her death sentence by telling the Shah stories nightly. She continues this for a thousand and one nights and in that time not only gives him three sons, makes him love and admire her and avoids her own death, but she also teaches the Shah that his blind hatred of womankind was destructive to the prosperity of his kingdom. The *1001 Nights* as a whole and in particular individual stories from the cycle are universally embedded in popular culture; Viola Shafik (1998) points out that the *1001 Nights* forms an inextricable part of Arab folk art.

Traces of the original oral diversity of the *1001 Nights* reveal storytelling devices that can be found in the structural and formal elements in Boughedir's *Halfaouine*. These devices include a moral attitude reflected in parallelism and metaphor; fragmentation, repetition, interruptions and embedding with the purpose of postponing conclusions; and the intricacies of detail, visualisation and framing. The film exposes a very rich, complex society within the medina of Halfaouine, where ogres roam the streets searching for boys, stories are a way of life and the division between the sexes is not as rigid and stable as an outside observer might believe. Neither the *1001 Nights* nor *Halfaouine* is in any way realistic in its representation of a historical period. Instead they are decidedly antimimetic and fantastic, a style that has become common and recognisable in Tunisian cinema. Roy Armes points out that after independence Tunisian filmmaking moved away from social realism into pure fiction and magic (2006: 65). In the 1980s and 1990s, personal memory and autobiography took centre-stage. *Halfaouine* is a product of these tendencies. Telling a story orally allows the screenwriter to prototype the story in real time in front of an audience. Techniques of omission, concision, juxtaposition, rhythm and repetition from the oral tradition remain at the heart of screenwriting practice. Cinemas with rich and active traditions of oral narrative are in a strong position to make use of these traditions in creating stories for the cinema, which are not written, but told. Through young Noura's character, the film delves into Boughedir's own experience as an adolescent and the setting – a medina city in northern Tunisia – is typical of many Tunisian films that include fantastical or magical elements, as the space of the labyrinthine medina lends itself perfectly to mystery and the supernatural.

The *1001 Nights* needs to be re-appraised as a representative of its own uniqueness and inconsistencies. Seemingly simple stories reveal great art and profound depth as incredible detail and superficial plot intermingle in almost all texts and tales. I am not suggesting that Boughedir directly based the story and form of his debut film on the *1001 Nights*. Rather, I would like to explore the possibilities for a more complex understanding of *Halfaouine* through an analysis of the structure and the form of storytelling devices offered by the *1001 Nights*. Behind the apparent superficiality so passionately emphasised by Boughedir himself lies a panorama of structural and formal tools that in their turn open up the immense depth of the challenge of transcultural cinema.

Boughedir was influenced by films from West Africa, the simplicity of which hides an entire universe of complex social structures (see Barlet 1998). For *Halfaouine*, he was influenced by Gaston Kaboré's *Wend Kuuni* (1982) and its illusory innocence. He was attracted by the purity of approach and an almost unique way of going straight to the essentials. Kaboré's style of framing countless semi-long shots with a motionless camera is applied here in sequences that last longer than is comfortable and shows more bodies and movement than was acceptable in Tunisia until the 1990s. Equally, Ousmane Sembène taught Boughedir that 'it is what is inside the fixed frame that counts: the movement, the space and the framing' (quoted in Barlet 1998).

Boughedir explains Tunisia's culture along the same lines: there is a ruling 'tendency to synthesize influences [...] transforming them in a nice, happy, moderated way. It's a culture that smoothes off the sharp edges' (ibid.).

The moral behind the story

One of the most pervasive aspects of oral storytelling is the moral behind the story. In the *1001 Nights*, many of the individual stories contain protagonist-focused lessons, but it is Shahriyar who learns the main lesson. However, there is no direct moralising on the part of Sheherazade. Instead, with the intertwining stories, she slowly but surely manages to open Shahriyar's eyes to the parallels between his own and the lives of the characters in the stories. She has found the most productive way of moralising indirectly through thematic patterning or recurrent concepts and moralistic motifs (see Pinault 1992: 22). With the repetition of motifs, plotlines and themes, it therefore dawns on Shahriyar that he is being taught something. Although *Halfaouine* thrives on magic and fantasy, the stories in the film and the story of the film do carry a didactic element for the protagonist. However, the directness of a few lessons forced onto him by his tyrannical father and the Sheikh of the medina do not establish anything fruitful for Noura. Severe punishment and sermonising do not have the desired effect on him.

Instead, the indirect lessons Noura learns from Salih, the medina's *bon viveur*, through observing and imitating what happens around him, are much more effective. As Armes observes, Salih's lessons in seduction are the model for Noura's sexual initiation (2005: 148) but the lessons go further than seduction. Noura turns to Salih for serious advice, and Salih, as wise as he is playful, refuses to lecture him. The first lesson he teaches Noura is impenetrable: 'a man proposes, a woman disposes' sounds as puzzling as the questions in Noura's mind. Instead, Noura learns through Salih's own actions and mistakes. The parallel situations through which the older and younger men go – together or separately – teach both of them about their sexually divided society. Noura also asks Salih 'when does a boy become a man?' and this time Salih plainly refuses to answer: he gestures and says 'my lips are sealed'.

Noura mirrors Salih by having an in-between status in society that allows him to transgress its moral codes. At the end of the film, what Noura has learnt is not how to belong to either the women's or the men's world, but how to be in-between: to be himself without having to be someone else's eyes and mind. As in the *1001 Nights'* frame story with Sheherazade and Shahriyar, the emphasis on parallel instances, metaphors and examples teaches him a lesson learnt through recognition of oneself in others' situations.

Fragmented storytelling

An often mentioned yet underrated structuring device of oral storytelling in general and of the *1001 Nights* in particular is fragmentation and the unfinished nature of the narrative act. In speech, the organic development of an argument can be interrupted by new thoughts and conclusions that make the stream of consciousness decidedly non-linear. These delaying devices postpone the ending of the story. In the *1001 Nights*, Sheherazade applies her own fragmented way of oral storytelling as she wishes to keep Shahriyar focused and curious. The fragmented nature of her stories ensures the continuation of her life. Some fragments, interruptions or anecdotes are vital for the development of the plot; the function of other fragments remains a mystery. Hints and motifs occurring several times in the plot, and particularly in the descriptions or visualisations, prepare the listener and viewer for what is to come. Formal patterning organises events, actions and gestures, giving shape to a story and anticipating the structure (see Pinault 1992: 22). Moreover, they offer a satisfying recognition pattern for audiences, who become participants in the telling. In *Halfaouine* the fragmentation forwards itself in the interruptions and seemingly insignificant anecdotes within the plot.

The most noticeable aspect of these interruptions and of the anecdotal nature of the subplots in *Halfaouine* is that they often come from the women. Like Sheherazade, by continuing to tell stories, Noura's mother tries to postpone time. Both avoid conclusions, perpetuate innocence and naivety, and keep the children safe so that they can avoid the influence of the men's world. The narrative voice therefore is a woman, the embodiment of the metaphoric and magical universe, instigator of the visualisation of the narrative.

Noura's mother desperately tries to postpone his growing up and wants him to remain an innocent boy belonging in the women's realm. She tells him terrifying ogre stories; their visualisations in the film, imagined by Noura, therefore become horrific symbolic instances in which Noura sees the severe effects of the rigidly segregated society of adults. Unbeknownst to her, Noura's visualisations of her stories ensure his inability to belong anywhere as he is terrified of the ogre and his companion, who are trying to 'scrunch' him. The two deformed characters are enacted by friends of his father's, thereby intensifying Noura's anxiety about the men's world.

The visualisations and the mother's stories can be seen as embedding, interrupting techniques that actually add to the fluidity of the development of the narrative. The mother's constant attempts to halt the slow forward movement of the narrative, through fragmentation, interruption, repetition and digression, ensure a slowing down of time. It stresses the momentary, the fluid, wavelike movement of the progression of time, constantly curving back time as it attempts another forward thrust. It transpires that plotline and narrative voices are constantly interrupted, subverted and left unfinished by women.

In order to formally parallel these many interruptions and fragments, the digressions and the repetitions, *Halfaouine* makes subtle use of long takes, slow montage and a fixed frame. These methods slow the narrative down considerably, such as the visualisations of the ogre story and the scenes in the *hammam*, where time seems to stand still and the viewer revels in bewilderment and wonder. In these instances, the camera zooms out slowly, giving the false impression of contextualisation. An important instance when the editing slows down drastically is when Noura turns inward, and he goes to the beach on his own to think. Sitting on a big rock, the camera zooms in on his face extremely slowly. It emphasises the standing still of time during moments of intense inner turmoil and reflection. Equally, the dramatic visualisations of the ogre stories give an intimate insight into Noura's mind. His innermost fears and anxieties about the men's sphere come to life before our eyes. The three instances of dramatic visualisation in the film, with their attention to detail and the absence of a voice-over telling the story or explaining what Noura sees, become individual climaxes within the film's overall development. In storytelling, 'visualisation is always reserved for the heart of the given narrative: the pace of the narration heightens the tension' (Pinault 1992: 25). The intensity of the experience of anxiety and the importance attached to details, colours and parallels in these visualisations are emphasised by the slowing down of the editing. The visual quality, the pacing and the sequence of montage therefore become more important than the actual storyline.

These interruptions fragment the plotline, halt the linear development and distract from Noura's difficulties in his development. A status quo is thus established, and time has not moved on (see Naddaf 1991: 98). The fearful symmetry that results from this 'contradicts and counteracts the forward-moving march of time, which necessitates the kind of change and potential for revolution that the [story] is apparently arguing against' (Naddaf 1991: 108). There is thus no closure, no ending, while orality has proven its potential for endless storytelling and childhood.

The development of the narrative is equally stalled by repetition and imitation in characters, events or descriptions. Not only does Noura socialise himself into the world of adulthood by imitating and paralleling Salih's seduction games, the repetition also establishes itself on a structural level. The polyphonic half-presence of the drunk on the streets of the medina at first seems inconsequential: he simply does not want Noura to collect his bottle in order to receive a few coins of pocket money. This character's 'repetitive designation reappears later to intrude suddenly on the narrative and become significant' (Pinault 1992: 16). Due to the repeated appearances of this figure and his role in Noura's visualisation of the ogre story, the audience recognises the relevance of the drunk/ogre and the anxiety this figure creates. Stories therefore become extraordinary through repetition: they generate recognition and involvement from the audience, while they provide a kind of control over the temporal movement for the teller. Moreover, 'by its very nature, repetition is an attempt to destroy its own essence' (Naddaf 1991: 95); linear time fails in its task of moving the story forward. Storytelling becomes a matter of life or death: kill time or be killed. That there is no satisfying conclusion to the story is a way out of threatening situations because as an involved, active participant in his mother's story, Noura is afraid the ogre will 'scrunch' him if he joins the men's space; therefore stalling time keeps him safe.

Fragmentation and *mise-en-scène*

The setting and descriptions in their turn stall the development of the plot in a formal way. Immediately after the opening sequence in the bathhouse, the camera offers a high-angle long shot, panning slowly over the city, setting the film firmly within the boundaries of this urban space. The introductory shot shows the rooftops and zooms in on the detailed structure of the suburb. As happens in storytelling, it not only clarifies the setting of the film, it also illuminates aspects of the form of the story. The high-angle overview not only shows the vastness of the city, it also shows the walled-in courtyards where the women hang up the washing or do other household work, mostly on their own. It subsequently pans over the mosque, where we see a large community of men praying together. It therefore sets out clearly the compartmentalised division between men and women and between scenes, stories and subplots. These tableaux form the initial suggestion that the *mise-en-scène* reflects the fragmented structure and is dominated by the separation of the sexes. The camera then focuses more clearly on the labyrinth of streets and playfully follows some of the women at the market. While they are walking along the street, the director chooses tracking shots that give the impression of handheld camerawork to follow the girls closely. During this sequence, we see the set-up of the city: separate shops, doors, windows, people looking in on shops and people looking out. The doors and windows serve as frames of their own miniature story within the frame narrative. The tableaux-like set-up of the scene introduces us to the busy market streets where Noura grows up. The playful camera movement highlights the young, male point of view and the handheld impression makes this viewpoint even clearer when Noura joins his older, adolescent friends Mounir and Moncef.

The exotic, unlimited possibilities of the world of the medieval medina offer a vivid background to the stories that are unfolding. The details are so well presented that they become almost tangible and distract from the plot: the *mise-en-scène* becomes as important if not more so than the actual plotline. This again is borrowed from the *1001 Nights*: the 'dazzling and amusing' aspects, colourful gardens, 'houses beyond description, sumptuous material nature of the description and scene setting make the fantasy that is about to unfold more tangible and steeped in materiality' (Sallis 1999: 71). It has been argued (for example by Shafik [1998]) that this could lead to an Orientalist gaze awed by mysterious objects and garments, but it is the fantastical elements of the stories and visualisations rather than the unfamiliar aspect of the materials in the *mise-en-scène* that are awe inspiring. The magic exuded by the medina is moreover experienced through the eyes of a child used to these things, which enhances a certain familiarity and recognition.

Nevertheless, the setting and story unfold in a 'decidedly Islamic milieu' (Naddaf 1991: 110) as the medina is culturally specific and the mosque places it firmly in a Muslim context. This is only relevant in so far as the artistic interests of Boughedir are concerned: the setting as well as the cultural and religious background of the place both serve as the context within which realism and magic easily intermingle. Naddaf explains that, historically, art in the Arab world consisted mainly of abstractions: Islam declares that Allah is the only image-maker, the only creative and shaping being with divine inspiration. Therefore the artist faced a problem with representational art. This resulted on the one hand in antimimetic, non-figurative art – Islamic art – and on the other hand in a constant insecurity about the level of realism in art. The willing suspension of disbelief is destroyed by the interruptive and distracting 'limitations placed on the figurative representation' (Naddaf 1991: 115) which results in a 'countering of the linear temporal progression, thereby suggesting a correspondence with the atemporal, infinite and eternal realm' (1991: 117). The non-development of the narrative is therefore reflected in setting and atmosphere, which are labyrinthine, illogical and unstructured on the one hand and fantastical or antimimentic and unrealistic on the other hand. Once again, the narrative recedes and the technical qualities are foregrounded.

Repetition as a narrative device

In spite of the delaying techniques and fragmentation or interruptions, which boycott or postpone the narrative development, there is a certain degree of forwardness. The repetitive nature of the delaying techniques has its own internal structuring layers: 'what one considers in an examination of narrative repetition is the larger correspondences within the text, the significantly similar though not exact textual recurrences that to a greater or lesser degree make the text cohere' (Naddaf 1991: 60). Ritualistic sequences of three dominate the *1001 Nights*. Although things are repeated, this repetition does not always occur without its own crucial minuscule but no less significant differences. In this respect, three is a strategic number in the narrative structure of *Halfaouine*: Noura tries to achieve his sexual goal with the beautiful housemaid Leila in three attempts, visualises a meeting with the ogre three times and goes to the baths three times. Each time one of these events is repeated, however, minute details change. These details therefore ensure an internal structuring device within the repetitive occurrences, which slowly forces certain aspects of the narrative forward in spite of the women's attempts to prevent this.

Noura visits Leila in her bedroom twice, trying to undress her in her sleep. Each time he tries, she turns while someone entering the room interrupts Noura. She tacitly encourages him by letting him go a little bit further each time. When she later leaves her necklace under his pillow, she gives him the confidence to continue to 'propose'. The third time, she has decided that she is going to 'dispose' – in Salih's words. This set of three sequences changes the dynamics of the male/female sexual relations, and redefines sexual politics through repetition.

The ogre story, as told by Noura's mother, initially serves as a distraction from the physical pain of his father's punishment. He has flashbacks to this image of the ogre three times. The flashbacks are expansions on the initial story: every visual flashback not only very slowly further develops the story within the story, but also alienates the viewer of the film due to the *verfremdung* aspect of this scene and the embedded repetitions, which distract quite forcefully from the plot. Moreover, it explains the implications of understanding womanhood. The fact that the ogre must prick Aïsha with a golden needle because she is a virgin, then follows the blood drops to her house where it turns out the orgre is only interested in 'little boys to scrunch', explains that women bleed, that men such as the butcher and the drunk are dangerous and that Noura is threatened by both genders because they imply adulthood and the loss of innocence. The embedded scene shown parallel to this visualisation is Leila being punished for bleeding onto her bed sheets, which has subtle but crucial implications for Noura's view on womanhood.

The three *hammam* scenes in *Halfaouine* illustrate the changing gaze of Noura and result in his expulsion from the women's space. This marks a social and spatial transition from childhood into puberty instigated by external forces: Noura's slightly older friends Mounir and Moncef, Salih, and Noura's father Azzouz. When the viewer is first introduced to him, Noura's gaze is innocent and observing without being intrusive or obstructive to the women in the baths. Noura has the audience's gaze – he looks with wide eyes, and with him, the audience enjoys the sensual (uterus-like) humidity of the baths and the safety of his mother's hands. The next time Noura goes to the baths this innocent observing gaze has changed: Mounir and Moncef insist that Noura investigate the breasts of the women. Their somewhat older, pubescent point of view of women is different from Noura's, but at this point Noura desperately wants to be accepted by them. Because he becomes their eyes, his gaze changes and when he is found out later on, the familiar and safe female nakedness suddenly becomes forbidden.

The subtlety with which his gaze changes from unobtrusive to invading and offensive illustrates the minute changes the pattern of three goes through to force the narrative forward in spite of the interruptive and fragmenting female forces at work. The development of this gaze can be linked to the art of cinema (Armes 2005: 147), the art of seeing in a different way, the selection of the object and the concentration of the gaze. Noura's gaze develops in three steps: from innocent observation to focused look to spying gaze.

The gaze as a framing device

But the film complicates the use of the gaze. On the surface, Noura seems to be the one through whose eyes the viewer observes the medina, its society and (sexual) fantasies. The camera often rests on Noura's eyes, in a close-up on his boyish face, to reveal innocence developing into a complicit male gaze. Nevertheless, even when his point of view is unmistakeably sexual and sensual, Noura *also* remains the focal point of the camera's gaze. In the second bath scene, the camera takes in what Noura is studying, while it also returns to his face in five quick close-ups. While Noura is observing, being the eyes for his friends, he is in turn being observed by the people around him.

The unrelenting presence of windows and doors also hints at the significance of the gaze. Watching from or spying through windows offers a fragmented view of what is going on outside. On several occasions he is seen secretly listening in on women telling stories or gossip, this always through a window. These windows therefore literally frame the stories he is eavesdropping on. The most interesting instance of a story framed by an ornate window is when his mother first tells him the ogre story. In this instance, the camera moves from her face to the left, to a window decorated with arabesques, through which for the first time the ogre and his companion are visually introduced. The arabesque is one of the typically non-representational (re-)generative Islamic decorative art forms that symbolise the eternal wave of forward and backward movements of the narrative development of the *1001 Nights* and *Halfaouine* (see Naddaf 1991: 119). Windows therefore not only exemplify the importance of the gaze, but also the magical framing of the stories and a dialogue between the inside and outside, between the genders. The slow, subtle transformations in time are illusory: Noura has changed, but he has not become integrated into the men's sphere. As Salih has been arrested and is now absent from his life, even he can no longer serve as an example. If anything, Noura now occupies Salih's in-betweenness, with a vantage point from which to observe the gaps in the world. He may no longer be part of only the female realm, but his mother and aunts have been successful in keeping him away from the rigidly defined men's realm too: he is outside of the female and outside of the male, *and* inside his own personal realm.

In this chapter I have tried to show how the intricacies of the storytelling devices used in the *1001 Nights* help to clarify some of the deceptively simplistic plotline issues in *Halfaouine*. Moralising techniques, elements of the narrative (non-)development and montage, gaze and *mise-en-scène* devices were analysed and paralleled to the *1001 Nights*, demonstrating that when the plot recedes to the background in *Halfaouine*, the storytelling devices and techniques gain centre-stage. Text and film refer back to themselves, instead of to a specific intrinsic plotline that develops slowly out of the myriad of fragments, interruptions, repetitions and detailed visualisations. The success of *Halfaouine* in Tunisia and abroad is therefore not merely due to its breaking of genre expectations and the subversive portrayal of women's bodies. It is most enchantingly a product of its own metanarrative and metafictional intricacies that intrigues audiences everywhere.

Bibliography

Armes, R. (2005) *Postcolonial Image: Studies in North African Film*. Bloomington: Indiana University Press.

_____ (2006) *African Filmmaking North and South of the Sahara*. Edinburgh: Edinburgh University

Press.

Barlet, O. (1998) 'The Forbidden Windows of Black African Film. Interview with Férid Boughedir'. *Africultures*.On-line.Available:http://www.africultures.com/popup_article.asp?no=5327&print=1 (accessed on 1 April 2009).

Naddaf, S. (1991) *Arabesque: Narrative Structure and the Aesthetics of Repetition in the 1001 Nights*. Evanston: Northwestern University Press.

Pinault, D. (1992) *Story-Telling Techniques in the Arabian Nights*. Leiden: E. J. Brill.

Sallis, E. (1999) *Sheherazade Through the Looking Glass: The Metamorphosis of the Thousand and One Nights*. Richmond: Curzon.

Shafik, V. (1998) *Arab Cinema: History and Cultural Identity*. Cairo: The American University in Cairo Press.

'Leaping broken narration': Ballads, Oral Storytelling and the Cinema

Adam Ganz

Writer and director Paul Schrader (in an interview with Mikael Colville-Anderson) has said: 'Screenwriting for me is part of the oral tradition. It's like telling a story. It's not like literature' (1998).

This chapter explores Schrader's contention that the screenplay is an oral medium by looking at it in the context of other oral media, specifically the ballad. Most often screenwriting manuals have used as a model the three-act structure first outlined by Aristotle as applied to, first of all, the nineteenth-century play, and then the classic Hollywood screenplay. Increasingly this model of screenplay structure has come to dominate the teaching and theorising of the screenplay, with writers like Robert McKee and Syd Field coming to dominate the way screenplays are analysed and developed.

I also want to speculate about the relationship between storytelling and the visual and suggest that for screenwriting, considering the ballad – as opposed to the Aristotelian drama – may offer more helpful models for thinking about and analysing screenplays, especially as shifting technology makes the screenplay more fluid and able to change during the making of the film, able to include chance and contingency as well as structure and planning.

In a book which looks at storytelling in world cinemas, it seems appropriate to rethink the relationship between storytelling and screenwriting. For too long one particular storytelling model has dominated the discourse about the screenplay – and more generally, the making of cinema – largely to the exclusion of other forms of narrative, which may be seen as poetic, episodic and much more linked to oral forms of narrative, of which the Scottish ballad series is just one example. The result has tended to be the separation of the story from the teller. As Adrian Martin has written, 'for many reasons, there has been a historical drift towards scriptwriting as an autonomous activity, breaking apart the ideal unity of script conception and screen realisation – an alienation that the current manuals help to reinforce' (1999).

There are many reasons why funding bodies and other gatekeepers of national cinemas might prefer a script-based cinema: as a means of retaining control, as a way of avoiding tackling the more difficult questions of what is involved in creating a national cinematic culture or simply from a desire to see the screenplay as 'literature'. But as digital technologies place the tools of storytelling back in the hands of storytellers, those cultures with strong oral traditions are in a peculiarly strong position to draw on a range of such traditions to make cinematic stories which can be integrated and hybridised with the range of influences from cinema, music and games from within and beyond any given culture.

This link between oral storytelling and cinema can be seen directly in for example Souleymane Cisse's *Yeelen* (1987) which draws on Bambara and Dogon oral traditions, or Zacharias Kunuk's *Atanarjuat, The Fast Runner* (2001) which is based on an ancient Inuit legend. But this is not just about the cinema in cultures with active oral traditions. Schrader's contention is that it is the screenplay itself which is close to the oral tradition. We should therefore acknowledge that the similarity to oral narrative is not only found in non-Western cultures. Quentin Tarantino's *Inglourious Basterds* (2009), for example, is structurally and thematically far closer to the ballad tradition than to literature. Indeed the very misspelling of the title marks out the work as something which is not from a 'literary' or even a fully literate tradition. Tarantino's film, in its borrowings and retellings, its relation to history, to plot and to other films, in its use of music, in the way it focuses on essential moments of action, expanding some, omitting others and compressing meanings, is much closer to the storytelling techniques of oral narrative. Its aim is less to tell a structured story than to create a series of unforgettable and vivid tableaux which are both hyper-real and symbolic, using the audience's active imagination to make these moments come alive in the 'now' of its audience.

The techniques of screenwriting should not be seen as coming from a European dramatic literary tradition but from something which is much older, and both more particular and more universal. Oral storytelling is improvisational, adaptable and collaborative as opposed to the model of the screenplay-as-text, envisioned as separate from the film which arises from it. Moreover, an oral model has the notion of visualisation at its very heart, an active audience complicit in creating the tale both from what the story they are told is and what they imagine as a result.

Ballads are not only oral narratives but rhythmic and time-based narratives which unfold in real time in front of an audience. Many storytelling techniques are shared between the two forms and for this reason I have chosen the ballad as a useful form to analyse.

Ballads: An early poetics of cinema

In January 1914 John Robert Moore, then a young graduate student, published what appears to have been his first academic paper, *The Omission of The Central Action in English Ballads* in *Modern Philology*, as he was completing his MA at the University of Missouri. He was 24 years old. In this paper, Moore attempts to engage with the sophistication which he finds in this form of dramatic storytelling, a sophistication which had not yet been recognised by other literary critics, and which seemed at the time to go against the grain of literary thinking. He is dealing with an unauthored and demotic form and he tries to engage with it. He meditates on the quality of anonymous art. 'In the case of the ballads', he points out, 'not only is the author unknown but the school itself is and in most cases has always been an anonymous one'; the ballads, he continues, constitute 'not merely an anonymous school of poetry but a school of anonymous poetry' (1914: 391, 393).

Moore makes explicit the link between the ballads and contemporary mass culture:

> We see something of the same sort today even now the personal element is everywhere so pronounced. Who writes the articles in a metropolitan newspaper? How many people know or care about the composer when they whistle an air from the music halls? Who makes the jokes of the day which are re-passed from mouth to mouth? (1914: 391)

Moore was undertaking this work at a time when the cinema was just starting to leave its early anonymity. By the time the article was written, the techniques of cross cutting, flashback, point of view and shot/reverse-shot cutting had all been used. What Moore is describing in this analysis about the ballads could be called an early poetics of the cinema. In particular, he makes reference to storytelling techniques of montage and elisions which have come to be seen as 'cinematic':

> In many of the best and most characteristic of the simple ballads, the central action of the story is omitted entirely, or else is withheld to furnish a climax at the end. Sometimes this suspense exists only for the characters in the story. [...] There is little effort on the part of the balladist to attribute speeches to the characters that utter them or to supply transition in the story. Leaping broken narration is characteristic rather than exceptional. (1914: 396)

It is interesting to think about how radical this form of storytelling appeared to a literate and literary culture, at the moment it was starting to re-examine its relationship to the popular and the non-literate and coming to understand that the approaches to literary texts it has at its disposal are no longer sufficient to fully comprehend the new dramatic form which is springing to life. Specifically, Moore recognises that he is dealing with storytelling through inference:

> Not only is the news of the death withheld but in many cases the death itself is to be inferred. [...] Is this omission a stronger device than detailed narration would afford? Obviously it is. The only objection to the method is that it may make the story too vague and obscure if carried to an excess. (1914: 400)

He puzzles over the absence of 'story' as it had been conventionally understood up until that time: 'It is the story which seems to drop out first; it is the situation ... which remains' (1914: 394). Stephen King, the contemporary author whose work has been responsible for more original films than perhaps any other working today, has written that 'plotting and the spontaneity of real creation aren't compatible' (2002: 164). Plot, he calls 'a dullard's first choice. The story which results from it is apt to feel artificial and labored' (ibid.). So instead of starting with plot, Stephen King puts his characters in a situation and likes to 'watch them try to work themselves free' (ibid.).

Moore observes that the ballads, which he recognises as a demotic form, differing from the written literature he has been studying, are nonetheless extremely sophisticated. As the new medium of cinema is beginning to attain its full potential Moore makes explicit the connection between the ballads and emerging modernist forms:

> The simple ballad with its selection of details, with its deliberately chosen situation with its antecedent action implied or but slightly expressed, with its resultant action merely foreshadowed is in close conformity with the modern short-story, the most highly developed form of the narrative art. (1914: 397)

Ballads and visualisation

The ballads always have had a relationship with the visual which goes beyond the vividness of their descriptions. Often balladeers made use of visual material – for example singers of German *Moritat* ballads (referenced by Bertolt Brecht in the *Ballad of Mack the Knife* [1928] – in German *Die Moritat von Mackie Messer*) used *Moritattäfel* or illustrative boards with pictures of key scenes. The singer would point to the appropriate scenes on the boards at the relevant moment. Elsewhere, particularly in Eastern Asian cinema, film became an extension of these links between the visual and oral traditions. In Japan the tradition of *benshi* meant that films were first shown with a narrator, who might use poetry as well as aspects of the *Noh* theatre and *kabuki* traditions to narrate the film to the audience.

But there is a more intriguing relationship between oral poetry and the visual: the importance of imagery embedded within the narrative to aid both the teller and the audience. These themes are explored in an interview with a Canadian balladeer:

> What do singers 'see' when they sing? The idea ... came to me from essays ... by D. A. MacDonald and Vivian Labrie. Both dealt with the way that storytellers could follow the

adventures of their protagonists, as they narrated, as though watching a film or set of slides projected on a wall in front of them … here is Clarence's response, which surprised and delighted me:

MJL: What do you think of when you see that song? Well do you see kind of a picture? In your mind when you sing a song?
CB: Well it's more like looking at a moving picture, or something like that you understand … you'd have to have just a picture in your mind going like a film, to really, really put the right music and everything to it, to do it right.
MJL: So each verse would sort of be a separate sort of a scene?
CB: Yes, it's like a motion picture … And it makes it so much easier if you can picture it. In your mind. And then that you can back it up with the music no matter how high or how low. (Quoted in Lovelace 1985)

The ballad, in performance, conjures up a series of vivid images, which in turn enable the storyteller to recall the ballad as they tell it. In the telling, these images are invoked in the mind of the audience. It is this dynamic invocation of images which is an essential element of oral narrative. Egbert J. Bakker states the difference between the two forms thus: 'the prose narrator fictionalises the act of perception, in order to represent the reality described, whereas presentation on the part of the epic poet is by itself an act of visualisation' (1996: 8). These ideas are also discussed in the work of Elizabeth Minchin: 'The storyteller's language serves as a prompt and a guide to stimulate us to perform the exercise of visualisation and to ensure that the picture which we build up is appropriate' (2001: 142).

Some of the characteristics of oral traditions noted by David Rubin in his analysis of memory in oral traditions are that they:

- exist in genres
- are transmitted in a special social situation
- are entertaining.
- are considered as special speech, either art or ritual
- transmit useful cultural information or increase group cohesion
- are poetic, using rhyme alliteration assonance or some repetition of sound pattern
- are rhythmic
- are sung
- are narratives
- are high in imagery both spatial and descriptive (1995: 8)

All of these apply to a greater or lesser degree to a film text. Other elements which ballads and screenplays share are a single storyteller and a rhythmically controlled dramatic story unfolding in real time with an active audience.

Rubin analyses the purpose of imagery in oral literature and its role in memory. In so doing he singles out some of the distinctive features of the oral tradition as making a narrative which is dynamic, specific and spatial. The role of the spatial in ballads is especially significant. As Rubin points out: 'There are no one scene epics, travel is the rule' (1995: 62). In film, certain genres, like the road movie, are dependent on journey.

This implied presence of the visual in oral narrative clearly has great implications when considering it as a model for writing for the screen. Ballads work with these invoked images and narrative points in a very different, more allusive and inductive way, which can be directly related to how film works with edited images. It seems to be self-evident that film is a visual medium. But this is often ignored in the poetics of screenwriting. Similarly Rubin also looks at the role of sound and music in organising the story. Rather than looking only at structure as an overall event, the use of the ballad as a comparative model for the screenplay allows structure to be considered as something that is constantly developing as ballads do, organising itself to retain audience attention moment to moment.

There are major narrative techniques which we can identify as being common to both genres. These techniques include juxtaposition, multiple interconnected narrative, expansions and contractions of time and omissions of action. Broadly, these can be defined as 'storytelling through editing', juxtaposing different story elements and requiring the audience to find the connection between them.

It is possible to think of editing as the process of asking and answering questions, in which a cut proposes a question about the connection between the two shots which follow each other. The next cut answers this question and poses a question of its own. The ability to cut away from action before it is completed, to leave questions unanswered and deal with a number of simultaneous events which occur in different locations or at different times but are placed in the same story space, are distinctive features both of film storytelling and of the oral tradition. In both film and ballad, the collaboration consists of a series of speculations about the possible relationship between the different story elements. Both forms make use of the audience's active imagination to deduce the story from what they are told. They do not explicitly tell the story; rather they invite the audience to deduce the story, which is created through the audience's active engagement with the story material. As Rubin writes, 'members of a culture have considerable knowledge about the kinds of routine that scripts describe and they can use this knowledge to make inferences and set expectations' (1995: 24).

It is the audience's speculation which enables the story to be recreated. It may be said that these techniques are also used in prose fiction, and to some extent that is true (though I would argue that these techniques are themselves greatly influenced by the cinema). But there are some crucial differences. Firstly, as Bakker states above, oral narrative involves an act of visualisation by teller and audience. Secondly, unlike a novel, where the audience is able to pick up or put down the text at will and explore it at their own pace, the ballad is a time-based medium, with a relentless forward narrative unfolding in real time in the presence of a real audience. As Walter J. Ong (1975) has said, the audience for the novel is always fictitious. In both ballad and screenplay, not only is the audience not fictional, it is required to become an active collaborator in making the story with the teller in real time.

Storytelling techniques in ballads

In a ballad, which has been sung many times, nothing irrelevant or extraneous should remain. It has been tested in the wind tunnel of audience response, constantly being remade in the interface between performer and audience. The text does not (or rather did not until collected) exist separate from its being performed (recited, sung, danced, acted). I would therefore like to look in a more focused way at the storytelling techniques the ballads employ and what kinds of comparison can be made between storytelling techniques in ballads and cinematic techniques and structure. I think that what I am talking about is relevant for oral and written epic poetry and for written epic poetry connected with the oral tradition.

I want to analyse in some detail these techniques in a specific ballad, and I have chosen for this purpose *Lamkin* (*Child 93*), a bloodthirsty revenge tragedy which still has the power to shock. The opening situation which generates the story is clearly and precisely described.

> 93A.1 It's Lamkin was a mason good
> As ever built wi stane;
> He built Lord Wearie's castle,
> But payment got he nane.

The first verse is the seed from which the story grows – 'the inciting incident' as it would be described in screenwriting terminology. Although the tone is apparently neutral, in the opening stanza we are told what the story seems to be about, and what it is not about. The subsequent conflict between Lamkin and Lord Wearie is not about the quality of the workmanship. At the beginning, then, our sympathies are with Lamkin who has been the victim of an injustice, and what immediately follows is the confrontation that arises from this injustice. After this first stanza we are in what Stephen King would call a 'situation'. A man owes another man money and is refusing to pay. We 'cut', from this piece of apparently uninflected reporting, to a dramatised scene in which these two characters argue.

> 93A.2 'O pay me, Lord Wearie,
> Come, pay me my fee:'
> 'I canna pay you, Lamkin,
> For I maun gang oer the sea.'

93A.3   'O pay me now, Lord Wearie,
        Come, pay me out o hand:'
        'I canna pay you, Lamkin,
        Unless I sell my land.'

93A.4   'O gin ye winna pay me,
        I here sall mak a vow,
        Before that ye come hame again,
        ye sall hae cause to rue.'

It is worth noting here that this transition does not need to be explained or described. The audience is able to make a narrative connection between the events, as they unfold rhythmically in real time. Indeed the audience has no choice but to make sense of them. They are not told what is happening; instead they are given the tools to reproduce the conflict for themselves. The first speaker is not introduced but deduced. It can only be Lamkin who is speaking. This is the Occam's razor of story-telling where the simplest solution is the best one. This supposition is confirmed in the subsequent couplet and the argument continues as three times Lamkin asks and twice Wearie refuses.

The rule of three is a well-established trope, identified by Vladimir Propp in his *Morphology of the Folktale* (1928) and Lewis Carroll in *The Hunting of the Snark* (1874). In *Lamkin* each repetition adds story information and prepares the terrain on which the story will be played out. Each version of Lord Wearie's excuse intensi-fies our understanding of the nature of the conflict between the two men and sets up the subsequent developments in the narrative. We learn that Lord Wearie will be leaving the country (and therefore out of reach) and we also learn about his pri-orities. Although there is no description of the two men, the exchange also reveals something of their characters. Wearie is a man of vacillation and excuses. Lamkin is direct and clear.

We learn about Wearie's priorities. He cannot pay without selling his land. The drama introduces elements of class conflict and dynastic obligation – the reason why land cannot be sold, traditionally, is that it must be passed on to the next generation – so the notion of Wearie's heir is subliminally introduced here. And here we see the sophistication of this demotic and pre-literate form. We are introduced to the way the story will subsequently develop without being aware that that is happening. This is the mark of very sophisticated storytelling. As Billy Wilder has said, 'the more subtle and elegant you are in hiding your plot points, the better you are as a writer' (quoted in Crowe 1999: 168).

The confrontation between Lamkin and Lord Wearie echoes a shot/reverse-shot structure. It's like a shoot-out. The word 'pay' is repeated six times in the first two verses, a word which will reverberate through until the end of the story, since it is Lord Wearie's refusal to pay which leads to his being called to account by Lamkin in such an extreme form. At the end of the exchange the word 'pay' is repeated once more, this time accompanied by the threat Lamkin issues, to which Wearie does not respond. Did this conversation happen once? Or on many occasions? It is not important; what is important is that we have left the world of real time and entered the world of narrative time, emotional time. There is a condensation of events. And the scene ends before the action does. The scene is left unresolved – it is through the cut to the next scene that the outcome is revealed.

We are informed of Lamkin's threat and we are left with two linked questions. How serious was the threat and how did Lord Wearie respond? What kind of people are we dealing with here? We discover who they are in what they do. Moreover this information is not imparted directly; instead it is left for the audience to deduce. This technique is an example of what screenwriting books call: 'Action is Character'. The phrase has been traced to screenwriter and novelist F. Scott Fitzgerald (see Bruccoli 1978: 332). We are also starting to establish a multiplicity of points of view and locations.

In time-based media (of which the ballads are a subsection), there are always questions about what will happen and what has happened in relation to what is happening. Here those cross-temporal connections are reinforced by thematic links about ownership and inheritance, which have resonance across the story. To pay for the castle, Wearie would have to lose his status – and that he is not prepared to do. His land – and the social distinction it confers – is what is at stake. In the next verse we see Lord Wearie's response to the challenge: he carries on regardless. There is no description of Wearie's state of mind. We are told what he does; in fact we observe it. And in taking the action forward we meet the next character, his wife. Every piece of story information is introduced dynamically, and we meet characters only as they directly become part of the narrative and are in direct interaction with characters we already know.

> 93A.5 Lord Wearie got a bonny ship,
> to sail the saut sea faem;
> Bade his lady weel the castle keep,
> ay till he should come hame

These lines not only contextualise that the conflict is about the castle, we are subliminally prepared for the conflict to take place in the castle. 'Home' is both the castle and what it contains – family and domesticity. Normally the home is attacked in order to get to the family. In the inversion which *Lamkin* explores, the family is attacked in order to get to the home. This incident contains a moment of unease. By invoking something it proposes the opposite. It reminds us of the castle as the origin of the dispute, and simultaneously, as a symbol of injustice and a place of protection. It is of course full of dramatic irony – since the castle is the only thing that will be 'kept' when he comes home.

93A.6 But the nourice was a fause limmer
        as eer hung on a tree;
        She laid a plot wi Lamkin,
        whan her lord was oer the sea.

93A.7 She laid a plot wi Lamkin,
        when the servants were awa,
        Loot him in at a little shot-window,
        and brought him to the ha.

In these next verses we meet yet another character: Lamkin's accomplice, the nurse. The nurse implicitly confirms the supposition about the existence of a child (although the child is still not explicitly mentioned), reinforcing the implied threat. We are being prepared for a shock which will not be delivered until several stanzas later. And our point of view shifts from Lord Wearie and back to Lamkin. It is this shifting of implicit point of view which is the distinctive quality of filmic storytelling – and which is a major component of the balladic form.

If we analyse these opening stanzas, we can see the narrative strategies used and the different implicit points of view and locations used.

Stanza 1

Location: none specified

Story Elements: exposition; introduction of protagonist and antagonist. Lamkin (L) and Lord Wearie (W); neutral POV

Action: L builds the castle and W refuses to pay

Stanzas 2, 3, 4

Location: none specified

Story Elements: conflict between L and W

Action: repeated demands for payment by L refused by W, L issues threat

Visualisation: unspecific location, but clearly using two points of view, shot/reverse-shot structure

---

Stanza 5

Location: port

Story Elements: introduction of third character Lady Wearie (LW)

Action: W goes abroad and ignores L's threat

Ironic inversion: LW enjoined to keep the castle till L returns

---

Stanza 6

Introduction of fourth character Nurse (N) and implication of fifth, baby (B)

Action: L and N conspire

Contextualisation: a reminder of the absence of W

Stanza 7

> Specific Location (castle)
> Action: L enters the castle aided by N
> Visual elements: L's entry to the Castle, from the inside

We enter the castle with Lamkin and – in a re-echoing of Lamkin's address to Lord Wearie – the rule of three is repeated, and the vow (which concluded the first rule of three) is made real. Lamkin is in the house, which he built, active and seeking revenge. What one would expect to be dramatic revelation or development is simply omitted. We are not party to his thoughts or his intention. The characters in the ballads, like those in film, rarely soliloquise. They act.

If we consider the first sequence to be shot/reverse-shot, this second is a more complicated sequence; in addition to Lamkin and the Nurse, the montage would include long shots of the different groups who are unable to help, confirming the isolation of the castle and those within it. They also indirectly show the power and wealth of Lord Wearie, and the extent of the lands he refused to sell.

At a moment of high drama, Lamkin asks the nurse rhetorical questions which emphasise the helplessness of Lady Wearie, and which deliberately slow down the narrative. But the very lack of action in this sequence means the change of pace which comes after the fourth stanza, 'we soon can bring her down' – which concludes and transforms the three verses preceding it – is all the more shocking. Moreover it is given an unforgettable visual equivalence, which acts as a powerful marker for teller and audience alike.

> 93A.13 Then Lamkin he rocked,
> and the fause nourice sang,
> Till frae ilkae bore o the cradle
> the red blood out sprang.

This visual image works on many different levels. Lamkin and the Nurse, singing and rocking the child with the blood pouring out at every corner of the cradle and ignoring the child's pain (which they have created), are the present false parents who are contrasted with the absent true parents who are also to some degree complicit in the child's suffering. And there is a third complicit absent present at the scene – the audience. We long to stop the child's suffering, and cannot. Instead we are forced to enjoy our complicated pleasure. We are in the room with the screaming child and those that are harming it. We are powerless. We are forced to know the awful secret of the fate of the child which the mother is excluded from. We see what she can hear. And it is this difference between seeing and hearing which gives rise to the subsequent question and answer scenes. In the confrontation between Lamkin and Lord Wearie culminating in Lamkin's vow of revenge, which concluded the fourth stanza, the men were confronting each other aggressively and face to face. The two women cannot see each other and are apparently friendly, but there is an enormous and terrifying difference between them which we, the audience, are party to. Dissembling is at the very heart of the scene. And we are present, complicit, in a scene familiar from numerous horror films. We know something terrible, which the victim does not, yet.

Lady Wearie is on the stair,s halfway between above and below. Though she cannot see what goes on, she is compelled to hear it. The difference between seeing and hearing is made terrifyingly apparent here. Hearing is speculation. Seeing is confirmation.

In the dialogue we are given an ironic reference back to the first conversation, and the reason for the conflict: 'he will not still for all his father's land'. If that first conflict ended with an ominous separation of the two participants, the second ends with a horrific coming together, building to the unbearable moment when Lady Wearie will be compelled to see with her own eyes what we have already visualised on her behalf: her dying child. And then that revelatory scene, which we have also already visualised, and which we are both anticipating and dreading, does not occur. We are faced, again, with uncompleted action. The story is moved on through a cut. Her decision to come down is expressed in her movement.

> 93A.18 O the firsten step she steppit,
> she steppit on a stane;
> But the neisten step she steppit,
> she met him Lamkin.

> 93A.19 'O mercy, mercy, Lamkin,
> hae mercy upon me!
> Though you've taen my young son's life,
> Ye may let mysel be.'

Here is an extraordinary shift of time – which is utterly filmic in its complexity and in the shifts of perspective and understanding it involves. In verse 18 she is on her way to see her dead child. In verse 19 she has already realised his life has been taken, and she is pleading for her own. All this happens in the gap between the verses, 'offscreen' so to speak. Any description of the key moment of this sequence, perhaps of the whole drama, is omitted. Between verses 18 and 19 Lady Wearie has moved from innocence to knowledge. She has realised that her son is dead and that her own life is at stake. The most significant change of all is that her position relative to the narrative and the audience has changed. From knowing less than us she knows more. And the question we were asking, how will she react when she discovers the terrible news?, has been replaced by another: will she live or die? And that has all been imagined in a breach, an absence, a moment of silence.

There now follows a very rapid unfolding of the story. Lamkin asks the nurse whether Lady Wearie should live or die, and in a reassertion of the class aspects of the drama, she is condemned to death because of the way she has treated her servant.

93A.20 'O sall I kill her, nourice,
   or sall I lat her be?'
   'O kill her, kill her, Lamkin,
   for she neer was good to me.'

93A.21 'O scour the bason, nourice,
   and mak it fair and clean,
   For to keep this lady's heart's blood,
   For she's come o noble kin.'

93A.22 'There need nae bason, Lamkin,
   lat it run through the floor;
   What better is the heart's blood
   o the rich than o the poor?'

And again we leave the scene before this act of violence is consummated. The murder of Lady Wearie, like that of her child, does not occur on screen. We leave the action not on the death, but on the decision to kill. Instead we cut to three months later.

93A.23 But ere three months were at an end,
   Lord Wearie came again;
   But dowie, dowie was his heart
   when first he came hame.

And it is not until this 23rd verse that we find the first piece of emotional description in the piece. Lord Wearie's heart is 'dowie' (sad).

93A.24 'O wha's blood is this,' he says,
   'That lies in the chamer?'
   'It is your lady's heart's blood;
   'tis as clear as the lamer.'

93A.25 'And wha's blood is this,' he says,
   'That lies in my ha?'
   'It is your young son's heart's blood;
   'tis the clearest ava.'

This moment shows the primacy of the visual in the storytelling. Clearly it is not in any sense 'realistic' that three months after the death, the blood was left for Lord

Wearie to examine. What this achieves is to make the exposition both dynamic and dramatic. What of course he is being asked to do is to confront the consequences of his own actions. The coming together of the blood with the building, whose construction led to this violent conflict, is expressed visually and symbolically. The two exchanges of question, and without the third we have come to expect from previous occasions, remind of us of incompleteness and loss. A reversion to normality is impossible for Lord Wearie now his wife and son are dead.

The final two verses conclude the story with, like the end of Alfred Hitchcock's *Psycho* (1960), a deliberately downbeat ending. They tell us that the killers faced justice – of a kind. By contrasting the death of Lamkin and the Nurse with the two birds who continue to sing after their death, our attention is drawn to the persistence of art, and to the ballad itself.

Conclusion

Stanley Kubrick has said 'a film is – or should be – more like music than like fiction. It should be a progression of moods and feelings. The theme, what's behind the emotion, the meaning, all that comes later' (quoted in Kagan 1989: 231). If we see film as like a ballad, we can conceive of many different forms of envisaging and recording the 'pre-film' process. We can think of its origins as originally written (as for example Rudyard Kipling's *The Ballad of Danny Deever* [1890]), we can think of it being a set of structured improvisations, given shape after recording, like Teo Mancero producing Miles Davis's *Kind of Blue* (1959), we can think of it as a retelling of a familiar story (like Davis's reinterpretation of *Someday My Prince Will Come* [1961]). What all these models have in common is that the ultimate focus is on the unfolding of a story in real time in conjunction with an audience. It does not see the writing and the telling as two separate practices but as one.

It is the nature of storytelling to improvise, to patch together, to juxtapose, in order to make its meanings. Rather than separating the screenplay from the film, we should see that it is the nature of storytelling to borrow and steal, to merge, to bring together, to combine. Any attempt to separate the tale from the teller does a disservice to both. As technology makes cameras almost universal, we can see the written screenplay as a form of notation – a necessary stage on the way to the creation of a film at a particular historical moment. As with recorded music, the relationship with the notation fundamentally changes when technology allows the work to be recorded directly. Notation allows different kinds of screenplays to be written as they allow different kinds of film to be written.

As Adrian Martin has said: 'Scripts, of course, are very important, though they're not necessarily the most important things in a movie. What's important in a movie is the movie. It's the cinema' (quoted in Michaels 2009: 28). Telling a story orally, as Schrader does, allows the screenwriter to prototype the story in real time in front of an audience. Techniques of omission, concision, juxtaposition, rhythm and repetition from the oral tradition remain at the heart of screenwriting practice. Cinemas with rich and active traditions of oral narrative are in a strong position to make use of these traditions in creating stories for the cinema, which are not written, but told.

Bibliography

Bakker, E. J. (1996) *Mimesis as Performance: Rereading Auerbach's First Chapter*. On-line. Available: http://www.philo.umontreal.ca/textes/Bakker_mimesis.pdf (accessed on 4 November 2009).

Bruccoli, M. J. (ed.) (1978) *The Notebooks of F. Scott Fitzgerald*. New York and London: Harcourt Brace Jovanovich/Bruccoli Clark.

Crowe, C. (1999) *Conversations with Wilder* New York: Alfred A. Knopf.

Kagan, N. (1989) *The Cinema of Stanley Kubrick*. New York: Continuum.

King, S. (2002) *On Writing*. New York: Pocket Books.

Lovelace, M. (1985) '"Down by this Laney Side": Clarence Bloise, Farmer and Singer', *Canadian Journal for Traditional Music*, 13. On-line. Available: http://cjtm.icaap.org/content/13/v13art2.html (accessed on 9 December 2009).

Martin, A. (1999) 'Making a Bad Script Worse: The Curse of the Screenwriting Manual.' *Australian Book Review*, April 1999. On-line. Available: http://home.vicnet.net.au/~abr/April99/mar.html (accessed on 9 December 2009).

Michaels, O. (2009) *Expanded Screenwriting, Expansive Cinema*: A review of *Screenwriting: History, Theory and Practice*, Steven Maras, Wallflower Press. RealTime issue 91, June-July, p. 28. On-line. Available: http://www.realtimearts.net/article.php?id=9467 (accessed on 24 August 2009).

Minchin, E. (2001) *Homer and the Resources of Memory*. Oxford: Oxford University Press.

Moore, J. R. (1914) 'The Omission of The Central Action in English Ballads', *Modern Philology*, 11, 3, 391–406.

Ong, W. J. (1975) 'The Writer's Audience is Always a Fiction', Publication of the Modern Language Association, 90, 9-21.

Rubin, D. C. (1995) *Memory in Oral Traditions: The Cognitive Psychology of Epic Ballads and Counting Out Rhymes*. Oxford: Oxford University Press.

Schrader, P. (1998) Interview with Mikael Colville-Andersen, 09 October 1998. On-line. Available: http://zakka.dk/euroscreenwriters/screenwriters/paul_schrader.htm (accessed on 25 May 2009).

Rethinking Storytelling
Forms in African Cinemas

Storytelling in Contemporary African Fiction Film and Video

Lindiwe Dovey

> *Every continent has its own way of telling stories.*
> – Senegalese film director Moussa Sene Asba

In 2009, a United Nations Educational, Scientific and Cultural Organization (UNESCO) report hailed Nollywood, Nigeria's home video industry, for overtaking Hollywood to become the world's second largest film producer. Nollywood has also 'closed the gap' on Bollywood, the world's largest film producer, with the former producing 872 films in contrast to the latter's 1,091 films in 2006 (UNESCOPRESS 2009). Nollywood is now Nigeria's second largest employer (*Peace Mission*, 2008), and has an annual turnover of more than US$150 million a year (*Nollywood Babylon*, 2008). However, the figures associated with Nollywood, although undeniably impressive and frequently cited, are perhaps the least interesting dimension of this industry. The ways in which Nollywood's powerful storytelling has captured not only the Nigerian audience but also audiences all over Africa and in the African diaspora are what merit much further exploration. Notably, the films are overwhelmingly popular in spite of their 'disjointed storylines', and the fact that the average Nollywood film is shot on a miniscule budget (averaging about US$10,000) in less than two weeks from a 'hurriedly written script' (Oguine 2004). In this context, then, disjointed storylines and quickly constructed scripts do not necessarily have the ability to sabotage the attraction of other elements of storytelling. The typical formula for success in Nollywood, according to Ike Oguine, is 'bold storytelling, a good dose of "black magic", and quick and easy distribution by video' (ibid.).

The popularity of Nollywood and its hold over the imagination of Africans in diverse contexts has brought about something of an impasse in African film studies, which has traditionally focused on 'African Cinema', constituted of 'art house' films that play at the large African and international film festivals, and which have conventionally been made on celluloid film stock rather than video. 'African Cinema' first appeared in 1963, the year in which the Senegalese director Ousmane Sembene produced the first film by a sub-Saharan African on African soil, *Borom Sarret*. In terms of its content, 'African Cinema' is widely seen to be a truly postcolonial cinema, engaging the history of colonialism, postcolonialism and neo-colonialism in Africa. Members of FEPACI (the Federation of African Filmmakers) initially insisted that this cinema be ordinary rather than spectacular in its aesthetic style, and pedagogical rather than commercial in its aims (see Diawara 1992). On the other hand, the digital commercial video films made by Nollywood (and other video film industries throughout Africa) have been seen, by many African film critics at least, to invoke unsavoury content, such as witchcraft, adultery, negative representations of women and excessive violence; to be of poor aesthetic and technical quality; and to compromise 'serious' African art owing to their commercial aims (see Anyanwu 2003; Popoola 2003).

Whereas the first films in the corpus of 'African Cinema' have been described as the 'child of political independence' in Africa (Cham 1996: 1), the first video films can, to some extent, be seen as the disillusioned offspring of the postcolonial period, with its failure to bring about real social and economic independence for the vast majority of people, as well as freedom from the constraints of neo-colonial financial institutions, African dictators and government corruption. The filmmakers of the documentary *Nollywood Babylon*, Ben Addelman and Samir Mallal, certainly suggest that the popularity of Nollywood is largely due to ordinary people's need for escapist and therapeutic narratives in the context of harsh and difficult lives. They suggest, via interviews with Nigerian scholars, that the video industries work in parallel to the Pentecostal Christian churches in that they both operate as 'therapeutic agencies'. These 'agencies' are seen to wrest blame for the disillusioning narratives of many people's lives from the people themselves and to lay this blame at the feet of occult or powerful forces; in opposing these forces in their narratives, the video films provide redemption, just as the churches offer redemption through Christ.

There are other narratives, however, that might be harnessed to explain the popularity of the video phenomenon in Africa. Video filmmakers largely hail from 'Anglophone' parts of the African continent that were colonised by the British and which were left, unlike the ex-French colonies, with scant funding in the wake of independence. When their governments showed no sign of being willing to support filmmaking, these filmmakers (many of them untrained) simply decided to pick up video cameras and fund themselves.[1] In this sense, the video films might also be seen as a response, if only a subconscious one, to 'African Cinema', which has largely been funded by the French Ministry of Foreign Affairs (formerly the French Ministry of

Cooperation) and other international funding bodies (such as the World Cinema Fund at the Berlin Film Festival and the Hubert Bals Fund at the Rotterdam Film Festival). This response has a political dimension to it, seeking autonomy for African film production. Whether this autonomy in funding structures has led to autonomy of perspectives in storytelling, however, is a separate issue. As Ngugi Wa Thiong'o has argued, while 'there has to be a decolonising of the economic resources' behind African filmmaking, 'decolonisation of the mental space has to go hand in hand with that of the economic and political space' (2000: 93). Some African scholars and African filmmakers have accused the video filmmakers of being racist in their figuring of certain characters as barbaric witches or monstrous murderers; certainly, Western viewers might recall Joseph Conrad's notorious line 'the horror, the horror' from *Heart of Darkness* (1899) when confronted with the violence in some of the video films which, while no more gory than Western horror films, play into old stereotypes of black Africans as bound to 'primitive', pre-modern modes of being – stereotypes which filmmakers in the 'African Cinema' tradition have long and consciously worked against. A question that needs to be addressed, then, is whether the video films are an instance of the 'subaltern speaking back' to the elite that attempts to speak on its behalf but is not in touch with its own imaginary and iconography – indeed, with its own *stories* – or whether the films are symbolic of the postcolonial state which 'is still suffering from all the colonial scars in its collective psyche' (Wa Thiong'o 2000: 95).

In this chapter, I want to explore this question through considering the content, forms and functions of African video films, while offering (limited) comparative analysis with the content, forms and functions of 'African Cinema'. Given the fact that a 'canon' of African video films has not yet emerged (and perhaps may not emerge, given the much faster production and consumption of video films compared to 'African Cinema'), my sample of video films is entirely random. My analysis, then, is not intended to be representative, but rather suggestive of the possibilities of drawing 'African Cinema' and video films into the same critical frame.

The power and performance of storytelling in Africa

Although video filmmaking in Africa would appear to approximate forms of popular culture anywhere else in the world (with many similarities, for example, with the Hollywood and Bollywood industries), it differs from these other forms in terms of its low aesthetic quality, something which audiences elsewhere would not be likely to tolerate. This seems to signal a different relationship to storytelling in the African (and diasporic African) context. As Nigerian video scholars Jonathan Haynes and Onookome Okome point out, 'audiences seem not to mind [the poor audiovisual quality of video films], being interested mostly in the *stories* the videos tell' (1997: 23–4; my emphasis). This suggests yet another narrative in terms of explaining the popularity of the video films, one that contradicts the idea that there needs to be a harmonious 'marriage of form and content' in African filmmaking (Wa Thiong'o 2000: 93). In Haynes and Okome's view, the stories in the video films shine through the grainy images and inaudible or inappropriate soundtracks.[2]

Certainly, the sheer importance of storytelling in diverse cultures across Africa cannot be denied. While the person (or persons) telling or performing the story differs greatly, from the *jeli* (*griot* or storyteller) in West Africa to the stories of a Zulu *gogo* (grandmother) in South Africa, communal oral storytelling is very much alive, unlike in the West, where it has virtually disappeared. Furthermore, in sub-Saharan Africa one finds, in addition to the oral tradition, songs imparting stories (see Scheub 2006), dance conveying narrative meaning (as in Zimbabwean writer-filmmaker Tsitsi Dangarembga's short film *Kare Kare Zvako* [2006], or in Senegalese filmmaker Joseph Gaï Ramaka's *Karmen Geï* [2001]), and the visual arts expressing narrative (see Winberg 2001). As Moussa Sene Absa says, film music is 'un trame narrative' (a narrative plot), 'un complément d'histoire' (a complement to the story), and he therefore always thinks about the development of his film soundtracks simultaneously to writing the film script (2003). Similarly, South African screenwriter Bhekizizwe Peterson has drawn attention to the fact that the narrative of the film *Fools* (Ramadan Suleman, 1997), which he co-wrote with Suleman, 'invokes the call and response patterns in African music and jazz. A theme is introduced, elaborated and then repeated in different ways. It's about looking at different facets of the same thing' (quoted in Bester 2004). Ian Rijsdijk and Adam Haupt (2007) have made a similar argument about the way in which music conveys much of the implicit narrative meaning of the South African film *Tsotsi* (Gavin Hood, 2005). Storytelling and the non-narrative arts are thus frequently brought into contact and inflect each other in myriad ways in a range of African contexts, revealing the close connection between storytelling and performance on the continent. The importance of storytelling is also evident when one considers that, although there has been a strong tradition of self-reflexive, counter-narrative films in North Africa that are influenced by the rhythms of Arabic poetry (for example, Algerian writer-filmmaker Assia Djebar's *La Nouba des femmes du Mont-Chenoua* [1977] or Tunisian film director Taïeb Louhichi's *Laylâ, ma raison* [1989]), many films made in sub-Saharan Africa have a strong storyline, regardless of the format in which they are made.

The centrality of storytelling is, of course, universal and it is one of the ways in which we as humans make sense of the otherwise disparate events and disjunctive nature of our lives (see Ryan 2001). However, whereas in many Western contexts, storytellers have increasingly become distanced from their audiences as a consequence of 'mechanical reproduction' (see Benjamin 1935), in many African contexts producers of narrative have tended to remain close to their consumers (Barber 2000: 5). It is therefore difficult to speak about storytelling in such African contexts independently of audience – the audience members are, in part, the storytellers, or they determine the nature of the stories. The popularity of African films certainly does seem to rely partly on the degree of 'closeness' between a filmmaker and his/

her audience. Ousmane Sembene has spoken of his need to remain close to his people, and after studying filmmaking in Moscow, he returned to Senegal to set up his own production company, Filmi Doomirew (see Murphy 2000). Unlike many other filmmakers of the 'African Cinema' tradition, Sembene continued to live in Senegal throughout his life rather than basing himself in France. This perhaps explains the popularity of his films in Senegal during his lifetime.[3] Many African video filmmakers also work within their local environments and have spoken of how their films reflect the desires of their audiences rather than their own beliefs. Filmmakers and audiences are thus both to be read as 'storytellers' in the context of African filmmaking.

Nollywood stories

The stories of Nollywood films are increasingly diversifying, evidenced by the wide range of genres of films advertised on Nollywood rental sites, which include action/thriller, Christian, comedy, drama, family/kids, history, horror, mythology, romance and war. Nollywood films have also dealt with serious issues around migration (for example, *Osuofia in London* [Kingsley Ogoro, 2004]), the epic past (see Meyer 2010), the traumas of war (for example, *Across the Niger* [Izu Ojukwu, 2005]), and the corrupting nature of power (for example, *Arugba* [Tunde Kelani, 2008]). The films that conform more to Western standards of production and that tackle issues more compatible with Western tastes are being incorporated into the film festival circuit, and certain directors, such as Kingsley Ogoro, Ladi Ladebo and Tunde Kelani, are being touted as those filmmakers who will 'take Nigeria to Hollywood' (AFI Silver 2006). While the diversification and 'development' of Nollywood was inevitable and anticipated, the creation of a canon of 'serious' intellectual Nollywood directors and the co-option of Nollywood into the film festival circuit risk overlooking some of the vital elements of what initially made Nollywood so popular in its own territory. As Birgit Meyer (1999; 2003; 2010) and other scholars have emphasised, and as Oguine points out in the quotation above, the stories in Ghanaian and southern Nigerian films with strong doses of the occult (or 'black magic', to use Oguine's contentious term) have had a particular hold on the popular imagination. These occult forces are banished in the narratives of many of the films via Pentecostal Christian practices (see Meyer 2003; Ukah 2003) in scenes that are often a source of amusement for secularised, Western audiences.[4] Such scenes have received descriptive (see Meyer 2003) and prescriptive (see Popoola 2003) responses from scholars, with some scholars suggesting that the battle between occult and Christian forces dramatises alternative modernities and the imbrication of magic and modernity in Ghana (see Meyer 2003), and, and with others arguing that although 'Pentecostalism speaks the language of traditional worldviews in terms of the emphasis on occultism, it is harnessed to a project of a Westernised system of commodity consumption' (Ukah 2003: 203).

The latter response highlights a second defining feature of the films that initially brought Nollywood widespread popularity: Nigerian-inflected 'rags to riches' stories. There has been much debate about whether the opulent wealth displayed in many of the films offers critique or approval of this wealth. While many of the stories possess a strong moral message that critiques material gain by occult ritual means, one scholar has argued that

> the stated moral intent of the films is to present a form of bad behaviour in order to discourage people from engaging in it, yet more than anything else the video-films validate the efficacy of rituals in the way and manner that the characters in the filmed 'rituals' are portrayed: fabulously rich and successful. (Okwori 2003: 7)

Perhaps too much scholarship has concerned itself, however, with the moralising stories (and imagined effects) of video films, and not on how these stories are hitched to questions of the audiovisual *medium* of film and its relationship to storytelling.

Mediums of storytelling

One of the definitions of 'medium' provided by the Oxford English Dictionary is 'a person claiming to be in contact with the spirits of the dead and to communicate between the dead and the living'. This definition is particularly pertinent to the medium of film/video in contexts where spectators may believe in the existence of the spirits of the dead. Here the medium of film/video is more than the 'intervening substance through which impressions are conveyed' (Oxford English Dictionary); it offers a 'revelation' (see Gabriel 2000: 97; Meyer 2003: 222) in the literal sense – the manifestation of the invisible as visible. In this sense, in these contexts, the audiovisual film medium itself becomes situated as a medium *of* magic, not simply a medium *in* which magic might be shown. Here the sensory human pleasures of seeing and hearing (in particular, seeing) are coupled with particular belief systems in which the film medium may be thought to make manifest the invisible realms.

Notably, such contexts are not restricted to certain places within Africa, but can be found globally. For a film scholar based in the West, the importance comes in recognising that the stories of the video films are not contrary to Western values in their representation and confirmation of occult and magic forces. As Meyer argues, the 'magic' in many video films simply 'realizes the magical potential of movies that is so often ascribed to this art form in the West' (2003: 203). Furthermore, as John Micklethwait has revealed in his *Economist* article 'In God's Name' (2007), a form of spiritual rationality in the exercise of politics is on the ascent not only in Nigeria, but everywhere in the world. Similarly, Hent de Vries has argued that the West has witnessed a resurgence in religious belief, 'the "return of the religious" within the geopolitics of "secular" modernity and its globalization' (2001: 23). De Vries' work is of particular relevance to this chapter in that he explores the 'interfacing of the religious and the medium, the theological and the technological' (ibid.). He does so through a focus on the relationship of 'miracles' to 'special effects', and he summons the magic of the film medium through positing that, perhaps, a miracle is a 'special effect', resembling the 'special effect' not only formally but also phenomenologically (ibid.). While providing the example of the *deus ex machina* in Greek literature (2001: 24), de Vries gives no cinematic example. His theory of the proximity of the miracle and the special effect can be productively applied, however, not only to the video films (which take and offer great pleasure in special effects), but also to many other films, both African and non-African.[5] The question thus arises as to how distinct Nollywood's spiritual anxieties, and investments in the material and audiovisual medium of film, are.

In cultures that have historically been more oral than visual (as in many African contexts), the relationship between sight, sound and the invisible becomes even more complex. Frances Harding makes an important connection between the video films and *fabu*, a term used to designate word-of-mouth stories and rumours; *fabu*, she points out, 'often focus on one mystery in particular: the changes in the lives of individuals which take them from poverty to wealth by *unseen* methods ... by means of exchanges and dealings *invisible* to the ordinary person' (2007; my emphasis). Thus, she notes that,

> Evidenced in visual, material features such as dress, cars, housing, furnishings, social behaviour, such manifestations [in the films] are part of the daily gossip of real people. Such features and behaviour are reiterated and re-presented in the characters in the video movies. The press – newspapers, radio, television – record strange happenings, strange disappearances and – whether they dismiss or believe them – people absorb them as part of the round of 'urban myths'. This is what constitutes the fabulous stories, the 'fabu' of conversation and incipient belief. The video movie gives the 'fabu' material, visual form. This form confers in turn, reality, on the fabulous, fantastical fiction. (Ibid.)

A particular kind of adaptation and visualisation of oral and spoken narratives is thus at work in the video films; rather than reading the video films only in relation to 'reality', then, what is required is an acknowledgement of their position within complex local and global webs of intertextuality and cultural transformation (see Dovey 2012). For not only are the video films engaged with local sources, such as 'fabu', Yoruba travelling theatre and Onitsha market literature, they are also in conversation with Latin American soap operas, Bollywood film and Hollywood film. That one finds video films titled *Sharon Stone* (Adim Williams, 2002), that the first Ghanaian video film (*Zinabu* [William Akuffo, 1985]) is an adaptation of H. Rider Haggard's novel *She: A History of Adventure*, and that one can find significant parallel scenes in Samuel Selvon's novel *The Lonely Londoners* (1956) and Kingsley Ogoro's *Osuofia in London*,[6] highlights the diverse sources of Nollywood stories. One can only imagine that the exogenous sources of Nollywood films have not received sufficient attention in the scholarship because they would seem to contradict characterisation of Nollywood as an autochtonous and autonomous cultural industry.

Telling stories

According to Haynes, Nigerian video films 'contain none of the visual poetry of true cinema. But in the aggregate they contain a staggering amount of narrative energy. Only the daily press rivals the videos as a medium for telling the story of Nigeria in the 1990s' (1997: 9). And yet, in both 'African Cinema' and the video films, storylines tend to be inflected by what might be called 'delayed temporality', resulting in a form that approximates the non-narrative rhythms of poetry or orature rather than prose. Many video films exploit their *mise-en-scène*, employ long takes, include connective scenes that are not intrinsic to the narrative (often involving characters driving from one place to another) and hold on a shot for a few seconds after the characters have departed. These types of storytelling techniques or strategies are not dissimilar to those used in much 'African Cinema', which gives preference to wide, long shots rather than close-ups, to minimal editing and to scenes which embellish narratives through visual and aural mood-setting and exposition. Malian-Mauritanian director Abderrahmane Sissako's *Waiting for Happiness* (2005), winner of FESPACO's Etalon de Yennenga, is renowned for the way in which it creates a deep sense of loss through holding the camera on each scene for several beats after all human presence has disappeared; video films such as *Potent Secrets* (Joyce Ashuntantang-Abunaw, 2001) and *My Promise* (Moses Ebere, 2004) might not conjure the same sense of loss by means of the same technique, but through their delayed temporality they reveal that, in this sense, their aesthetic is quite different to that of soap operas, a genre to which video films have frequently been compared.

Harding sees similarities between the video films and soap operas in terms of their imitative representations of sex and treatment of gender. She points out, how-ever, that 'one oblique feature working against this imitative thrust is the prolonged duration of the video movie which, it could be argued, situates it alongside accept-able cultural norms of verbose public orature' (2007). Furthermore, whereas soap operas are edited in such a way that they cut on moments of emotion and melodrama, with close-ups of faces and action emphasised, the way in which the video films are edited often decreases and deflates the melodrama one finds within the narratives. The effect of these hiatuses or deflation is one of introducing an atmosphere of failed dreams and expectations: it is in these flat, liminal moments that social realism over-takes melodrama in the video films and reproduces the pace of everyday life in these African cultures. The long connective scenes, which conjure a neorealistic aesthetic in their 'slice of life' approach, further contribute to this liminal atmosphere.

Social realism is the acknowledged genre and aesthetic of much 'African Cinema', but one finds it in ample supply in video films as well. The opening sequence of *My Promise* imparts the pain of childbirth through the excruciatingly long take in which we watch the pregnant Basilia as she is escorted to a clinic by her husband and friend; and the scene in which Anne and Obidisi drive from his parents' village back to the city allows us to experience in 'real time' the Nigerian landscape and the interactions of a romantic couple. The fact that the video films are made, like much 'African Cinema', with non-professional actors and in natural locations magnifies this social realist aesthetic. In some cases, the viewer feels that s/he has more access to 'African cultures' through watching video films rather than 'African Cinema', in spite of the frequent melodramatic themes and acting in the former. This access is perhaps the consequence of an immediacy created through certain modes of production – for example, few rehearsals and much improvisation (see Haynes and Okome 1997).

Editing requirements also often play a significant role in determining the over-arching aesthetic of a video film. Ghanaian filmmaker Socrate Safo (2007) has, for example, critiqued Senegalese art filmmaker Djibril Diop Mambety's classic film *Touki Bouki* (1973) for its recurrent images of the sea and waves. Safo has said that the exigencies of fitting his films onto VCDs (video CDs, which hold sixty minutes of information, and which are cheaper to produce than DVDs) would have forced him to cut all such shots from one of his own films. On the other hand, in many video films certain scenes are fleshed out so as to fill up time to generate money, to ensure that the film lasts for the length of time of a bus journey, or delays the narrative for the purpose of creating a serial narrative played out across a set of sequels. While the social realist aesthetic of video films may not, then, be intentional, it nevertheless undeniably exists.

The quote from Haynes and Okome above suggests that narrative supersedes aesthetics in terms of audience desire when it comes to the video films. Are there instances of 'beauty' in these films, however, to which the non-local eye is oblivious? The South African model and fashion editor Nakedi Ribane (2006) has written about the very different aesthetic of bodily beauty that exists in many African cultures compared to the West and this is certainly apparent in the beauty of Nollywood's female stars; much more research is required to explain conceptions of beauty in Africa in general. That a non-local viewer obtains immediate access to 'African cul-ture' through the video films has been taken for granted by scholars, and this implies that the films are useful as anthropological objects and allow for anthropological readings. However, the fact that the study of video films has, to date, been dominated by anthropologists means that the films risk being read only in ethnographic terms and not also in aesthetic terms. As Nigerian scholar J. A. I. Bewaji argues:

> Most texts discussing African and African Diaspora arts have been mainly descriptive, exploring mostly historical aspects of the phenomena of arts in Africa and its Diaspora; that is, dwelling mainly on issues of when certain identified works of art … were made, how they were made, for whom, for what purpose(s), etc. These discussions have ignored the critical, analytic and philosophical implications of the artistic objects of their study in any serious depth. (2003: 2)

As Haynes has argued, 'we need much deeper readings of the [video] films, approach-ing them as works of art with adequate interpretative sophistication' (1997: 10).

Haynes has also set a precedent by making an attempt to do this himself, in a study of the films of Nigerian director Kenneth Nnebue (2007b). He has spoken of the difficulty of this attempt, however, acknowledging that he felt himself 'on spongy ground as [he] tried to make claims about Nnebue's originality and his personal accomplishments, because those claims depended on a reliable, detailed general history that does not exist' (2007a: 10). A further difficulty arises when one considers the very different modes of production of 'African Cinema' and the video films, with the former films tending to take more than five years to make. It is difficult, therefore, to find the kind of aesthetic and narrative integrity in the video films that one finds in 'African Cinema', and this does, perhaps, suggest that socio-anthropological approaches to the video films are more apt than critical-aesthetic approaches. Socrate Safo has even gone so far as to question the broader academic project of studying the video films, which tend to be made by and for people who do not share the intellectual concerns of 'African Cinema' directors and viewers (2007).

If we are to find a way of engaging in deeper readings of all African films – regardless of the format in which they are made – perhaps one of the key conceptual frameworks needed is precisely that of integrity. A video film such as Hammie Rajab's *Kolelo* (2007) may not have the integrity of the visual motifs that one finds in Sissako's *Waiting for Happiness*, but it offers, on one level, aural integrity, through the eerie repetition of a musical refrain and electronic sound effects which are well-suited to the subject matter and which work to create a particular viewing atmosphere for the audience. A Nigerian video film such as *The President's Daughter* (Chico Ejiro, 2001), with its crude acting and loose storyline, may have none of the narrative integrity that Sembene's *Guelwaar* (1992) owns, but in that it was entirely produced by Nigerians, the theme of political self-reliance preached within the film's storyline is integral to its mode of production. *Guelwaar*, on the other hand, which shows the Senegalese populace rebuking foreign aid within the film's diegesis, but later reveals in its credits that it was itself the recipient of foreign aid, displays internal hypocrisies that are difficult to reconcile. The narrative meaning of a film such as *To Part No More* (Sunday Nnajiude, nd) is partly built around the aesthetic choices of the director: a bright pink colour is used throughout the film (in terms of costume and décor) to suggest the casting of a curse on Ugo by Tessie, and the subsequent infiltration of this curse into Ugo's life and the lives of those around him. Films that have multiple layers of meaning that may be apprehended by different spectators in different contexts (such as Sembene's *Xala* [1974]), and films with 'symbolic narratives' (see Givanni 2000) that create integrity through images and sounds that require decoding, are films that merit deeper readings.

Conclusion: the ends of storytelling

The most common way in which the function of 'African Cinema' and video films has been distinguished is by contrasting the pedagogical nature of the former with the commercial nature of the latter. Sembene's well-known refrain, in which he said that cinema was a 'night-school' for his people, has been much rehearsed in African film studies. Filmmakers in the 'African Cinema' tradition, such as Mambety, Absa and Cheick Oumar Sissoko, have stressed the educational functions of filmmaking. As I have argued elsewhere, the history of 'African Cinema' is largely the history of a cinema of critique, not only of colonialism and Western imperialism, but also of Africa and its autochthonous practices, a tradition inaugurated by Sembene (see Dovey 2009). On the surface, African video films are not made with the aim of offering critique, but with the aim of providing entertainment for viewers and profit for producers (see Ogunleye 2003).

However, if one studies the concerns of particular video filmmakers a little more closely, one does find filmmakers engaging in critiques of ethnic violence, HIV/AIDS and neocolonialism (for example, in Nigerian director Ladi Ladebo's *Heritage* [2003], and Kenyan director Bob Nyanja's *Malooned* [2007]). Karin Barber points out that there are 'openly political videos' made by the Yoruba (2000: 261) and Haynes has devoted much attention to the ways in which certain Nigerian films are beginning to offer serious socio-political critique (2003; 2006; 2007b). According to Harding, individual video films 'can be simultaneously reactionary, liberating, validating or even therapeutic' (2007). In fact, many video filmmakers refer to their work as 'edutainment' (*This is Nollywood* 2007).

Rather than seeking to identify the 'progressive' and 'educational' elements of video films and thereby rehearsing the moralising discourse that has dominated African film studies, perhaps it is time for 'African Cinema' scholars to start learning from the pleasure generated by African video films. In seeking a new path, we might follow the lead of the Congolese filmmaker Mweze Ngangura (1996), who has talked about the importance of entertainment to African filmmaking. Similarly, Wa Thiong'o has stressed that

> Any discussion of African cinema inevitably calls into question the role of art in society, for cinema is an art, as Professor Teshome Gabriel put it, 'making the invisible visible'. [...] It is not of course a matter of just making the invisible visible, it is doing it in such a way that it does not come out as simply instruction. It has to come out as delight also. Delight and instruction become intertwined in such a way that they are part of each other. [...] African cinema has to pay equal attention to both the principle of instruction and that of pleasure (2000: 93).

In the end, and once upon a time, in all societies, the main function of storytelling has without doubt been to instill delight and pleasure, and that is what – for the present at least – the video films seem to be successfully offering their audiences.

Notes

1　The first video films were made in 1985 by Ghanaians who, irritated by the lack of financial support from the Ghana Film Industry Corporation (GFIC) and having no previous film training, started to make their own films (see Meyer 1999; 2003; 2010). The first film to be released on VHS in Ghana was William Akuffo's *Zinabu* (1987). As Samuel Benagr points out, 'in a kind of neorealist tradition, *Zinabu* and subsequent video films made depicted for the most part the lives of ordinary people living ordinary lives and in an entertaining manner cross-examine society' (2007: 8–9). Notably, the film is an adaptation of H. Rider Haggard's problematic novel *She: A History of Adventure* (1886–7). Yoruba travelling theatre practitioners began to make their dramas on video in 1988, finding the publicity that the videos attracted for their theatre work very useful (see Haynes and Okome 1997: 23–4; Barber 2000). In 1990, *Turmin Danya* (Sulaiman Katsina), the first Hausa-language video film was made in predominantly Muslim northern Nigeria. As Hausa film expert Abdalla Uba Adamu has pointed out, *Turmin Danya* is based on the traditional *tatsuniya* folktale. The film, which is about a forced marriage, reflects the 'social realities of conservative Muslim northern Nigeria in which parents, using one particular aspect of Islamic Shari'a, interpret that they have the right to choose a life partner for their female (rarely male) offspring. The success of this first video film was more on its portrayal of daily realities of many women in forced marriage situations' (Adamu 2007: 7–8). Today, with the Hausa video film industry well established, two narratives abound: the aforementioned forced marriage story, and the love triangle narrative (see Adamu 2007). All Hausa film scholars concur that, in addition to Hausa oral tales and novels being popular sources for films, Hindi ('Bollywood') films are an undeniable influence on the form of the films' storytelling (see Adamu 2007; Larkin 1997; 2003); as Adamu points out, 'over 98% of Hausa video films must contain at least two to three song and dance routines' (2007: 8). Although the Hausa video films are unique in their use of Hindi films as sources, they share Ghanaian and southern Nigerian films' interest in social realities. In 1992, the first southern Nigerian ('Nollywood') film appeared: Kenneth Nnebue's *Living in Bondage*, a film which, according to Nigerian video film expert Jonathan Haynes, 'started the video boom' and 'to an extraordinary degree … contains the seeds of almost everything that followed' (2007a: 10). Haynes has pointed out that the film's source was stories people told Nnebue, or stories that he read in the newspapers (ibid.). Video film industries in other 'Anglophone' areas of the continent soon sprung up. Mfuh Ebenezer's *Love Has Eyes* (1998) inaugurated the industry in Anglophone Cameroon by Cameroonians (see Ashuntantang 2007) and Judy Kibinge's *Dangerous Affair* (2002) was possibly the first video film in Kenya. Matthias Krings (2007) has done important work in tracing the origin of video films in Tanzania. Work is needed on South Africa's recent video film industries, 'Nandawood' and 'Joziewood'.

2　The music used in many of the video films sounds like synthetic 'elevator' music, and is repeated throughout the films even if the mood of a particular scene does not warrant it. There are, of course, exceptions. The soundtrack for *Osuofia in London* (2004) was composed by local musicians specifically for the film, and offers ironic commentary rather than bland background noise.

3　Unfortunately today there are not many venues in Senegal in which Sembene's films can be shown, with only two rundown cinemas remaining in Dakar, the capital of Senegal (see McClune 2010).

4　When I have shown such scenes to my students on African film and video courses at the University of Cambridge and at SOAS, University of London, they are often met with laughter.

5　The verisimilitude with which Christ's miracles are represented in Mel Gibson's *Passion of the Christ* (2004), establishing the relation of special effect to miracle of which de Vries speaks, can, for example, be contrasted with the ways in which such a relationship is self-consciously treated in the South African film *Son of Man* (Mark Dornford-May, 2006), a startlingly original adaptation of the New Testament. In the latter film, the mediatisation of miracles is foregrounded, with characters using various mediums (video, song, art) to narrativise and authorise Christ's miracles.

6   I would like to thank Edward Teversham for pointing out the similarity in the scenes of the pigeon 'hunting' to me.

Bibliography

Absa, M. S. (2003) Filmed interview with author, 2 March.

Adamu, A. U. (2007) 'Islam, Shari'a and Censorship in Hausa Video Film', unpublished conference paper, delivered at the African Film Conference, University of Illinois (Urbana-Champaign), 9–10 November.

AFI Silver (2006) CinemAfrica. On-line. Available: http://www.afi.com/silver/new/nowplaying/2006/v3i4/cinemafrica.aspx (accessed on 16 December 2009).

Anyanwu, C. (2003) 'Towards a New Image of Women in Nigerian Video Films', in F. Ogunleye (ed.) *African Video Film Today*. Manzini and Matsapha, Swaziland: Academic Publishers, 81–90.

Ashuntantang, J. (2007) 'Cameroon Video-Film in English: Real Deal or Copy Cats?', unpublished conference paper, delivered at the African Film Conference, University of Illinois (Urbana-Champaign), 9–10 November.

Barber, K. (2000) *The Generation of Plays: Yoruba Popular Life in Theater*. Bloomington: Indiana University Press.

Benagr, S. (2007) 'Promises of Digital Technology in Ghanaian Video Production', unpublished conference paper, delivered at the African Film Conference, University of Illinois (Urbana-Champaign), 9–10 November.

Benjamin, W. (1935) 'The Work of Art in the Age of Mechanical Reproduction', rpt. in L. Braudy and M. Cohen (eds) *Film Theory and Criticism: Introductory Readings* (1999). Fifth Edition. New York/Oxford: Oxford University Press, 731–51.

Bester, R. (2004) '*Fools*: Review for New York African Film Festival 2000–2001'. On-line. Available: http://www.africanfilmny.org/network/news/Rbester.html (accessed on 27 September 2008).

Bewaji, J. A. I. (2003) *Beauty and Culture: Perspectives in Black Aesthetics*. Ibadan, Nigeria: Spectrum Books.

Cham, M. (1996) 'Introduction', in I. Bakari and M. Cham (eds) *African Experiences of Cinema*. London: British Film Institute, 1–14.

De Vries, H. (2001) 'In Media Res: Global Religion, Public Spheres, and the Task of Contemporary Comparative Religious Studies', in H. de Vries and S. Weber (eds) *Religion and Media*. Stanford: Stanford University Press, 3–32.

Diawara, M. (1992) *African Cinema: Politics and Culture*. Bloomington: Indiana University Press.

Dovey, L. (2009) *African Film and Literature: Adapting Violence to the Screen*. New York: Columbia University Press.

_____ (2012) 'Film and Postcolonial Writing', in A. Quayson (ed.) *Cambridge History of Postcolonial Literature*. Cambridge: Cambridge University Press.

Gabriel, T. H. (2000) 'The Intolerable Gift', in J. Givanni (ed.) *Symbolic Narratives/African Cinema: Audiences, Theory and the Moving Image*. London: British Film Institue, 97–102.

Givanni, J. (ed.) (2000) *Symbolic Narratives/African Cinema: Audiences, Theory and the Moving Image*. London: British Film Institute.

Harding, F. (2007) 'Appearing Fabu-lous: From Tender Romance to Horrifying Sex'. *Film International* 28 (August). On-line. Available: http://findarticles.com/p/articles/mi_7135/is_200708/ai_n32249687/pg_3/?tag=content;col1 (accessed on 16 December 2009).

Haynes, J. (1997) 'Preface', in J. Haynes (ed.), *Nigerian Video Films*. JOS: Nigerian Film Corporation, 9–10.

———— (2003) 'Mobilizing Yoruba Popular Culture: *Babangida Must Go*'. *Africa* 73(1): 122–38.

———— (2006) 'Political critique in Nigerian video films'. *African Affairs* 105(421): 511–33.

———— (2007a) 'What Is To Be Done? Film Studies and Nigerian and Ghanaian Videos', unpublished conference paper, delivered at the African Film Conference, University of Illinois (Urbana-Champaign), 9–10 November.

———— (2007b) 'Nnebue: The Anatomy of Power', *Film International*, 28, 30–40.

Haynes, J. and O. Okome (1997) 'Evolving Popular Media: Nigerian Video Films', in J. Haynes (ed.) *Nigerian Video Films*. JOS: Nigerian Film Corporation, 21–44.

Krings, M. (2007) 'Nollywood beyond Nigeria: The Localization of Nigerian video films in Tanzania', unpublished conference paper, delivered at the African Film Conference, University of Illinois (Urbana-Champaign), 9–10 November.

Larkin, B. (1997) 'Indian Films and Nigerian Lovers: Love Stories, Electronic Media and the Creation of Parallel Modernities', *Africa*, 67, 3, 406–40.

———— (2003) 'Itineraries of Indian Cinema: African Videos, Bollywood, and Global Media', in E. Shohat and R. Stam (eds) *Multiculturalism, Postcoloniality, and Transnational Media*. New Brunswick, New Jersey and London: Rutgers University Press, 170–92.

McClune, B. (2010) 'In Search of Sembene', *Journal of African Media Studies*, 2, 1, 107–20.

Meyer, B. (1999) 'Popular Ghanaian Cinema and "African Heritage"', *Africa Today*, 46, 2, 93–114.

———— (2003) 'Ghanaian Popular Cinema and the Magic in and of Film', in B. Meyer and P. Pels (eds) *Magic and Modernity: Interfaces of Revelation and Concealment*. Stanford University Press, 200–22.

———— (2010) 'Tradition and Color at its Best: "Tradition" and "Heritage" in Ghanaian Video-movies', *Journal of African Cultural Studies*, 22, 1, 7–23.

Micklethwait, J. (2007) 'In God's Name', in *The Economist*, Special Report on Religion and Public Life, 1 November. On-line. Available: http://www.economist.com/specialreports/displaystory.cfm?story_id=10015255 (accessed on 27 September 2008).

Murphy, D. (2000) *Sembene: Imagining Alternatives in Film and Fiction*. Oxford: James Currey; Trenton, NJ: Africa World Press.

Ngangura, M. (1996) 'African Cinema – Militancy or Entertainment?', trans. Paul Willemen, in I. Bakari and M. Cham (eds), *African Experiences of Cinema*. London: BFI, 60–64.

Nollywood Babylon (2008) Dir. Ben Addelman and Samir Mallal. Canada/Nigeria. 74 min. English. Prod. AM Pictures (film).

Oguine, I. (2004) 'Nollywood looks to the future'. *New Internationalist* (October). On-line. Available: http://findarticles.com/p/articles/mi_m0JQP/is_372/ai_n6353196/ (accessed on 15 December 2009).

Ogunleye, F. (ed.) (2003) *African Video Film Today*. Manzini and Matsapha, Swaziland: Academic Publishers.

Okwori, J. Z. (2003) 'A Dramatized Society: Representing Rituals of Human Sacrifice as Efficacious Action in Nigerian Home-video Movies', *Journal of African Cultural Studies*, 16, 1, 7–23.

Peace Mission (2008) Dir. Dorothee Wenner. Germany/Nigeria. 80 min. English. Prod. Pong (film).

Popoola, I. S. (2003) 'Nigeria and the Challenges of Violent Video Films', in F. Ogunleye (ed.) *African Video Film Today*. Manzini and Matsapha, Swaziland: Academic Publishers, 129–40.

Ribane, N. (2006) *Beauty: A Black Perspective*. Scottsville, South Africa: University of KwaZulu-Natal Press.

Rijsdijk, I. and A. Haupt (2007) 'Redemption to a kwaito beat: Gavin Hood's *Tsotsi*', *Journal of the Musical Arts in Africa*, 4, 29–46.

Ryan, M. (2001) *Interactivity in Literature and Electronic Media*. Baltimore: Johns Hopkins University

Press.

Safo, S. (2007) Discussion at the African Film Conference, University of Illinois (Urbana-Champaign), 9–10 November.

Scheub, H. (2006) *Storytelling Songs of Zulu Women: Recording Archetypal Rites of Passage and Mythic Paths*. Lewiston, N.Y. and Lampeter: Edwin Mellen Press.

This is Nollywood (2007) Dir. Franco Sacchi and Robert Caputo. Nigeria/USA. 56 min. Distr. (DVD) California Newsreel (USA) (film).

Ukah, A. F. K. (2003) 'Advertising God: Nigerian Christian Video-Films and the Power of Consumer Culture', *Journal of Religion in Africa*, 33, 2, 203–31.

UNESCOPRESS (2009). 'Nollywood Rivals Bollywood in Film/Video Production'. *UNESCO Website*. On-line. Available: http://portal.unesco.org/en/ev.php-URL_ID=45317&URL_DO=DO_ TOPIC&URL_SECTION=201.html (accessed on 16 December 2009).

Wa Thiong'o, N. (2000) 'Introduction', in J. Givanni (ed.) *Symbolic Narratives/African Cinema: Audiences, Theory and the Moving Image*. London: BFI, 93–6.

Winberg, M. (2001) *My Eland's Heart: A Collection of Stories and Art*. Claremont, South Africa: David Philip.

That's Entertainment?:
Art, Didacticism and the Popular
in Francophone West African Cinema

David Murphy

Sub-Saharan African cinema was born in the era of decolonisation in the 1960s. Consequently, it comes as no surprise that many within the first generation of Francophone West African filmmakers (who dominated this early period of sub-Saharan cinema) conceived of their work in explicitly political terms: in effect, they were engaged (or so they believed) in a process of decolonising the cinema screens of the continent, which were largely dominated by cheap imports from the West. (Egypt was the other main source of films, largely melodramatic potboilers, in the period from World War II until the 1960s.) For many critics and filmmakers of this period, African cinema was at the cutting edge of a politically and artistically radical 'Third Cinema', which explicitly rejected the capitalist world order of the West.

Essentially, then, sub-Saharan African filmmaking from the 1960s and 1970s has been viewed as an inherently political, and frequently didactic, art form, the work of highly committed cinematic *auteurs* who envisage cinema as part of a wider social, political and cultural struggle. In turn, directors from the 1980s onwards, it is argued, have created a more 'authentically' African form of filmmaking through greater engagement with oral narrative traditions. This latter form of filmmaking was also seen to have begun the move away from the ideologically inspired cinema of the first wave of African films, and, from the late 1980s onwards, this process would go even further with the emergence of a new generation of directors who would express the complexities and ambiguities of contemporary Africa in films that would mix styles, genres and influences. Although this acts as a useful overview of the general evolution of sub-Saharan African filmmaking, I would argue that it is excessively general and imposes a sense of homogeneity where in fact there has always been a great diversity of approach. The maverick talents of a pioneering figure such as the Senegalese director Djibril Diop Mambety, who made one of the most acclaimed African films, the unclassifiable *Touki Bouki* (1973), cannot be contained within any specific ideology, just as there is no shortage of political commitment amongst many contemporary filmmakers. Consequently, it is one of the aims of this chapter to challenge the ways in which African film criticism has constructed its object of study: which filmmakers and which modes of filmmaking have been positioned as central to an emerging African film tradition, and how might the development of a more complex genealogy of African cinema help to enhance our understanding of cinematic storytelling in West Africa?

The other main aim of the piece is to interrogate another truism of African film criticism, namely that the African filmmaker is a contemporary *griot*, a direct descendant of the traditional guardians of the oral heritage in West Africa. (Although often used as a generic term to refer to filmmakers from across sub-Saharan Africa, the specific historical figure of the *griot* has been a feature of life solely in those countries that formed part of the Mali Empire.) In this conception, the filmmaker, like the *griot*, is seen as a guardian of important communal values, who maintains the traditional bond between storyteller and audience. However, although it is a critical commonplace that African filmmaking is deeply influenced by the oral narrative tradition, there is no consensus as to how this influence translates into actual filmmaking practice. At the heart of the conflicting arguments about narrative structure lie (often unspoken) assumptions about the popularity of African cinema: the basic position on the various sides of the argument is that for an African film to reach, make sense to, and for some critics, to 'teach', a wide African audience, it must utilise narrative structures with which its local audience is familiar. As Francophone African films have struggled to maintain a presence on African film screens (due to complex issues of film production and distribution), this debate has often been cast in highly abstract terms about 'what African audiences want'. However, there has been little consideration of the weight that the critic should accord to audiences' familiarity with the narrative codes of Kung-Fu movies or more latterly Bollywood musicals, which have proven so popular in many parts of Africa since the 1970s. For more than half a century, there has been a vibrant cinema-going culture in Africa, which has shaped popular African expectations and understanding of how film narratives operate. (For an important introduction to the 'geographies' of film spectatorship, see Jancovich et al. 2003.) Consequently, I would contend that a more productive critical approach to African cinematic narratives must attempt to explore the confluence between Western (modernist) artistic practices and 'modernising' ideas on the development of Africa, between the influence of 'popular' urban African culture and African oral narrative devices, and this chapter will examine the work of some leading sub-Saharan African filmmakers (Ousmane Sembene, Gaston Kaboré and Jean-Pierre Bekolo) in order to explore the complexity of the narrative structures found in their work.

African cinema and Third Cinema

The radical ethos that informed the work of many African film directors of the 1960s and 1970s is illustrated through the various charters produced by the corporative union, FEPACI (Fédération Pan-Africaine des Cinéastes), which consistently sought to promote the development of an 'authentically' African form of filmmaking. For instance, in its most radical mission statement, the 1975 'Algiers Charter on African Cinema', FEPACI claimed that:

> To assume a genuinely creative role in the process of development, African culture must be popular, democratic and progressive in character, inspired by its own realities and responding to its own needs. It must also be in solidarity with cultural struggles all over the world. [...] Within this perspective the cinema has a vital part to play because it is a means of education, information and consciousness raising, as well as a stimulus to creativity. The accomplishing of these goals implies a questioning by African film-makers of the image they have of themselves, of the nature of their function and their social status and of their general place in society. The stereotyped image of the solitary and marginal creator which is widespread in Western capitalist society must be rejected by African film-makers, who must, on the contrary, see themselves as creative artisans at the service of their people. (Cited in Bakari and Cham 1996: 25)

In this agenda, African filmmakers are explicitly perceived as radical artists who are engaged in a dialectical relationship with their audience, a process that clearly echoes the work of Frantz Fanon, one of the most important theorists of decolonisation (see Fanon 1967). Films have an educational role but their form and content must be found in the societies from which they emerge. They must be 'popular' in the sense of engaging with and emerging from 'the people', but they must resolutely refuse a 'popularity' based on what is perceived as the top down success of a commercially successful 'product'. For the French critic André Gardies, African directors, in their desire to break with Western images of Africa, constructed an 'ideal spectator' to whom they would 'show' the 'true reality' of Africa, as opposed to the process of 'telling' them stories (1989: 14–16). Essentially, the popular was defined by what African directors chose to represent and how they chose to represent it: there was no dialectical relationship between filmmaker and audience.

This vision of African filmmaking is inextricably bound up with the notion of 'Third Cinema', which emerged from Latin America in the 1960s but which soon came to refer to most cinematic work emanating from what was then called the Third World but which has subsequently morphed into the 'Global South' (amongst other terms). Although critics of 'Third Cinema' rarely agreed on precisely what constituted the governing aesthetics of such work, there was a general consensus that it was different in style and content both from the dominant Hollywood cinema and from (mainly European) *auteur* cinema. For the influential Ethiopian critic, Teshome

Gabriel, this meant that Third Cinema was an inherently (Fanonian) revolutionary artistic practice (see Gabriel 1982; 1989). On the other hand, Paul Willemen plays down the politically radical nature of Third Cinema, and instead emphasises its capacity to represent the complexity of postcolonial societies. For Willemen, Third Cinema practitioners, such as Ousmane Sembene (Senegal) and Souleymane Cissé (Mali) acknowledge the 'many-layeredness' of African culture, and their films 'exemplify a way of inhabiting [this] culture which is neither myopically nationalist nor evasively cosmopolitan' (Pines and Willemen 1994: 4).

Willemen's carefully constructed critical formula neatly smoothes over the potential opposition between a radical, avant-garde cinematic practice (top down) and a 'popular' cinematic practice, steeped in the culture from which it emerges (bottom up), and, in so doing, he allows us to think in more complex ways about our understanding of the relationship between the popular and the avant-garde. Unfortunately, the tension between the radical and the popular has more often led to highly polarised appraisals of the work of both major and minor African directors. So, for example, Souleymane Cissé's *Yeelen* (1987) or *Yaaba* (1989) by Idrissa Ouédraogo (Burkina Faso) find themselves cast by turns as an authentic expression of an African mode of storytelling or as an escapist and retrograde plunge into a mythical pre-colonial world. (For in-depth analysis of the opposing critical evaluations of both films, see Murphy and Williams 2007.)

I will examine a number of case studies below in order to trace the critical manoeuvres that position these works as variously avant-garde, popular or populist. However, as a prelude to these case studies, I would first like to explore the ways in which African film criticism has created genealogies of African filmmaking via the processes of inclusion and exclusion inherent in the creation of a cinematic canon.

Genealogies of African cinema

The late emergence of sub-Saharan African filmmaking and the desire on the part of both critics and practitioners to differentiate this new body of work from dominant (i.e. US) film practice led to what might be termed a 'critical exceptionalism' in the discussion of African filmmakers' work, an exceptionalism that dominated the field until the late 1990s. In the film histories by Manthia Diawara (1992) and Nwachukwu Frank Ukadike (1994), for example, African films are classified on an almost entirely thematic basis (social realist films, colonial confrontation films, return to the source films), which emphasises content over form. Certain critics, such as Clyde Taylor (1989) go even further, calling for African film critics to abandon aesthetic considerations completely, for such an approach is fatally compromised by what he perceives as the Western imperialist notions of universal value that underpin them.

While more recent criticism has attempted to provide a stronger focus on questions of form (see Thackway 2003; Armes 2006; Harrow 2007; Murphy and Williams 2007), there often remains an unquestioning acceptance that African cinema of the

1960s and 1970s was marked almost entirely by a didactic social realism, while film-making from the 1980s onwards has adopted more varied styles, often perceived as more 'authentically' African than the early work of Sembene or Med Hondo, for example. This perception of early sub-Saharan African cinema as didactic, realist and primarily interested in the exploration of social and political issues accompanied it from its beginnings, and was clearly fostered by many directors themselves, not least through documents such as the fiery Algiers Charter cited above. This view became entrenched as critical orthodoxy with the publication of two pioneering histories of African cinema in the early 1990s: Manthia Diawara's *African Cinema: Politics and Culture* (1992) and Nwachukwu Frank Ukadike's *Black African Cinema* (1994). However, as Lizelle Bisschoff and I have argued at length in our ongoing project that aims to recover the 'lost classics' of African film (see Bisschoff and Murphy 2007), this perception of African cinema is both excessively limited in its reading of the work of the likes of Sembene (whose work was always far more complex than the tag of social realist allowed), and also extremely partial in its choice of films deemed to be 'representative' of African filmmaking practice. (See Ruelle 2005 for further reflection on the history of Francophone African cinema.)

Sembene's short film *Borom Sarret* (1962) is generally described by critics as the first film made by a sub-Saharan African on the continent itself. Its neo-realist tale of a poor cart driver in 1960s Dakar has been perceived by many critics as having laid down a template that virtually all African directors would follow until the 1980s. However, some African film historians have argued that *Aouré*, also made in 1962, by Mustapha Alassane (Niger) predates *Borom Sarret*. Alassane has played a marginal and largely maverick role in African film history. His short film *The Return of an Adventurer* (1966) is an exuberant and innovative parody of the cowboy movie, in which the African émigré returning from the USA, is literally 'Westernised' as he and his friends don cowboy outfits and proceed to terrorise the local community. Throughout the 1960s and early 1970s, Alassane passed through a range of styles (fable, parody, social satire) and later became one of the first African filmmakers to move into the field of animation, a form in which he still works. He has thus quite clearly played something of a pioneering role in African cinema but he is nonetheless generally overlooked in historical accounts of the field: it is Sembene who became known as 'the father of African cinema' but what of Alassane's playful form of film-making and its gleeful mix of high and low styles? Where does such filmmaking practice fit within the dominant genealogy of African cinema?

The promotion of alternative genealogies of African cinema, in which the work of pioneers such as Alassane is given its long overdue recognition, undermines the idea that a radical, politicised cinema of the 1960s and 1970s gave way to a less explicitly political, more 'personal' and more 'African' style from the 1980s, for the existence of parallel aesthetics already present in that early period is highlighted more clearly. A brilliant African director such as Djibril Diop Mambety has long found himself cast in the middle of tortuous critical debates characterising his work as either typically

African or as mere copies of a Western avant-garde due to the perceived need to fit directors of that early period into a single African aesthetic. (Similarly binaristic views have informed much criticism of the early films by the Mauritanian director, Med Hondo.) However, when viewed alongside the work of Alassane (and other early pioneers such as the Ivory Coast director Désiré Ecaré), Mambety can be seen as part of a general movement within this early period of African filmmaking, which explored less directly political or realist cinematic paths. Looking at African cinema in terms of its diversity rather than within a restrictive, monolithic framework opens up genealogies that link early directors such as Mambety to contemporary figures such as Jean-Pierre Bekolo who explicitly expresses his debt to Mambety's work. In place of a 'stagist' view of African film as a whole slowly adopting, then moving beyond, certain styles and narrative structures, we can develop a sense of African filmmaking practice as always already plural in form from its very beginnings.

The popularity of African cinema

In her highly influential essay on 'Popular Arts in Africa', Karin Barber defines popular African culture as a 'cultural brokerage between Western culture and folk culture' (1987: 12). In this exhaustive study of popular cultural forms in contemporary Africa, it is interesting to note that Barber makes no mention of African cinema as a popular art form; however, she does list Western films under the heading of 'arts consumed but not produced by the people' (1987: 25). In essence, Barber's argument is that there exists in Africa a popular 'consumption' of film but that there is no popular African cinema as such. Barber's article was first published in the late 1980s at a time when indigenous film production in Nigeria, the main geographical focus of her work, had yet to take off, but there had by then been almost three decades of Francophone African film production, which she effectively (by omission) deems not be a 'popular' form. As mentioned above, many critics have traced the use of oral narrative elements in African films, seeing in this process an attempt to embed film narratives within a narrative tradition familiar to the audience. (Melissa Thackway's study from 2003 is by far the best account of the influence of orality on African filmmaking, although her desire to read orality into this body of work often leads her to neglect other influences.) However, the significance if any to be accorded to the audience's familiarity with the narrative codes of Bollywood musicals, Kung-Fu films or Western action movies has constituted a critical blindspot. One of the few critics to think through the issues relating to the popularity (or lack of it) of African cinema is Pierre Haffner who called in the late 1970s for a popular African cinema that would marry those film techniques that worked best with cinema audiences he observed in Mali with local performance-based arts such as the *koteba* (see Haffner 1978: 55–65). Haffner's comments seem highly prescient when one considers the success of Nigerian and Ghanaian video films (often generically termed 'Nollywood'), which are often made by local theatre troupes, who forge a syncretic mix of local performance techniques and narratives with some of the more spectacular elements from foreign film styles that have enjoyed success in Africa. (For analysis of Nollywood filmmaking, see Haynes 2000; Barrot 2005; and Dovey in this volume.) In so doing, Nollywood has in fact followed a model that was already established by the small number of non-Western countries that have managed to create genuine film *industries*, which have enjoyed success both at home and abroad: the filmmakers of Egypt, India, Japan, Taiwan and Hong Kong have successfully combined elements of local narrative tradition with melodrama and the visually spectacular.

To what extent then can Francophone West African cinema be considered a popular cultural form? In the remainder of this chapter, I will examine three case studies, spanning three decades, in order to explore the varying extents to which art, didacticism and the popular have informed Francophone West African filmmaking. The three films in question are Ousmane Sembene's *Xala* (Senegal, 1974), Gaston Kaboré's *Wend Kuuni* (Burkina Faso, 1982) and Jean-Pierre Bekolo's *Aristotle's Plot* (Cameroon, 1997), and they all pose in very different ways crucial questions about the form and the content of African films.

Xala is a scathing satire of the emerging African bourgeoisie, who are depicted as a literally impotent version of their Western counterpart, and it has been hailed as a classic of Third Cinema (see Gabriel 1982; for a more in-depth analysis of *Xala*, see Murphy 2000: 98–123). The film opens with a symbolic ten-minute sequence in which a group of African businessmen chase their French counterparts from the Dakar Chamber of Commerce, cheered on by the masses. However, the French soon return carrying brief cases laden with cash; the masses are dispersed, and the cash is distributed to the grateful African businessman. In essence, this opening sequence depicts what Sembene perceives as the 'reality' of African independence, namely the creation of an African elite that would continue to govern the newly independent nations on behalf of their former colonial masters: this is 'realism' in the Brechtian sense of depicting the underlying facts of history that often remain hidden beneath the surface reality of everyday events.

However, the film does not fit solely within a modernist, avant-garde style, for Sembene situates his deeply political story within an oral narrative structure with which his audience is highly familiar, that of the arrogant, foolish male who undergoes a series of public humiliations. In a highly influential article, Mbye Cham (1982) traces the influence of oral narratives on the structure of Sembene's films. For Cham, *Xala* is primarily a 'trickster' narrative in which the protagonist, the corrupt businessman El Hadji Abdou Kader Beye, is set a series of tasks in order to find a cure for his impotence; but, in this modern version of the trickster tale, it is the trickster himself who is brought down by the deceit and lies of those he encounters: his wives, the fake 'witch doctors', his fellow businessmen. The film also revels in the earthy and bawdy humour evoked by its subject matter, as El Hadji is subjected to an endless stream of sarcastic comments on his failed manhood. In many ways, *Xala* sets down

the parameters for a form of filmmaking that would marry modernist aesthetic practices and oral narrative structures and tropes, and it proved highly popular with
West African audiences: for instance, in Senegal, it managed to attract audiences
in similar numbers to the Kung-Fu movies that were at that time dominating the
screens of local cinemas. (Posters of Bruce Lee are still to be found on bedroom and
shop walls throughout West Africa.) As both a critically acclaimed film and a genuine popular success within Africa, *Xala* stands as an example of the possibilities of
a popular, radical African cinema in which art, didacticism and entertainment are
equally balanced.

Despite the importance of oral narrative strategies within a film such as *Xala*,
Francophone African filmmaking of the 1960s and 1970s has primarily been considered in terms of its realism and of its modernising agenda. It was with the release of
Gaston Kaboré's film *Wend Kuuni* in 1982 that African cinema was deemed by many
critics to have forged a new and authentically African style, which engaged in a more
profound fashion with the continent's oral storytelling heritage. It was also subsequently deemed to have launched what became known as the 'return to the source'
genre in African filmmaking, that is a body of work that explicitly took its inspiration from the oral tradition, and the action of which was often set in rural African
locations in the pre-colonial era. Although varying greatly in style, films such as
Wend Kuuni, Souleymane Cissé's *Yeelen* (1987) or Idrissa Ouedraogo's *Yaaba* (1989)
enjoyed considerable commercial and critical success both in Africa and beyond.
Supporters saw in these films the development of a new and specifically African aesthetic that would replace the Western-inspired modernism of Sembene and others
like him, while hostile critics saw in them a shift away from the necessary radicalism
of Third Cinema towards the essentialist aesthetics of a timeless Africa. This debate
often involved a rather confusing and generally unsubstantiated set of assumptions
about the audience being addressed by these directors. For instance, Ukadike praises
Yeelen's inventiveness in imitating the structures of orality but he is wary of its 'universalism', which is seen to be the result of the targeting of 'foreign' (i.e. Western)
audiences (1994: 254–62), while Diawara acknowledges that Ouédraogo's films are
beautiful but argues that they are imbued with a 'bourgeois humanism', which is
designed to attract a Western audience (1992: 162). However, it is significant that
neither critic attempts to account for the success of both directors at the box office
in Africa itself.

What exactly is it then that might explain why a film such as *Wend Kuuni* has
proven popular and why it has been deemed more specifically 'African' in form than
the films of a Sembene? Diawara's important article on *Wend Kuuni* identifies three
'classic' oral tropes that would normally constitute separate narratives: the missing husband; the wanted son; and the emancipated daughter (1989: 205). Diawara
deftly analyses Kaboré's highly complex interweaving of these stories – opening with
the missing husband narrative, but then veering off into the tale of the lost child
who is taken in by a kindly family in whose home he encounters the emancipated

daughter – and he writes convincingly of the very slow pace and often wordless narrative, which attempt to reflect the pace and rhythm of African rural life. However, Diawara's overall assessment of the process involved in adapting the oral narrative tradition to contemporary cinematic practice is far less convincing: 'From simple and linear narratives which serve to maintain the status quo, Kaboré has created a complex plot turned against the repressive forces of tradition' (1989: 206). This statement is problematic on a number of levels: firstly, the assertion that oral narratives are deeply conservative and always advocate 'a return to law and order at the end' is an excessive generalisation that simply does not stand up to sustained scrutiny; secondly, to describe oral narratives as 'simple' and 'linear' is to offer a very partial view of this mode of storytelling, which is often highly complex, ornate and digressive in character; and, thirdly, although the film is deemed to be more embedded within the oral tradition, it is ironic that the critic simultaneously underlines its 'modernising' critique of African society. Indeed, if the 'return to the source' movies maintain a didactic slant that is in part informed by a modernising perspective, one is left to wonder if the main difference between a film such as *Xala* and *Wend Kuuni* resides largely in the rural setting of the latter. Josef Gugler writes convincingly of the idealised representation of the country found in some African films (in particular, those of Kaboré and Ouédraogo), which he interprets as an urban perception of a lost rural paradise, an exoticisation designed to appeal to Africans in the cities (2003: 29–36). Africa is a continent that urbanised rapidly in the second half of the twentieth century and it is understandable both that directors should wish to engage with a 'lost' rural world and also that recently urbanised audiences should find such work appealing. Essentially, films dealing with a (more or less) romanticised and untouched African countryside constitute both a form of escapism and a necessary attempt to come to terms with the profound transition that Africa is undergoing.

Jean-Pierre Bekolo is one of the most significant figures in the wave of Francophone African film directors who have emerged since the early 1990s. Far from the didacticism, politics, slow pacing and rural settings that marked previous forms of African filmmaking, his embrace of elements of urban African youth culture and a global 'pop' aesthetic has led to a series of highly innovative and exuberant films such as *Quartier Mozart* (1992) and the sci-fi movie *Les Saignantes* (2005). Bekolo's second feature film, the highly complex film-essay *Aristotle's Plot*, offers a fascinating analysis of the situation of film in Africa. In its bravura opening, two men confront each other at a railway crossing, held at arm's length from one another by the mediating presence of the policeman; one man announces himself as a 'Cineaste', while the other claims to be called 'Cinema':

Cinema: They call me 'Cinema' because I've watched 10,000 films.
Cineaste: Oh yeah? How many of them were African?
Cinema: Very few … because they're shit!
Cineaste: If they are shit then you are shit because you're African!

In this sequence, Bekolo establishes a clear tension between the African filmmaker and the African audience. Which of them might be said genuinely to represent the state of cinema in Africa? Is it the director whose work is deemed 'shit' by 'Cinema' and his gang? Or is it the gang, who are interested only in Hollywood-style action movies and Kung-Fu films? After the confrontation with Cineaste, Cinema is asked by the policeman to produce his ID, and, seemingly to his own bemusement (given the look on his face), he presents a series of ID cards that feature his photograph and the names of several of the most feted African film directors: Mambety, Kaboré, Sembene, Hondo, Cissé. Is Bekolo suggesting (echoing Cineaste's own words) that African films are part of Cinema's identity whether he likes it or not? Or, more prosaically, are these the names of the 'very few' African filmmakers whose work is not 'shit'? The film offers no easy answers to any of these questions but, in its exploration of the tensions between the expectations of director and audience, it provides an important reflection on the future of the film on the continent. Will Francophone African cinema ever manage to find an audience on its home turf?

Conclusion

This chapter has attempted to trace some of the complexity of the filmmaking that has emerged from Francophone West Africa over the past few decades. In place of the monolithic vision of African cinema that has dominated certain accounts of the field, I believe it is vital to trace the series of distinct but intertwining paths that have been followed by filmmakers. These various cinematic approaches may or may not have reached a wide, popular audience in Africa or elsewhere but their popularity or lack of it tells us little or nothing about the supposed 'authenticity' of their cinematic vision. The concept of the 'Screen Griot' may emphaise continuity with the past but, as Barber has argued, popular art forms in Africa – such as cinema – have created brand new audiences and new forms of community:

> [Popular arts] can be said to attract a public rather than a community. Thus, though the prevalent use of popular implies limits, in another sense it points to the rise of a populace of a different range altogether from what was known in the traditional world. (1987: 15)

Cinema has created a new forum in which a form of communal storytelling takes place. The varying blend of oral motifs, didacticism and entertainment contained in these films is evidence of the ongoing evolution of the continent: for what may appear to be fixed modes of receiving or narrating films are in fact inevitably subject to change. As cinematic forms and audience expectations evolve, African films will continue to search for their local audience in complex and innovative ways.

Bibliography

Armes, R. (2006) *African Filmmaking North and South of the Sahara*. Edinburgh: Edinburgh University Press.

Bakari, I. and M. Cham (eds) (1996) *African Experiences of Cinema*. London: British Film Institute.

Barber, K. (1987) 'Popular Arts in Africa', *African Studies Review*, 30, 3, 1–78.

Barrot, P. (ed.) (2005) *Nollywood: le phénomène vidéo au Nigeria*. Paris: L'Harmattan.

Bisschoff, L. and D. Murphy (2007) 'Africa's Lost Classics', special dossier in *Screen*, 48, 4, 493–527.

Cham, M. (1982) 'Ousmane Sembene and the Aesthetics of African Oral Traditions', *Africana Journal*, 13, 1, 24–40.

Diawara, M. (1989) 'Oral Literature and African Film: Narratology in Wend Kuuni' in J. Pines and P. Willemen (eds.) *Questions of African Cinema*. London: British Film Institute, 199–211.

_____ (1992) *African Cinema: Politics and Culture*. Bloomington: Indiana University Press.

_____ (1996) 'Popular Culture and Oral Traditions in African Film', in I. Bakari and M. Cham (eds) *African Experiences of Cinema*. London: British Film Institute, 209–18.

Fanon, F. (1967) *The Wretched of the Earth*. Harmondsworth: Penguin.

Gabriel, T. H. (1982) *Third Cinema in the Third World: The Aesthetics of Liberation*. Ann Arbor: University of Michigan Research Press.

_____ (1989) 'Towards a Critical Theory of Third World Films', in J. Pines and P. Willemen (eds) *Questions of Third Cinema*. London: British Film Institute, 30–52.

Gardies, A. (1989) *Cinéma d'Afrique noire francophone: l'espace miroir*. Paris: L'Harmattan.

Gugler, J. (2003) *African Film: Re-imagining a Continent*. Oxford: James Currey.

Haffner, P. (1978) *Essai sur les fondements du cinema africain*. Abidjan and Dakar: Les Nouvelles Editions Africaines.

Harrow, K. W. (2007) *Postcolonial African Cinema: From Political Engagement to Postmodernism*. Bloomington: Indiana University Press.

Haynes, J. (ed.) (2000) *Nigerian Video Films*. Athens, OH: Ohio University Centre for International Studies.

Jancovich, M., L. Faire with S. Stubbings (2003) *The Place of the Audience: Cultural Geographies of Film Consumption*. London: British Film Institute.

Murphy, D. (2000) *Sembene: Imagining Alternatives in Film and Fiction*. Oxford: James Currey; Trenton, NJ: Africa World Press.

Murphy, D. and P. Williams (2007) *Postcolonial African Cinema: Ten Directors*. Manchester: Manchester University Press.

Pines, J. and P. Willemen (eds) (1989) *Questions of Third Cinema*. London: British Film Institute.

Ruelle, C. (ed.) (2005) *Afriques 50: Singularités d'un cinéma pluriel*. Paris: L'Haramattan.

Taylor, C. (1989) 'Black Cinema in the Post-aesthetic Era', in J. Pines and P. Willemen (eds) *Questions of Third Cinema*. London: British Film Institute, 90–110.

Thackway, M. (2003) *Africa Shoots Back: Alternative Perspectives in Sub-Saharan Francophone African Film*. Oxford: James Currey.

Ukadike, N. F. (1994) *Black African Cinema*. Berkeley: University of California Press.

Intriguing African Storytelling:
On *Aristotle's Plot* by Jean-Pierre Bekolo

Matthias De Groof

'Who is this man called cinema?' Jean-Pierre Bekolo asks Djibril Diop Mambety, the great Senegalese filmmaker. 'Why should it be a man?' Mambety replies, and continues: 'For me, it is a storytelling grandma, as all grandmas do. It could be also another sort of grandma (grammar) the kind that wants you to say things in one way, and not another. But Grandma herself allows us to betray grandma. She will let you contradict grandma. This means that the ABCs you get taught at film school can be absolutely transformed. Grandma wants us each time to reinvent her grammar. Grandma wants us to tell her story in a different way each time. [...] Sometimes she is lazy and tells it in the same way. Then I get angry and say "grandma, come on!" She replies: "go and talk to Grandma". Grandma asks me to always reinvent her discourse, to recreate it for her own durability.'

This short interview between Mambety and Bekolo turned into the film *Grandma's Grammar* (*La Grammaire de Grand-Mère*) in 1996 and was initially intended as a part of *Aristotle's Plot* (1996). Although *Grandma's Grammar* was not inserted, it remains nevertheless of great significance for understanding *Aristotle's Plot* and new African storytelling in cinema. The ambition of Djibril Diop Mambety to 'reinvent the grammar' of storytelling and so to 'reinvent her discourse' is the main thing that made the Cameroonian filmmaker Bekolo the heir to Mambety. The most relevant present-day example of this heritage is *Aristotle's Plot* itself because of its investigation into the roots of the most influential storytelling technique – the one featured in Aristotle's *Poetics*, 'the bedrock of European storytelling' (v.o.)[1] – while at the same time being strongly oriented towards African realities.

In our reference to both Mambety and Aristotle we can distinguish the cultural contexts in which Bekolo's storytelling exists and which shaped *Aristotle's Plot*. The film and its storytelling come out of the tradition of African filmmaking as well as by interaction with the West. On the one hand, Bekolo is often portrayed as a filmmaker praised for his renewing of African cinema by his emancipation from the didactic social realism of his progenitors. *Aristotle's Plot* therefore serves as a case in point for new African storytelling. While leapfrogging over the *griot*-narration that characterises African cinema, he is nonetheless preoccupied with storytelling that is *African*. On the other hand, Bekolo is deeply rooted in the tradition of African struggle against Western imagery and therefore rethinks Western storytelling. In a tension between the popular and the experimental, Bekolo deconstructs Aristotelian storytelling by questioning its claims and by exerting different strategies to give narrative alternatives. Bekolo encounters Western conventions, puts them in perspective, alternates, frustrates and parodies them to remind us not to become or remain trapped in someone else's constructed plot. This two-sidedness, which is definitely not oppositional, is a negotiation – expressed in most diverse ways – that is common to most contemporary African filmmakers.

This chapter will elaborate mainly on narrative aspects evoked by *Aristotle's Plot*. The thematic and aesthetic aspects of the film will be discussed solely in light of the storytelling they are strongly related to. In the first part, entitled 'plot', the chapter will analyse the context Bekoloian storytelling interacts with. This context is constituted both by Aristotelian narrative techniques in classic storytelling and by mimetic realism of the early films of African cinema. The second part, entitled 'counterplot', examines six ways Bekoloian storytelling deals with this multifaceted context. We can recognise strategies Bekolo adopts in dealing with the context in, for instance, avant-garde cinema. The unicity of his strategic storytelling, however, resides in its relation to and concern with the African continent and African cinema, as the chapter will conclude in the last part, entitled 'complot'.

Jean-Pierre Bekolo – born in 1966 in Yaoundé – features as an exemplar filmmaker of the post-independence generation (see Harrow 1999, 2007; Barlet 2000; Ukadike 2002; Armes 2006; Murphy and Williams 2007). At the age of twenty-four, after having made video clips, he was awarded the Prix Afrique en Creation at the 1992 Cannes Film Festival and nominated for the British Film Awards for his first feature film *Quartier Mozart* (1992). This success was followed by the realisation of *Aristotle's Plot* in 1996, intended as the African entry in the British Film Institute's 'Century of Cinema' series but which was never included. Ceaselessly ironic towards African authenticity, Bekolo tells the spectator: 'I was in my bush of Africa chewing kola nut with my grandfather when I heard the drums telling me I had a phone call from London. The BFI wanted me to make a film to celebrate the centenary of cinema. I asked them who else was on the list. Martin Scorsese, Stephen Frears, Jean-Luc Godard ... Then I started wondering why me?' (v.o.).

Plot

How many times have you heard a story of a cop and gangsters? How many times have you heard a story of a filmmaker? This railway crossing you have already seen, witnesses an old quarrel between filmmaker, cinephile and government, all represented by these three individuals. I call it now 'the railway crossing of the three deads', a tribute to all the dead victims of Aristotle's plot. In his time, the happy ending was necessary. Aristotle's disciples understood that the rules they thought were immutable would be changing soon. Death did not exist anymore and the idea of ending a story had to be reinvented. (v.o.)

Essomba Tourneur – also abbreviated ET (extra-terrestrial) – is the protagonist in *Aristotle's Plot*. He is also called 'Cineaste' and nicknamed 'Silly-ass' by local moviegoers, his antagonists, called the Tsotsis. ET returned to his homeland to be an African film purist declared insane by the government. Notwithstanding, he uses a policeman to fight this mob of blockbuster-watching gangsters named Tsotsis. Essomba thinks the only way to save himself and to raise hope for African cinema is to let the government think he stands on their side by pulling the Tsotsis out of their movie theatre which is considered a gangster university. The gang of trash-talking filmgoers, led by the character 'Cinema', ingests the latest imported B-movies in the theatre 'Cinema Africa' and is in conflict with 'Cineaste'. The voice-over by Bekolo, who was asked to make a film celebrating the centenary of cinema, is accompanied by a cameraman who eventually appears to be absent. 'When the camera stops shooting, what remains is storytelling' (Bekolo 1997).

Essomba Tourneur stands for the Westernised African filmmaker. The context *Aristotle's Plot* reflects on is the dependence of African film on northern funding (mostly from Paris but in this case also London) which shaped African cinema into a *cinéma d'auteur*, Westernised and disconnected from popular genres and African audiences. Audiences – symbolised by the Tsotsis – turn towards Hollywood films, the product which is most widely distributed on the African continent, together with Bollywood in the 1970s, 1980s and 1990s and increasingly Nollywood and Ghanaian video films nowadays (see Barlet 2008; Diao 2009). Bekolo's cinematic allegory in *Aristotle's Plot* reflects upon the outsider status of the African filmmaker, the distribution monopoly of foreign films in Africa and their consumption, or in other words, upon the tension between the African filmmaker and the African audiences and the alienation of the former from the latter. 'I put a lot of narration to give a voice, in a way, to the predicaments of African cinema' (Bekolo 1999: 78).

In accordance with these hard realities of African filmmaking that we perceive through Essomba Tourneur's eyes, *Aristotle's Plot* reflects on the Western imagery of Africa that ET carries out in his homeland and that is put on stage by the Tsotsis' comments: 'They project Africans like some aliens from another planet, extraterrestrials without ET's space technology. [...] A goat chasing chickens and chickens chasing goats ... with traditional music! And they call that culture, African culture.' African cinema challenged this exotic imagery throughout its history but was also influenced by it, and by formal aspects of storytelling that go along with Western imagery. Thus, Bekolo questions this aspect not only through his characters in the film, but also through the storytelling of the film itself. *Aristotle's Plot* questions those classic Western scenario structures by using parody of hegemonic storytelling in an allegory of cinema:

> We as Africans, what is cinema for us? Courses of scenario writing, whether it is Syd Field or Robert McKee, say that 'a good story should arouse pity and fear'. Aristotle said this. What do we do of Aristotle? Does a story have to generate pity and fear also in Africa? Do I embrace this formula or do I interrogate it in order to redefine what cinema is? (Bekolo 2006).

The very first words of *Aristotle's Plot* are 'ABC Cinema' that we hear as lyrics on its soundtrack. They refer to the necessity of reinventing hegemonic storytelling taken to heart by Mambety in 'Grandma's Grammar'. 'The idea is to go back to the smallest unit, the word and to assemble them in a way that makes sense' (Bekolo quoted in Latanich 2003). 'How do we tell the story differently? The challenge is to create a new language, a new semantic actually. The moment we create a new semantic, we will be able to speak' (Adesokan 2008).

Aristotle's Plot very clearly puts forward the notion that the challenge of difference relates to the nature of hegemonic storytelling. Bekolo, amongst others, relates the storytelling of, for example, Syd Field or Robert McKee to Aristotle who, in his *Poetics*, defines tragedy as an imitation of an action which achieves, through the representation of pitiable and fearful incidents, the catharsis of such incidents.[2] This catharsis, which is located in every imitative art, is a pleasure which can paradoxically be constituted by, for instance, images of misery. The paradoxical combination of pity and fear in looking at tragedy evokes catharsis – the pleasure which is the very function of tragedy and its storytelling. 'I name that a theory of the bitterness and sweetness of a kola nut. Violence needed for humanity's wellbeing. To inspire fear and pity, that's the mission.[3] Because without fear and without pity, no redemption' (Bekolo 1996). But it does not have to be like that. 'When we made films in the third century B.C., we didn't need a formula. White men call that improvisation, to minimise us. Yet, it is the basis of cinema' (v.o.). The formula is thus not a law, but is considered as a particular 'storytelling technique', that of which the spectator becomes aware throughout the film. 'The formula, for me, is the problem. It is what I believe Africa is suffering from – the Western formula and the content that we are appropriating' (Bekolo 2002).

A plot according to Aristotle is the arrangement of incidents in the storytelling, whereas Bekolo considers Aristotle's plot as an intriguing arrangement of incidents or as collusion. 'Essomba Tourneur reveals us [sic] the greatest plot of all time,' says the narrator. We will try to understand how 'Aristotle's plot' can be seen as a great conspiracy by means of storytelling. In this Aristotelian storytelling the 'pitying in others what we fear for ourselves' contains a purgation of fear: catharsis is achieved by the externalisation of our fear by an image and story which evokes our pity. This storytelling technique, which brings pleasure through – for example – depicting suffering and grief often attributed to Africa through its image, is regularly condemned by African filmmakers.[4] Mimetism in the representation of calamity, and thus its fiction according to a Platonic realism, allows the spectator's pleasure. Representations are nonetheless 'structuring' reality, as Valentin Y. Mudimbe (1998) puts it strongly. The structuring effect on Africa by those images is evoked too by African filmmakers, and Bekolo in particular: 'Tragedy is pushed on Africa' (Bekolo 2002); 'Africa becomes imprisoned by all these recitals about Africa' (Bekolo 2007c); and 'If Africa is shown in a dramatic way, she ends up being it because we integrate drama, we integrate misery, and then we become it' (Bekolo 2006). Essomba Tourneur does not understand his country to which he desired to return. 'Invented stories took the place of reality,' says the narrator.

The externalisation of our fear by a projection (image or/and story) on a mimetic other (pity) brings along with it a pleasure and redemption (catharsis). In the process from fear and pity through its exteriorisation to pleasure, the 'other' serves as our relation to its image and through its function in the story. Exteriorising fear to a mimetic other does not differ from doing it to a real other, as the other only exists as a projection i.e. as an invention reducing the alterity of the other firstly as 'difference' and secondly as a representation. The Aristotelian storytelling technique – in which the representation of otherness brings catharsis – results consequently in an involvement of the spectator which is contra-intuitively derivative and produces a blindness in its appeasement and which is accessory to maintaining the suffering from which the spectator gets pleasure. In other words, mimesis does not necessarily produce catharsis of fearful and pitiable incidents outside of their imaginary representation. The plot in this way becomes a *complot* because the feeling of appeasement is not resolving the pitiable incidents but is rather an accomplice in maintaining pitiable incidents.

> If today the world arouses grief and pity, fear ... it is not by accident. Aristotle, as an alchemist, thought that the mix of these two ingredients would produce a catharsis that would save humanity. Look at the results today. The formula of Aristotle produces gangsters, forgers, illusionists, damned artists, corrupt governments, thieves, killers ... All this is not too bad, because the sweetness of the kola nut comes only after the bitterness. Aristotle has trapped the world by this formula, the 'how to'. And his less inspired modern disciples, like Syd Field, maintain the big lie. [...] If I had to pass my time chewing on a bitter kola nut, hoping there will be a sweet aftertaste, I understand the man who invented candy (v.o.).

In its gaining of appeasement – i.e. the catharsis of pitiable and fearful incidents in their representation while conserving these incidents in reality – mimetic and linear storytelling offers at the same time an impression of a re-instalment of a just symbolic order. A plot functions namely as an understanding of events (see Halliwell, in Aristotle's *Poetics* 1987). It gains insights, clarifications, gives perceptions of coherent relations and alleviates (Hardison, in Aristotle's *Poetics* 1968). This storytelling 'in which the hierarchy amongst the discourses which compose the text ... is defined in terms of an empirical notion of truth', as Colin MacCabe defines 'classic realist text' (1974: 8), 'deceives by producing things like the truth', according to Empedocles.[5]

This deceit – or 'blindness in the appeasement' as it was called above – causes an involvement of the spectator which is not only derivative, but which is thus all the more remote from 'truth' – a truth which is precisely looked after by the 'traditional committed African filmmaker' symbolised on screen by Essomba Tourneur. By putting a character like ET on screen, Bekolo reflects upon the 'quest for truth' through storytelling which characterises the political and socially engaged African cinema of the 1960s and 1970s (that put Ousmane Sembene as father of African cinema) as well as ethnographic filmmaking. Thus, Bekolo not only reassesses the Aristotelian storytelling technique which is present in Hollywood movies that produce alienating imagery of Africa and that are constantly watched by the African audience symbolised by the Tsotsis, but he also eschews the mimetic realism in representational patterns of the tradition of African cinema which seem tributary to Aristotelian conventions.

Mimetism considers reality as knowable and comprehensible (see Harrow 2007: 140–1). Yet ET's presumable use of mimesis in his film style as a quest for truth paradoxically creates a distancing effect from the truth. As Plato puts it in the tenth chapter of the *Republic*: 'the tragic poet [the filmmaker] is an imitator, and therefore, like all other imitators, he is thrice removed from ... the truth'. 'Instead of imitating life, they were imitating an imitation of life', Bekolo tells us about his characters who become filmmakers at one point. The cinema of commitment of Sembene and his contemporaries presented in their representational cinema a veracity residing in the authority of the images (see Diouf 1996). 'The truthful image or voice that presented social problems, that gave voice to the wretched of the earth, to the oppressed masses, emerged as though by itself, as though without any mediating actions' (Harrow 1999: xvi). By his storytelling, Bekolo distrusts the rhetoric of mimesis 'that took its *prises de conscience* to be self-evident, transparent, while ignoring the implicit self-justification involved' (ibid.). Referring to the narrative and aesthetics of video clips, Bekolo defies a non-problematic representation of reality by opting for a style that does not allow the spectator to identify too easily with characters or with the story. Although Bekolo continues, in a way, the evolution of Sembene concerning his thematic choices (from the distant to the local, from extern to intern, from anti-colonialism to the rejection of African elites),[6] he follows his own path on the narrative viewpoint, attracted by the urban cinema (*Badou Boy*, 1970;

Touki Bouki, 1973) and cyclical screenplays (*Le Franc*, 1994) of Diop Mambety.[7] In order to be able to enter into urban phenomena and hybrid experiences, Bekolo uses fragmentised and non-linear recitals. He adopts a narration which does not claim to convey the truth through simply representing the real. More fundamentally, Bekolo continues to do what Grandma asked Djibril Diop Mambety: always to reinvent her grammar. In respect to mimetic social realism of the beginnings of African cinema, 'the game of the contemporary African filmmaker with his spectator gains subtlety. Rather than leading him on a beaten track, Bekolo pre-eminently frustrates the spectator in order to get him elsewhere, towards an understanding out of didacticism' (Barlet 1996: 192).

Counterplot

In our attempt to discern strategies that Bekolo's alternative storytelling adopts in order to repostulate the Aristotelian conventions of linear narrative, mimetic realism, conflict rising to a climax and catharsis, we perceive how these strategies turn towards a certain *Africanité* and particularism. We will refer more deeply to strategies of fragmented storytelling; the function of invisibility; the use of the voice-over and the importance of its fiction status; the strategy of 'blurring'; the setting of the future; and finally the recovery of the second chapter of Aristotle's *Poetics* ('The Comedy') in the revaluation of African imagery and its appropriation of cinematic technique.

The key question of the film – why actors who die in one film reappear alive in another – remains unresolved. The *dénouement* is absent. *Aristotle's Plot* has no evolution to a final plot which could bring catharsis by giving the spectator access through incidents to an intelligible totality. 'My ambivalence with Aristotle's poetics is trying just to follow the formula, and at the end getting lost because those rules do not apply to who you are' (Bekolo 1999: 77). The plot turns back on itself, scenes are repeated and the storyteller is not sure whether he 'occupies the beginning, middle or the end of the plot' (v.o.). This narration prevents the revelation of a coherent order which would bring the spectator sham truth. On the contrary, Bekolo opts for presenting reality as contradictory by showing narrative disparities, contradictory incidents, elements and situations.[8] For instance, when ET's own audiences – those who relate more to Clint Eastwood than to Kocumbo – are killed by him, Bekolo decides he does not like that turn of events – continuing the key question. So he re-starts the story, and now the fight takes place Kung-Fu style in the setting of a western. 'As my grandfather used to say, "Death has never killed nobody." [But] I was already trapped in the narrative my grandfather warned me to avoid. I decided then to stop following Aristotle's principles, to bring the dead back to life and change the rule of the game' (v.o.). The desire for the representation of misfortune by fearful and pitiable incidents fails to appear in this sequence in which the imaginary order completely takes over any reference to the real. Incidents do not construct the plot anymore but lay the plot. 'The imagination is the solution', Bekolo repeats. After this sequence, the already ambivalent and eclectic storytelling falls apart, leads astray, splinters into variations on the theme of the artificiality of film and the actualisation in reality of news from Hollywood that 'no one is dying anymore' in a resurrecting sequence.

The empirical notion of truth in the classic realist text and the assignation of social meaningfulness to materiality by mimetism of pioneering African cinema are countered not only by the structure of the storytelling, but also by the importance of the presence of absence and the invisible which is never revealed in *Aristotle's Plot*, not even at its end. 'Aristotle's Plot may best be considered in the light of what it does not say' (Dye 1998). The invisibility constitutes the 'organising principle of the film, [which] makes all relations possible' (Harrow 2007: 141). Shown hidden in cans and only indirectly by the reflection of their projection on the faces of the spectators, movies make perception possible and constitute the object of desire. This absence not only points at the lack of African films in today's cinema landscape, but is also the framing principle of reality, according to Kenneth Harrow's Lacanian-Žižekian inter-pretation of *Aristotle's Plot*. In this manner, Bekolo refers once again to Mambety, who makes of invisibility his axiom. 'If you want to see, you have to close your eyes. This is the way I make my films' (Mambety 1998). The perspective of the film on reality itself is in this way put at stake. Bekolo wonders: 'Is an image meant to expose reality? Doesn't it conceal more than it reveals?'

The use of voice-over differs deeply from *griot* narration. By questioning his own position as a narrator through a voice-over reflecting on the plot, Bekolo throws himself constantly out of the status which is classically attributed to the omniscient narrator. In this specific and deliberate use of the medium of voice-over – by which Bekolo goes against the grain of a quest for truth – he rather attributes a 'self' to his voice. 'For *Aristotle's Plot*, I couldn't use anything else but fiction in which I have put a lot of voice-over, that is, I have given voice to the "I", a technique unfortunately missing in African cinema. I was once told that no one ever hears what Africans say or what they think. And by extension such a statement would deem to suggest that Africans don't think at all' (Bekolo 1997). Since for the West, Africa is already an imaginary space, Bekolo prefers not to reproduce this imagination by doing documentary or ethnography, he says, but opts for the creation of an alternative imaginative process (see Murphy 2007: 188–204). This process of reinventing, which belongs inherently to African storytelling, is the key to the future of African cinema, according to Bekolo (see Ukadike 2002). *Aristotle's Plot* relies on fiction, even when the fictitious gets eventually transgressed by the blurring of its boundaries.

Blurring reality and the imaginary order (both on an intradiegetic as well as an extradiegetic level); blurring reality and mimesis; reality and cinema; the repre-sented and its representation; urban and rural, modern and traditional, the good and the bad, blurring identities, characters, genres are other examples of Bekolo's strategies. Considering himself at once as a Tsotsi, Bekolo tells us at the beginning of the film: 'By hanging around in front of the movie theatre and seeing films, we ended up finding an imaginary double. It took me [sic.] only a short time for the double taking over the real being you thought you were once' (v.o.). The Tsotsis identify themselves with characters from Hollywood movies[9] and 'take on names like Bruce Lee and Schwarzenegger (sic.) and start envisioning themselves inside the action' (Shea 1998). 'This isn't Aristotle, but Plato – it's Plato's cave, the difference being that when they leave the cave, they take their monikers with them. They have become the shadows in a world with no ideal forms' (Harrow 2007: 145). 'Can we tell the fiction from the real?' (v.o.) Cinema empties out distinctions. As the film continues, ET transforms into a character from the type of film that he despises. Essomba Tourneur, an African as we can hear by his first name, is yet an outsider. He's a 'Tourneur', an equivocator, a *sham*, as is Aristotelian storytelling according to Bekolo. It takes ET two years to understand reality. And in this process, he is changing as a true turner. Essomba Tourneur, the committed African filmmaker, becomes Billy the Kid: '"cinema" has overtaken him' (Harrow 2007: 146). 'Bloodshed transformed once again Essomba who didn't stop changing. [...] He proved by this that a coat can have more than two sides' (v.o.). His change occurs towards the behaviour of the Tsotsis, even though they continue to call him 'Silly-ass'. Yet the further we get into the story the more we become aware that ET resembled the Tsotsis from the very outset. This is already suggested at the beginning of the film when 'Cinema' and 'Cineaste' are both handcuffed by the police. 'Cinema' hands over to the cop several ID cards that feature famous African directors like Hondo, Mambety, Kaboré, Cissé, Gerima, Sembene.[10] 'Filmmakers are gangsters who lack sufficient personality to be real gangsters', according to Bekolo's grand-father (v.o.). The Tsotsis, whose imagination has completely taken over their sense of reality due to their idolatry, correspond in fact with ET who sticks with the image taking over the real. Their struggle to find an identity is their reality (see Dembrow 2008) which is satirised by Bekolo, pointing out the folly of emulation of such facile, second-hand iconography (see Dye 1998). The banishment of the Tsotsis into the jungle causes them to change from their audience position into producers, filmmakers and actors all at once. The heroes are making a film, pushed by the lack of African self-representation. The spectator of *Aristotle's Plot* observes people interacting with and being affected by the medium the spectator too is watching. A shift thus also occurs on an extradiegetic level where the spectators become characters, as they are addressed, and become an important subject of the film, experiencing a 'tragedy'. The viewer's gaze is returned back as object of that gaze. 'Because we are watching a film about people watching the film, *Aristotle's Plot* purposely becomes its own contradiction. It refuses to pretend to be above the contradictions which seem almost inescapable to any film' (Shea 1998). The narrator's parodic voice-over as an intra-diegetic character holds an extradiegetic position questioning his own role and the context of the film, its distribution and reception. Reflecting on his own story, he jumps on a metadiegetic level. Characters prance around like narrator's pawns. Yet the narrator tells the audience his 'characters were out of control'. They complain about the lack of action in the movie and get to insult 'that fucking Jean-Pierre Bekolo' when they call for 'African movies that kick ass'. Bekolo himself feels like a pawn of the BFI after they invite him to contribute to the series commemorating one hundred years of cinema (Bekolo 1997). 'Is it Christian charity or political correctness?' Bekolo thereupon makes a film reflecting the theme of the project, but it gets out of control. At the end of the movie, he addresses us: 'Where has the cameraman gone? He ran away from the spectacle. He neither understood that it was cinema.'

In this cinematic hall of mirrors, Bekolo confronts the spectator with his own gaze also by adopting a strategy of storytelling referring to the future.

> I think putting things in the future is more interesting because the prevalent discourses house Africa in the past. [In *Aristotle's Plot*] the past and present unite in a somewhat funky vision of the future. It may not be a skyscraper but it is something built by those kids towards a kind of vision ... a projection which metaphorically stands for cinema and Africa. (1999: 80)

Bekolo explores the idea of a cinema of anticipation and projection: 'We lost our dreams and that is what we are suffering from actually' (2007a). In the jungle, Cinema contemplates his makeshift movie theatre 'New Africa' which the Tsotsis built, and says: 'This is the real Africa.' When the Tsotsis are building 'New Africa', Cinema says: 'We take what we can get. If it's old: that's good. If it's new and it fits? Excellent!' About his oeuvre, Bekolo writes that he tries to 'structure the narration in the sphere of the S.F., the fantastic' (1999: 74). Yet, in his predilection for the science fiction genre, the virtual is in the service of the real (see Bekolo 2007b). The concept for his television project *Evénement 4* (2005) is REATUAL: the combination of REAL and VIRTUAL. *The Bloodettes*, Bekolo's film from 2005, constitutes one of the first African science fiction movies. In reaction to the cinematic representation of Africa and to the Occidental imagery which situates Africa in the past, the events in *The Bloodettes* occur in 2025 in the dystopian city of Yaoundé. 'Talking about yesterday is difficult when it comes to the subject of Africa', Bekolo tells us; 'talking about today is already too much – that's why I want to talk about the future' (Bekolo 2006). He pursues this theme in his video installation *Une Africaine dans l'espace* (2007) and in his book *Africa for the future* (2009). Parallel to the movie theatre 'New Africa' in *Aristotle's Plot*, the video installation is a UFO which hosts people from the Diaspora seeking a space in which to materialise their dreams.

Not accidentally, when he talks within the film about his filmmaking activity, Bekolo refers to the 2,300 years of African filmmaking. 'My grandfather explains to me that a long time back we knew that thing they call cinema in Africa' (v.o.). By referring to African storytelling twenty-three centuries ago as an answer to the task he received from the BFI to celebrate the hundred years of cinema, Bekolo wants to give a different image of his continent. 'Our task consists in giving an understanding that whites lied with their images', says Souleymane Cissé (Kotlarski and Münch 2001). If the storytelling of *Aristotle's Plot* relies on pitiable and fearful incidents, it is only on an ironic and reflexive level. Bekoloian storytelling resists 'the aesthetics of despair and absence of purposiveness' which characterise some patterns in African cinema preceding Bekolo (Diouf 1996: 33–4). As stated above, Bekolo takes an ambivalent position towards the social critique and political contestation of the committed cinema such as that of Sembene. He considers indeed that this school of social critique essentially recycles the idea of a chaotic, unstable, desperate and despondent Africa. In these films, according to Bekolo, Africa is full of tragedies tending towards the negative (1999: 77). On the contrary, Bekolo translates a pride in being African in his way of filming. Bekolo integrates comedy, satire and humour in his stories. 'I lived in a universe which – according to me – is rather funny' (Bekolo 1992). The voice-over complains that African films do not represent Africa's glory. Bekolo does not tell the dramas of the past, but projects his narrative accounts into the future. He does not lock Africa up in an image of grief and misery but makes the characters of *Aristotle's Plot* build 'New Africa'. In this way, Bekolo hopes to 'counterbalance some prevalent ideas that were formed of what is called "African cinema"' (Bekolo 1992) and which were ingrained in its storytelling, themes and aesthetics. The revaluation of his image is not built with pitiable and fearful incidents and is even maybe only possible when abandoning this storytelling technique. 'Formula is for those who do not have any imagination, and we don't need it. [...] As I was reading the *Poetics* I realised something was missing – comedy' (Bekolo 2002), which is an approach inherent to African narrative traditions, according to Bekolo. This revalor-isation of the African representation through filmmaking comes from the thought that the image and the story are the quintessential solution to what the intervention of the other meant to Africa: its reduction and negation. 'Africa has only one problem: how it's represented all over the world. ... If the problem is the image then the solution is also the image' (Bekolo, quoted in Paramoer 2008).[11] Can Africa emerge from the shadow that made it 'the dark continent' in Western eyes by the light of cinema? We can understand the new ways of storytelling, and also the proposition which Bekolo advances (that African cinema is the oldest cinema) combined with Bekolo's parodic image of Hollywood (the depiction of Modernity as defined by the West in all its ridiculous glory) as hyping up the image of Africa that Europe keeps inventing. Remarkably, Bekolo is not alone in his position of defending the presence of cinema in Africa's history. Mambety states that 'cinema was born in Africa, because the image itself was born in Africa. The instruments, yes, are European, but the creative necessity and rationale exist in our oral tradition. [...] Oral tradition is a tradition of images. [...] Imagination creates the image and the image creates cinema, so we are in direct lineage as cinema's parents' (quoted in Ukadike 1999). Congolese filmmaker Balufu Bakupa-Kanyinda Kanyinda says: 'I made a film called *10,000 Years of Cinema* because I'm convinced that 10,000 years ago, here in Africa, a *griot* made cinema. The *griot* is the narrator, the storyteller. Even though there is no camera, when he tells stories, we can see images' (in Kotlarski and Münch 2001).

> Cinema wasn't born twice. It was in Africa twenty-three centuries ago. [...] What is an initiation ceremony? People in pursuit of a goal, whose actions form scenes divided into crisis, confrontation, climax and resolution. All wrapped up with pictures and sound. Stories, images, sounds, narrations, rhythms. Is there anything here that is not African? Fantastic and mystic? Walt Disney, we got; *Lion King*, we got; sex, action, violence, we got; massacres, we got; comedy, music, we got; Paul Simon, we got; dance and dancers, we got; beauty, ugliness, we got; thinkers, we got; Aristotle, catharsis, kola nuts, we got; to make it short, what don't we have? (v.o.)

Bekolo does not only purport that cinema has been invented in Africa twenty-three centuries ago – which is approximately when Aristotle wrote his *Poetics* – to emphasise that African storytelling is an alternative as valid as Aristotelian storytelling. By his claim, he also puts an image of Africa with a history. This strongly counters the Occidental idea of a backward Africa without a past (Basil Davidson, G. W. F. Hegel, Joseph Conrad) and constitutes a prompt response to the invitation of the BFI which – in the eyes of Bekolo – 'casts African cinema as a "belated gesture", vainly attempting to catch up with the rest of the world, destined only to copy rather than to innovate' (Murphy 2007: 201). 'Was I accepting a challenge from someone already standing on the finish line?' wonders Bekolo. 'I suspect the decision to invite me ... could only be a subplot, twenty-three centuries old; Aristotle's Plot' (v.o.). Of course, African films were only recently born, and this in a situation of oppression and marginalisation in which the African is understood as 'the "other" than' ... (*La noire de...*, Sembene). This situation of *alienation* forced the African to make an attempt to think of the self by way of the image and stories which were imposed by the centre, and in extension, by the technique which the coloniser possessed (see Elungu 1984). The appropriation of the image, the mastering of the (Aristotelian) storytelling and the (cinematographic) technique is the neutralisation of that situation of alienation. In this perspective, referring to twenty-three centuries of African cinema metaphorically advances the assertion that African (filmic) storytelling does not *inevitably* and *necessarily* have to be a reaction to the intervention of the other anymore. The other is not *indispensable* for the African to define himself.[12] Our analysis of *Aristotle's Plot* as a 'reaction towards Occidental storytelling' has now been reversed by African filmmakers who argue that cinema is part of an African essence and is intrinsic to their culture. Claiming the invention of cinema is, furthermore, related to a certain openness already mentioned above, although this may seem paradoxical at first sight. How can Bekolo state – apparently with Mambety, Kaboré and others – that cinema is born in Africa while cinema in its technical aspects at least, is clearly a non-African invention but comes from abroad as Med Hondo ironically states in *Les 'bicots-Nègres' vos voisins* (1974)? This allegation seems to Westerners objectionable due to a false opposition between adaptation and authenticity.[13] The un-authentic imitation, perceived as arrogation, is for Western thinking a condemned value, because it is not original, authentic, creative. Still nowadays, this kind of appropriation is 'rejected in a monstrous succursal of Occidentalism', write Jean Baudrillard and Marc Guillaume (1992: 57).[14] Yet cinema has not been borrowed and cannot be a derivation. African cinema is the result of hospitality towards the technique and its narrative potentialities, an absorption and transmutation/transformation of its use, which implies a total liberty of storytelling. 'What is film – the content or the container? Although the container can have some content, I felt that the content should be invented in Africa' (Bekolo 2002). The 'integration' of foreign technique or signs means a 'recycling' by the filmmakers for their own motives and purposes. Hospitality is no arrogation: it preserves integrity and the integration results in something which is not reducible anymore. Technique is not a vehicle for/of unilateral universalism, as *Aristotle's Plot* shows. African cinema goes beyond its technical reality to go in a kind of extra-territoriality of the cinematographic technology which frees itself from it. 'To me', concludes Bekolo, 'what makes a good film is not the camera or technique. One has to master and control the basic elements of cinema. To me, the narrative is a critical choice. Why are you telling this story but not the other?' (1999: 73).

Complot

The polyphonic storytelling of Bekolo corresponds with an important claim of the Third World cinema that the condition to be understood is to make audiences understand that a different cinema is possible. This understanding refutes claims of universality by classic film language and Aristotelian narration, along with its pitiable and fearful image. 'The issue of universal films ... means that some people have a specific idea of what Africa or an African is. These contradictions are the key elements that inform my work', says Bekolo (1999: 72). He achieves the refutation not only by presenting a particular or 'different' cinema in order to offer alternatives to imagery of Africa constructed by fearful and pitiable incidents, but also by putting this 'conspiring imagery' on stage. Notwithstanding the fact that classic texts can be universally understood, those texts are unmasked as particular, or in other words, Occidental. 'Hollywood is just a place' (Bekolo 2002). Bekolo consequently counts on a universal understanding of his particular films and filmmaking, and in extension, of a *unique* 'yet to come' African film language in which he believes. Pointing to the particularism of Aristotelian narration coincides with the thought that his particular and unique narration can be universally accessible. This ambition comes already into force in Cameroon: Bekolo tells a story using image (film) – which is the mode of communication in this country consisting of two hundred populations – and the common languages (French and English) while the use of the *lingua franca* is not at all an evident choice amongst African filmmakers. 'I exploit the everyday to make a universal language out of it' (Bekolo 2006); 'My main interest is in mastering and manipulating the medium to create a [relation] with the audience so anybody can understand the film. The challenge is to experiment with cinema language. [...] I try to find a logic, premised on some African elements' (Bekolo 1999: 73).

In his concern that the contextual and particular has a universal reach, the film-maker inevitably meets the question 'how is he perceived?'. The cultural framework in other words is enlarged. Bekolo's project turns by no means upon its 'difference' or its differentiation, but on the contrary throws open difference by the interaction of the gazes. From this follows the openness of African cinema, confirmed by Abderrahmane Sissako. 'We are more universal than Europeans are. [...] The Other is less different for the African as is the African for the Others' (quoted in Gavron 1995). Bekolo's practical answer to the question 'in how many ways can cinema tell a story?' goes back to the necessity of dealing with the intervention of the other. The presence of the other is an undeniable part of African history and shapes the self-representation and auto-conception of Africans which is evoked in their artistic expressions. Even though these arts cannot be reduced to this confrontation, which is for that matter not oppositional, they cope with the intervention of the other which is a negating one, by expressing the need for affirmation of the self and thus the will to being understood. Storytelling, and in particular cinema, is one of the ways in which this negating gaze can be returned by self-representation and by ascribing to the self the right to own a proper gaze on the 'other', as *Aristotle's Plot* does explicitly. Hence the necessity of 'speaking ideally to everybody': reaching the universal other is the ideal affirmation of the self. Creating the possibility of universal understanding is the condition of reaching the other in his alterity, an alterity which the African filmmaker wants to be acknowledged for, contrary to being reduced to a mere negation or variation of the self and as the other's pitiable and fearful imagery. Comprehension of 'different' cinema needs thus comprehension of 'difference': an understanding that goes beyond a particular system of knowledge. This idea of the possibility of understanding alterity is thus based on (a certain notion of) universality. The escape from the imprisoning image places its hope in this shared comprehension.

Notes

1 This abbreviation (v.o.) used throughout the chapter indicates the voice-over in *Aristotle's Plot* spoken by Bekolo as narrator.

2 This notion of tragedy must be distinguished from 'the tragic' and is closer to our modern understanding of the dramatic and – more generally – to storytelling. See Hardison's commentary on Chapter VI in Aristotle, *Poetics*, 1968.

3 For Bekolo – contrary to Hardison's comment on the *Poetics* (1968: XIV1.17) – pity and fear do not intrinsically belong to the incidents nor are the relations between the incidents universal. Bekolo considers – along with someone like Bywater (see Aristotle's *Poetics* 1909) – that the experience of catharsis is related to the psychology of the spectator, rather than to what happens in the tragedy itself. Moreover, the response of the audience is not only related to emotions, rather than to

incidents – but is also relative. This scepticism towards attributing pity and fear to the nature of tragedy, together with the consideration that catharsis and the experiences of pity and fear are not emotional imperatives, allows Bekolo to put these elements in a cultural perspective.

4 See the documentary Kotlarski & Münch, *Les Fespakistes*, and Ouedraogo, *Les parias du cinéma*.

5 Empedocles, *The Two Arguments* in Aristotle, *Poetics*, introduction, commentary and appendixes by D. W. Lucas, Oxford, Clarendon Press, 1968, XIX.

6 See M. De Groof, La critique Saignante, 'La critique saignante', in *Les films d'Afrique et la critique*, S. Lelievre (ed.), coll. Images plurielles, L'Harmattan, Paris, to be published.

7 We can find Sembene's legitimation of his choice not to transgress mimetism in his critiques of the participatory anthropological film practice of Jean Rouch. 'He considered us as being insects', Sembene said about Rouch once, the latter always defending that an anthropologist could not be an entomologist anymore. The shared anthropology and interactive documentary – where the film objects participate in making storytelling and aesthetic choices, and becoming film subjects – wants to nuance the perception on alterity by breaking the invisibility of the observator/ filmmaker. Sembene argues that the making explicit of interaction and revealing of the influence of perception conceals argumentation and hierarchy which are still present in Rouch's imagery. 'When we are portrayed in a style which is more realist than realism, it is even more dangerous, because one would believe in it more easily.' Paradoxically, we could consider the Brechtian motives in Bekolo's narration and storytelling 'more realist than realism', falling into the trap that Sembene always avoided.

8 See the first essential feature of MacCabe's definition of the classic realist text: 'the classic realist text cannot deal with the real as contradictory' (1974: 12).

9 This phenomenon has an old history in African cinema. Oumarou Ganda has taken the name 'Edgar G. Robinson' and his friends the names of other American stars, in Rouch's *Moi, un noir* (Haynes 1999: 35). Other African filmmakers such as Dany Kouyaté (*Ouaga Saga*), Bouna Medoune Seye (*Bandits Cinema*), Moussa Sene Absa (*Ça twiste à Popenguine*), Pierre Yameogo (*moi et mon blanc*), and others have pictured these identity quests by African audiences through imported media as well.

10 The main idea, however, is to show that African cinema has many identities.

11 The belief Bekolo has in the power of the image is indeed visible in the extreme influence of Hollywood upon the Tsotsis (Shea 1998).

12 A paradox is occurring here. Bekolo shows contemporary young urban Africans in their need to find their identity through identification with Hollywood heroes. On a surface level, those quests for identities are represented by Bekolo in an ironic way, according to the use of comedy in the tradition of Cameroonian storytelling and popular theatre (see Murphy & Williams 2007). Identification with foreign influences appears as alienating (see Haynes 1999: 39) which mirrors on a second level the spectators' preconceptions. On a third level, taking a hero as your alter-ego reflects the desire to identify with some characters that challenge the system, which gives you a cathartic release. On a fundamental level, however, Bekolo shows those imaginary quests as reality. Bekolo can maintain the idea that the need for defining in reference to the 'other' and the tradition of militant cinema has been surpassed (an idea which is symbolised by the status he ascribes to African cinema as the first cinema) because the universality he attributes to his own films are projected onto those of Hollywood and because the Tsotsis give their own meaning to those films which are played in 'cinema Africa' without being swallowed by them: this appropriation (which is not an arrogation) implies that the process of constituting the identity does not rely anymore on the (creation of) the other, but on the proper imagination. Using (the invisible) Hollywood movies to visualise this identity process makes Bekolo even more a character in his own film.

13 For an account of this aspect, see M. De Groof, *La critique Saignante*, 'La critique saignante', in *Les*

films d'Afrique et la critique, S. Lelievre (ed.), coll. Images plurielles, L'Harmattan, Paris.
14 This reasoning is inspired by a text of Baudrillard (1992) on Japan. Baudrillard himself argues that his reflection on Japan is exemplary for 'all other cultures, different than ours [i.e. the European]'.

Bibliography

Adesokan, A. (2008) 'The challenges of Aesthetic Populism: An Interview with Jean-Pierre Bekolo', *Postcolonial Text*, 4, 1. On-line. Available: http://postcolonial.org/index.php/pct/article/view/771 /538 (accessed on 5 November 2009).

Akudinobi, J. G. & Bekolo, J. P. (1999) 'African Cinema and the Question of Meaning. An interview with Jean-Pierre Bekolo'. *Third Text*. 48: 71-80.

Aristotle (1909) *Poetics*. Trans. and comm. I. Bywater. London & New York: Oxford University Press.

_____ (1968) *Poetics*. Trans L. Goldon; Comm. O. B. Hardison. New Jersey: Prentice-Hall.

_____ (1987) *Poetics*. Trans. and comm. S. Halliwell. London: Duckworth.

Armes, R. (2006) *African Filmmaking North and South of the Sahara*. Edinburgh: Edinburgh University Press.

Barlet, O. (1996) *Les cinémas d'Afrique noire, le regard en question*. Paris: Images Plurielles.

_____ (2000) 'Les nouvelles écritures francophones des cinéastes afro-européens'. *Cinémas*,11, 1, 113–32.

_____ (2008) 'Bollywood et l'Afrique: le divorce?'. *Africultures*. On-line. Available: www.africultures. com/php/index.php?nav=article&no=8107 (accessed on 14 October 2008).

Baudrillard, J. and M. Guillaume (1992) *Les faces de l'altérité*. s.l.: Editions Descartes.

Bekolo, J. P. (1992) 'La parole à Jean-Pierre Bekolo. « Il ne faut pas réduire la vision d'un peuple à la réalité »'. *Ecrans d'Afrique* n°2 : 14-17.

_____ (1996) *La grammaire de grand-mère*. Afrique du Sud, 9'. (film)

_____ (1997) 'Comment on *Aristotle's Plot* by Jean-Pierre Bekolo' in M. N. Eke, K. W. Harrow and E. Yewah (eds) *African Images, Recent Studies and Text in Cinema*. Asmara: Africa World Press, 19–30.

_____ (1999) 'African Cinema and the Question of Meaning, An interview with Jude Akudinobi', *Third Text*, 48, 71–80.

_____ (2002) 'interview with Ukadike' in N. F. Ukadike, *Questioning African Cinema: Conversations with Filmmakers*. London: University of Minnesota Press, 217–38.

_____ (2005) *Bekolo at the Historical Black College Panthers*. On-line. Available: bekolocourses.blog-spot.com (accessed on 11 December 2005).

_____ (2006) Bekolo in a Workshop on the Thematic and Aesthetics of African Cinema, unpublished. Brussels: La coopération par l'éducation de la culture (CEC) & Afrique Taille XL, EM.

_____ (2007a) 'Les chantages identitaires, interview avec Jean-Pierre Bekolo', *France 3*. On-line. Available: http://www.dailymotion.com/video/x1g4o3_adsl-tv-20070314-235621-france-3-na_ events (accessed on 15 March 2009).

_____ (2007b) 'Un cinéaste pratique. Interview de Jean-Pierre Bekolo Obama par Jean-Marie Mollo Olinga', *Africiné*. On-line. Available: http://www.africine.org/?menu=art&no=6838 (accessed on 19 August 2007).

_____ (2007c) 'Parole à Jean-Pierre Bekolo', *Dailymotion.com*. RIFF Production. On-line. Available: http://www.dailymotion.com/video/x3k8ml_parole-a-jeanpierre-bekolo_news (accessed on 23 November 2007).

_____ (2008b) 'Jean-Pierre Bekolo à Kumasi, Ghana'. *Technorati.com*. On-line. Available: http://www. youtube.com/watch?v=SkD-SeJ4YHc (accessed on 24 February 2008).

_____ (2009) *Africa for the Future. Sortir un nouveau monde du cinéma*. Yaoundé: Collection Mondes en Mouvement – Cinema, Dagan & MedYa.

Boughédir, F. (1983) *Caméra d'Afrique*. Tunisie-France, 95'. (film)

De Groof, M. (forthcoming) 'La critique saignante', in S. Lelievre (ed.) *Les films d'Afrique et la critique*. yet unpublished, Paris : coll. Images plurielles, L'Harmattan.

De Groof, M. (unpublished) 'Representation of African film audiences in African film. How text reflects on context & the case of Aristotle's Plot'.

Dembrow, M. (2008) 'Program Notes for *Aristotle's Plot*', in Ninth Annual Cascade Festival of African Films.

Diao, C. (2009) 'Le cinéma africain vu par les spectateurs maliens', *Africultures*. On-line. Available: http://www.africultures.com/php/index.php?nav=article&no=8294 (accessed on 13 January 2009)

Diouf, M. (1996) 'Histoires et actualités dans *CEDDO* d'Ousmane Sembene et *HYENES* de Djibril Diop Mambéty', in S. Niang (ed.) *Littérature et cinéma en Afrique francophone*. Paris: L'Harmattan, Images Plurielles, 15–34.

Dye, M. (1998) 'Aristotle's Plot: Lampooning Cinema and Identity', *African Media Project*. Michigan: Michigan State University. On-line. Available: http://ccms.ukzn.ac.za/index.php?option=com_content&task=view&id=184&Itemid=43 (accessed on 7 November 2009).

Elungu, P. E. A. (1984) *Eveil philosophique africain*. Paris: L'Harmattan.

Gavron (1995) *Y a pas de problème !, Fragments de cinémas Africains*. (film)

Harrow K. W. (ed.) (1999) *African Cinema: Post-Colonial and Feminist Readings*. Asmara: Africa World Press.

_____ (2007) *Postcolonial African Cinema: From Political Engagement to Postmodernism*. Bloomington: Indiana University Press.

Haynes, J. (1999) 'African Filmmaking and the Postcolonial Predicament: *Quartier Mozart* and *Aristotle's Plot*', in K. W. Harrow (ed.) *African Cinema: Post-Colonial and Feminist Readings*. Asmara: Africa World Press, 21–44.

Kotlarski F. & E. Münch (2001) *Les Fespakistes*, Burkina Faso, 52' (film)

Latanich, K. (2003) 'The Cameroonian Connection'. *The Chronicle*. On-line. Available: http://dukechron-icle.com/node/131930 (accessed on 13 November 2003).

MacCabe, C. (1974) 'Realism and the Cinema: Notes on some Brechtian Theses', *Screen*, 15, 2, 7–27.

Mambety, D. D. (1998) *Entretien avec Djibril Diop-Mambety*, Médiathèque des trois mondes, 12'. (film)

Mudimbe, V. Y. (1988) *The Invention of Africa: Gnosis, Philosophy and the Order of Knowledge*. Indianapolis: Indiana University Press.

Murphy, D. and P. Williams (2007) *Postcolonial African Cinema: Ten Directors*. Manchester: Manchester University Press.

Ouedraogo, I. (1997) *Les parias du cinéma*, Burkina Faso, 6' (film).

Paramoer, E. (2008) 'On Africa's Input', *Inputblog*. On-line Available: http://inputblog.wordpress.com/2008/04/03/on-africas-input/ (accessed on 3 April 2008).

Shea, M. (1998) 'Aristotle's Plot' in *African Media Project*. Michigan: Michigan State University. On-line. Available: http://ccms.ukzn.ac.za/index.php?option=com_content&task=view&id=304&Itemid=44 (accessed on 7 November 2009).

Ukadike, N. F. (1999) 'The Hyena's Last Laugh, A Conversation with Djibril Diop Mambety'. *Transition* 78 8(2): 136-153. Reprinted in *California Newsreel*, On-line. Available: http://newsreel.org/articles/mambety.htm (accessed on 23 June 2010).

_____ (2002) *Questioning African Cinema: Conversations with Filmmakers*. London: University of Minnesota Press.

Storytelling and
Visual Forms

Pirosmani's Passion: Narration and the Aesthetics of Pirosmanashvili's Paintings in Georgian Film

Gesine Drews-Sylla

In Georgian and Soviet-Russian culture, Niko Pirosmanashvili's paintings play a very important role: for Russian avant-garde art, they became part of the 'Russian' primitivism (just as Rousseau's paintings did for the French avant-grade). His paintings were originally displayed at Tret'yakov Gallery in Moscow (see Rakitin and Rakitin 1988: 27; Curiger 1995: 16) and after they were removed from the gallery under Stalinism they were later re-displayed there. For Georgia, Pirosmanashvili and his paintings have become one of its primary national symbols. Today, most of his paintings are displayed at the Georgian National Museum (Shalva Amiranashvili Museum of Fine Arts) in Tbilisi.

His life and paintings have inspired two films in Georgian-Soviet film history which both work with intermedial differences between film and painting: *Pirosmani* by Giorgi Shengelaya (USSR, 1969) and *Arabeskebi Pirosmanis Temaze* (*Arabesques on the Pirosmani Theme*) by Sarkis Ho'vsep'i P'arach'anh'anc, also internationally known as Sergei Paradzhanov (USSR, 1985). In both films, film language closely follows visual elements of Pirosmanashvili's paintings: in *Pirosmani* we find scenes that were restaged in accordance with his paintings, forming the main elements of the artist's narrated biography. In *Arabeskebi Pirosmanis Temaze* the complicated and highly elaborated arabesque structure lacks a distinctive plot, mainly circling around elements of Pirosmanashvili's oeuvre in a self-reflexive manner. It is mostly Pirosmanashvili's paintings themselves that form a filmic arabesque.[1]

For this reason, Pirosmanashvili's biography, his works and the specific film narration form an inseparable unit that must be contextualised within Soviet-Georgian film history. The Soviet-Georgian cinema developed a unique narrative film language which was based on Georgian literature, art and music and was told in parables, myths, and so on, partially in order to avoid Soviet censorship when dealing with contemporary problems.[2] This chapter will concentrate on the narration of the film *Pirosmani* within its overall historical, biographical and aesthetic contexts and aims at opening hidden layers beyond the quasi-biographical narration of the artist's life that are introduced in the film by means of an aesthetic principle based on Pirosmanashvili's paintings themselves.

Niko Pirosmanashvili: life, work, myth

The painter Niko Pirosmanashvili (also internationally known as Pirosmani) lived the homeless life of a poor bohemian artist in the Georgian capital of Tbilisi at the turn of the twentieth century, then still part of the Tsarist empire. As an autodidactically trained painter, he made his living by wandering through shops and bars, painting everyday paintings commissioned by the local petit-bourgeois such as trade signs, mural paintings, panels or individual portraits in exchange for food, shelter and alcohol. His work was outstanding though, and Pirosmanashvili excelled in his local environment artistically as much as he did intellectually. His style was unique; he painted representatives of different social classes (pedlars, small tradesmen, the rich and the poor, fishermen, artisans, children), scenes from Georgian history, animals, vast landscapes, rural scenes, Georgian festivities and folk customs such as simple picnics, grape harvests, weddings or still lives as well as religious themes, especially Easter motifs or church festivities. Even though he received no formal education[3] neither in classical nor in traditional styles of painting, his own style is far from naïve or primitive. Mostly painted on black wax cloth, his work combines influences ranging from folk art to monumental medieval frescos, from aesthetic traditions such as religious icons to local painting traditions of the eighteenth and nineteenth centuries which were preserved in the traditional local painters' guilds, and in European realistic painting or early photography (see Rakitin and Rakitin 1988: 26; Okroshvaridze et al. 1995: 88; Smolik 1995). His paintings often show static figures that are either presented by themselves or in groups in front of vast landscapes or otherwise receding backgrounds in an aesthetic fashion that is reminiscent of the depiction of saints in orthodox icons (see Smolik 1995: 99). Pirosmanashvili had his own elaborated aesthetic principles, for example regarding the use of colours such as black and white, in order to depict the contradictions inherent in life (see Okroshvaridze et al. 1995: 94). He was highly aware of the artistic and material value of his paintings even though the price he sold them for hardly ever came close to this value.

His life, about which relatively little is known,[4] is surrounded by a whole range of myths that are sometimes based on facts and sometimes belong to the realm of legends, which are both essentially inseparable from the recipient. It is a well-known fact that the Russian avant-garde artists Mikhail Le-Dant'yu and the brothers

Kirill and Il'ya Zdanevich 'discovered' Pirosmanashvili. One of the reasons why many of his paintings were preserved is his contact with members of the Russian futurist movement, yet simultaneously this is one of the legends surrounding him. As a result of this acquaintance, his paintings were included in Mikhail Larionov's and Natal'ya Goncharova's epoch-making exhibition *Mishen'* (*Target*) in Moscow in 1913 along with paintings by Larionov, Goncharova, Malevich and Chagall (see Rakitin and Rakitin 1988: 20–1) and other newly 'discovered primitivist' painters. Subsequently, in 1916, the recently founded Society of Georgian Artists acknowledged Pirosmanashvili as an artist and invited him to an assembly (see Zdanevich 1965: 35; Okroshvaridze et al. 1995: 92). However, Pirosmanashvili withdrew completely from this milieu after a caricature appeared in the newspaper *Sakhalkho Purceli* which presented him painting one of his masterpieces (that in the aftermath, has often been associated with him) the *Giraffe* (1905) (see Curiger 1995: 90).[5] The caricaturist lamented Pirosmanashvili's lack of formal training and suggested he visit an academy before daring to exhibit his paintings again. This complete withdrawal led to the formation of the myth of the doomed artist Pirosmanashvili who gave up society for a life completely dedicated to his art and who is said to have died forgotten and alone in 1918.

Of his estimated two thousand or so pictures, about two hundred have been preserved (see Okroshvaridze et al. 1995: 95). Their reception has always been closely associated with Georgian culture and forms a myth in itself. Grigol Robakidze (1882–1962), a Georgian contemporary of Pirosmanashvili's and well-known Georgian author, is even quoted as saying 'who sees Pirosmani, sees Georgia' (Rakitin and Rakitin 1988: 24).

It is this complex mythologically enriched background against which the film *Pirosmani* – as a quasi-biography – has to be read.

Georgian-Soviet film traditions

The film tradition within which *Pirosmani* was filmed and produced is inexorably linked with Russian and Soviet film history, as Georgia was part of the Soviet Union beginning in 1922 and had already been part of the Tsarist colonial empire since 1783; independence was only regained in 1991 after the demise of the Soviet Union. During Soviet times, Georgian cinema formed a highly aesthetically productive part of Soviet film history within which the Shengelaya family played a significant role. In the early Soviet Union, Giorgi Shengelaya's father Nikoloz was the director of two influential silent films, *Éliso* (*Eliso* or *Caucasian Love*, 1929) and *Dvadtset' shest' komissarov* (*Twenty-Six Commissars*, 1933).[6] Both films were made under the influence of and within the hopes of early Soviet ethnic policies that treated the Caucasian historic national liberation movements as resistance against Tsarist politics. *Éliso* which is set in Chechnya is aesthetically interesting. Under the influence of the stage director Mardzhanivshvili, the filmmaker Shengelaya implemented Caucasian theatre traditions in the film, especially in modelling its characters which seem to step out from a choir. Forceful Tsarist resettlements carried out in Chechnya in 1864 formed the quasi-documentary backdrop for a melodramatic love story between a Christian and Muslim. The style was shaped significantly by the Russian co-writer Sergei Tret'yakov (1832–1939) who was the editor of the Soviet factographic avant-garde journals *LEF* (1923–25) and *Novy LEF* (1927–28) (see Amiredžibi 1988: 54). He started the film with a historic Tsarist document commanding the beginning of the deportations. The quasi-documentary style is reinforced by an elaborate presentation of local costumes and customs (see Zorkaya 2005: 175–6).

At the time that the film *Pirosmani* was made forty years later, the situation was different. During this time the Soviet avant-garde had been subjected to Stalinist suppression as much as the self-conscious representation of ethnic and national identities of the early Soviet Union had. Both had been replaced by a centralised Russian-Soviet policy that brutally persecuted any political or aesthetic deviations. The post-Stalinist thaw had brought some relief and at the time that *Pirosmani* was filmed, the depiction of the multicultural Soviet Union was officially encouraged again within certain limits.[7] The Soviet cinema of the stagnation period was generally characterised by a retraction from social problems which had shaped earlier periods, such as the cinema of the early 1960s, which was still searching for 'socialism with a human face', or even the immediate post-Stalinist thaw films of the late 1950s, the main topic of which was the depiction of individual fate within the tumult of war. The period of 1967 and 1968 was generally characterised by an apolitical, uninvolved author cinema that turned to art as such (Zorkaya 2005: 395). Thematically, *Pirosmani*, with its description of an individual artist's struggle for life and free expression set in a Georgian nationalist context, fits into this overall scheme very well.

Thus, *Pirosmani* should be considered within the context of the 'poetic' or 'archaic' school in Soviet cinema inaugurated by Sergei Paradzhanov's *Tini zabutykh predkiv* (*Shadows of Forgotten Ancestors*, 1964).[8] During the 1960s and 1970s this school was developed mostly by non-Russian directors like Yury Illyenko and Leonid Osyka from Ukraine, Eldar Shengelaya (Giorgi Shengelaya's brother), Tengiz Abuladze and Otar Ioseliani from Georgia, Bolotbek Shamshiev and Tolomush Okeyev from Kyrgyzstan, Artavazd Peleshyan from Armenia and Andrei Tarkovsky as a Russian exception (see Marshall 1992; Oeler 2006: 479–80).[9] Films of the 'poetic' or 'archaic' school often accentuate the cultural specificities of the respective republics and therefore feature 'the folklore, costumes, decorative arts, and music of particular ethnic groups' (Oeler: 2006: 479).[10] The term 'poetic cinema' alludes to the 'distinction between a cinema built primarily around the symbolic and the graphic "rhymes" of its images and a cinema dominated by narrative cause and effect' (Oeler 2006: 480), as Karla Oeler explains referring to Roman Jakobson's (1958) famous definition of the poetic function. In his influential essay 'Arkhaisty ili novatory' ('Archaists or Innovators', 1970)[11] Mikhail Bleiman (1970) coined the term 'archaic school' as a distinctive indication of this special direction in Soviet film history. It describes those Soviet films from the 1960s and 1970s that 'began treating the problem of artistic creation and depicting the writers, poets, musicians and painters of the past: Chekhov, Tchaikovsky, Vazha-Pshavela, Andrei Rublev, Sayat-Nova, Pirosmani' (Marshall 1992: 175) and thus started deflecting from the ideological norms of Socialist Realism. 'Above all, the artist appears in these films as a kind of catalyst of moral principles. Creative art is seen not as a vehicle of political propaganda, but first of all as a means of moral expression reflecting the responsibility of an artist to himself, to his talent and to his calling' (Marshall 1992: 176).

Shengelaya's *Pirosmani*: a Georgian passion

Giorgi Shengelaya's film *Pirosmani* was shot and released in Georgia in 1969.[12] Critics praised it, especially in the West (see Elley 1974; Glaessner 1974; Gow 1974; Capdenac 1975; Horton 1978–79; Aidan 1989),[13] and it is regularly included in encyclopaedias on Georgian film history (see Freunde der deutschen Kinemathek e.V. 1975: 31–4; Radvanyi 1988). Although articles or books on Soviet and Georgian or Caucasian film history generally emphasise the tremendous meaning of the Soviet Republic's contribution to Soviet film history, *Pirosmani* is usually only mentioned in passing (see Liehm and Liehm 1977: 331; Marshall 1992: 178; Dallet 1992: 312; Zorkaya 2005: 428). Despite its success with film critics, especially in academic discussions, it seems to be overshadowed by the overwhelming craftsmanship and ingenious perfection of the films by Sergei Paradzhanov. And indeed, the film was released one year after Paradzhanov's *Sayat-Nova* (*Nran guyne/The Colours of Pomegranates*, 1968) which is aesthetically much more daring.

Sayat-Nova is the film in which Paradzhanov perfected the 'tableaux style' which he had developed earlier on in *Shadows of Forgotten Ancestors* (1964). One of the aspects of the 'tableaux style' is the frequent reference to traditional or older media techniques, such as medieval manuscript illumination, ritual, silent cinema or, in this context, painting. The effect is a very self-reflexive one, an effect that can be attributed to intermediality. Joachim Paech defined intermediality as the inscription of one medium into another, such as creating a fracture which ultimately makes the medium in itself observable (2002: 303), which is exactly what is happening here.

According to Frank Curot (cited in Papazian 2006: 305), the 'tableaux style' is characterised by:

i) prolonged, frequent and repetitive use of close-ups;
ii) organisation of images based not on temporal and spatial continuity, but rather on pictorial and figurative coherence among relatively autonomous shots (such as stages in an exemplary destiny, or mythological symbolism);
iii) flatness, shallow depth of field and planar disposition of objects and actors, who address the camera directly (without 'penetration' into the image by depth

perspective or by shot/reverse-shot sequences), resulting in spatial indetermi-
nation between shots and even within the shot;

iv) autonomy of sound from image, for example in dialogue in voiceover attached
to seemingly mute figures;

v) frequent use of title cards and nondiegetic still lives.

These features more or less explain how the 'poetic' or 'archaic' school organises
film language. The focus seems to be on the organisation of images based on pictorial and figurative coherence rather than on temporal and spatial continuity, which
seems to paraphrase Jakobson's poetic function. Others clearly show the proximity
of 'tableaux style' to painting, e.g. the autonomy of sound from image, the creation of
nondiegetic still lives, the renunciation of decidedly filmic techniques such as shot/
reverse-shot sequences, the explicit combination of relatively autonomous shots or
the flatness and shallow depth of field, the planar disposition of objects and actors
who address the camera/viewer's gaze directly. Although the last point is not true of
painting in general, it is certainly true for Pirosmanashvili's style of painting. Many
of these elements are true of *Pirosmani* as well: for instance, Shengelaya does show
a very distinctive use of close-ups, the introduction of title cards and still lives, the
organisation of images based on pictorial and figurative coherence or a particular flatness of the image, all of this based on the aesthetics of Pirosmanashivili's oeuvre.

Artistically, *Pirosmani* is the final point of a long filmic acquaintance for Shengelaya.
The life of Pirosmanashvili had already been the subject of his documentary, *Niko
Pirosmanashvili* which was his diploma project in 1959 as he graduated from the
State Institute of Cinematography (VGIK). It was screened at the first major post-
Stalinist show of Pirosmanashvili in 1961 (Zdanevich 1965: 45–6).[14] Kirill Zdanevich
praised this film as aesthetically exceptional:

> He succeeded in creating an outstanding coloured documentary film. It bravely and
> ingeniously displays its pictures. The director did not refrain from any difficulties. The
> film gathers more than fifty of Pirosmani's pictures and many fragments, thus rediscov-
> ering those features that the spectator tends to miss on a grand scale. The aggrandized
> fragments seem to show and open up a new Pirosmani. [...] The pictures gathered are
> perceived as an exhibition. (Zdanevich 1965: 4; translated from Russian by the author)

The extraordinary familiarity that Shengelaya seems to demonstrate in his gradu-
ation film is more than present in his later feature film *Pirosmani* which oscillates
between documentary and filmic biography as well as mythological and allegorical
readings of both Pirosmanashivili's life and his paintings. On the surface it is a rather
simple and straightforward narration of the artist's mystified life, told in a film language that reiterates the aesthetic principles of Pirosmanashvili's paintings. At a
second glance, however, the film develops a very sophisticated way of integrating
both Pirosmanashvili's life and works into a distinctive poetic structure that circles

around mythologemes of Georgian culture, an individual artist's fate, Christian resurrection myth and filmic experiment. As a part of the 'poetic' or 'archaic' school, the
film is arranged by means of rhymes, analogies and similarity rather than a purely
narrative syntagmatic structure.

The focus of both structural elements, i.e. the syntagmatic film narration and
the poetic function, forms Pirosmanashvili's work; it is the driving force of his life
as demonstrated by the narrative, but it is just as important as the central poetic
element of the film's aesthetics. Pirosmanashvili's paintings are present on a whole
range of different layers within the film, thus forming the set of similarities around
which the film language circles.

The film starts and ends with a fragment of the painting *Shest' peizazhei* (*Six
Landscapes*),[15] forming the background of the film's credits at the beginning and
of the word 'Konec' ('End') at the end, thus introducing the paintings as the film's
framing principle. Within the film we are presented with different paintings that are
introduced as title cards (*Giraffe*, *Lion*, *Easter*) typical of silent films. In this way the
mostly temporally arranged sequences of the depiction of Pirosmanashvili's life are
separated thematically. Time is not shown to pass, only apparent in the protagonist's
greying hair and beard and his continued physical deterioration. Thus, a timeless-
ness often attributed to Pirosmanashvili's paintings is introduced into the film and
reiterated just as a certain essentialism that lies beyond the realm of time.

On the syntagmatic narrative layer, single sequences are structured by mythologemes that surround the fate of Niko Pirosmanashvili. This includes his voluntary
dismissal from the rich Georgian family where he grew up as a poor relative, his
failed dairy shop business and wedding, his life as a free bohemian artist, his love
story with the actress Margarita, his invitation to join the Society of Georgian Artists
and the subsequent catastrophe with the incriminating caricature, and, finally, his
dying in a derelict shed.

Within the diegetic world of the narrative, Pirosmanashvili's paintings are present in a variety of ways: they are shown while being painted, while hanging on walls
in taverns, shops or homes, while being carried around and discussed; they are present as *topoi* in conversations Pirosmani[16] is engaged in; and finally they are present
as filmic arrangements of scenes that act as models for Pirosmani, who is depicted
as painting.

The arrangement of the narration follows the Aristotelian dramatic structure
of *protasis* (introduction), *epitasis* (including *peripeteia*) and *catastrophe* which is
reminiscent of his father's oeuvre who had already experimented with drama structures in *Éliso* (Nikoloz Shengelaya, 1928). Even though many films are arranged by
Aristotelian conventions, in *Pirosmani* this arrangement is consciously foregrounded
by the demonstrative introduction of every single act by the above-mentioned 'title
cards' which are essentially Pirosmanashvili's paintings. Pirosmani's failed bourgeois
life is outlined in the exposition, his growing fame as an artist is the rising action, his
experience with the Society of Georgian Artists and the subsequent caricature marks

the climax and turning point of his individual fate. After the climax, the classical drama structure requires a falling action which is often accompanied by a moment of final suspense, which the film realises by subsequently depicting Pirosmani's personal decline in bleak colours and omitting Pirosmanashvili's paintings in the *mise-en-scène*. The momentum is decelerated by showing Pirosmani wandering through a vast landscape and visiting the sites of the motifs that inspired his work, such as flailing peasants, the harvest of grapes, flocks of sheep with a shepherd, a poor peasant woman with children, and so on. The film's end, which in accordance with dramatic structure must either result in a catastrophe or a solution to the dramatic conflict, manages to realise both of them. While on one hand Pirosmani dies as a result of the ultimate resentment brought onto him by society, he is carried away on Easter Sunday on the other, opening the depiction of his life up to an analogy with Jesus Christ.[17]

Narratively this analogy is foregrounded through many elements. The film opens with Pirosmani reading the story of Jesus entering Jerusalem (Matthew 21: 1–11), the symbol of which is palm leaves. In the film Pirosmani is shown sitting on palm leaves while reading the psalm. In Christian and especially Orthodox traditions, Palm Sunday is the first day of Holy Week which ends with Christ's passion. In an analogous manner the film ends with the symbolic death of Pirosmani and his paintings and their subsequent resurrection. The last of the 'title cards' is one of Pirosmanashvili's paintings with Easter as the subject of the picture. It is introduced after the symbolic death of Pirosmani as a painter, realised in the film by a complete disappearance of his pictures from the *mise-en-scène* in all its possible dimensions. Within these narrative sequences we can also find Judas's betrayal re-enacted by a bartender who was shown to be one of Pirosmani's supporters and repudiates him after the appearance of the fatal caricature. The scenes that follow show Pirosmani being locked into a room in the cellar and forced to paint an overall panoramic view of Georgian landscape, similar to the one that frames the film as a background for credits and the word 'End'. While Pirosmani is painting, his paintings reappear in the *mise-en-scène* of the diegetic world: we are confronted with a whole range of groups of people sitting at tables and celebrating outdoor picnics, reiterating one of Pirosmanashvili's themes which is again a 'Georgian topos'.[18] On the other hand, the film insists on this motif at this point because of the Sabbat of the biblical Easter events. In the end, Christ's burial and resurrection are also restaged by the film as Pirosmani is shown dying in his shed. However, the film does not end with such a symbolic and/or factual death. Just as his paintings have reappeared in the filmic representation after the introductory Easter painting, the film suggests that Pirosmani is carried away from his tomb-like shed possibly to die. These are the myths surrounding Pirosmanashvili's life, yet a second layer in the film suggests a Christ-like resurrection. Thus, Christ's passion becomes Pirosmani's passion. So, the biographical depiction indicates death and consequently tragedy while at the symbolic level salvation is indicated in resurrection.

The overall presence of paintings in Shengelaya's *Pirosmani* does indicate a medial self-reflexive element typical of the 'tableaux style' of the 'archaic' or 'poetic' school. Just as with English, the Russian language can render the film as a 'picture' ('kartina'). The inscription of paintings onto film by way of an intermedial operation performatively operates on the ontological level of the medium of film itself. At this point the argument approaches the poetic principle of the film which lies beyond the syntagmatic narration of Pirosmanashvili's life.

In her discussion of *Sayat-Nova* as a film of the 'poetic' school, Oeler refers to André Bazin who used the metaphors of the window and the picture frame in order to distinguish the specific quality of filmic representation compared to theatre. Bazin maintains that the window frame is comparable to filmic representation in as much as the spectator imagines the world to continue beyond the window (or filmic) frame whereas the picture frame is similar to theatre within which the world ends beyond the stage, i.e. frame. 'What is framed is all there is' (Oeler 2006: 483). She states that in Paradzhanov's *Sayat-Nova* the framing is so similar to theatre framing, that 'with few exceptions, the film does not construct, with such common devices as the pan or the point-of-view sequence, a diegetic world beyond the edges of the frame' (ibid).

Much of this is also true for Shengelaya's *Pirosmani*. Firstly, it reiterates a dramatic structure which brings it closer to theatre. Secondly, taking Bazin's argument into consideration, this theatrical structure is comparable to Pirosmanashvili's art itself which is omnipresent within the film. And even though the film does construct a diegetic world, it is exceptionally modest in using specific filmic techniques such as shot/reverse-shot. In such cases, it usually confronts the film language with Pirosmanashvili's paintings. For instance, in one scene people are being painted by the film's Pirosmani and thus the painting is 'reformulated'. In the next scene the finished painting is shown in response to the demands of people who have been painted. Thus, the film language and Pirosmanashvili's paintings mirror each other, consequently introducing another major self-reflective cinematic element: the metaphor of the screen as a mirror (see Elsaesser and Hagener 2007: 77).

Even in its clear narrative sequences, the film seems to function more as a montage of Pirosmanashvili's paintings than a quasi-documentary feature film about Pirosmanashvili's life. It not only integrates original paintings into the montage or uses them within the actual *mise-en-scène* of the diegetic world, but many of his paintings are also restaged on the film screen, as described above. The film does not stop at merely restaging existent paintings; it even creates 'new ones' by using Pirosmanashvili's aesthetics in order to arrange filmic motifs.

Very often, it is the painter Pirosmanashvili himself who becomes the central focus of such a restaging. Metaphorically, he consequently becomes part of his own pictures so that the painter and character Pirosmani stares back at the spectator.

We are presented with tableaux, complete in themselves, that often, through the eyes of the characters, look back at us. Through framing and through images that gaze back at the beholder, the film presents a highly mediated world, ultimately arriving at a representation of consciousness that frames, allegorises and symbolises, using a long collective tradition. (Oeler 2006: 483)

Again, what Oeler writes about *Sayat-Nova* is true for *Pirosmani* as well, and again, we are dealing with one of film theory's major issues, the question of the gaze (see Elsaesser and Hagener 2007: 103). When taking into consideration the poetic principle of the film narration, we arrive at a symbolic level already present within the syntagmatic narration which parallels Pirosmanashvili's life with that of Christ.

A look at the aesthetic principles of Pirosmanashvili's paintings, which are partially derived from Christian orthodox icons, enhances this symbolic level.

It was these motifs, this formal vocabulary that had a seminal influence on Niko Pirosmani. It was from icons that he learned his treatment of space, of movement and transience, of light and colour. Above all, icons taught him that, contrary to the assumption of realistic painting in Western Europe, art does not necessarily have to reproduce reality but can create one of its own. (Smolik 1995: 103)

The transfer of Pirosmanishivili's aesthetic principles directly into the film language essentially also transfers the aesthetic access of religious icons. One could say that the poetic principle thus enables film language to create a reality of its own which is deeply influenced by Christian mythology; 'Icons do not aim to reproduce the visible world but rather to oppose this world by creating another that is lasting and absolute' (Smolik 1995: 105). Within the poetic film language Pirosmani becomes the Messiah of this opposite world, his pictures become the expression of his message, the film self-reflexively spreads this message into the world.

What could the message of this opposite world be? I would suggest it to be constructed threefold. According to Christian mythology, it would be some kind of salvation which lies deeply rooted in Georgian culture. Georgia was already Christianised in the fourth century, and icons were 'the most intense artistic expression' (Smolik 1995: 103) of this cultural tradition. So firstly, mediated by the poetic film language, it seems as though the cultural traditions of this long history are staring back at us. Pirosmanashvili's paintings are commonly interpreted as conveying the mythology of Georgian culture with a tragic salvation, and Pirosmanashvili is its prophet. With respect to his art, Pirosmanashvili seems to be incorruptible and willing to die tragically rather than make any concessions with regard to his independence. At the same time his death is linked with resurrection. Subsequently one could interpret Georgian culture to be independent and incorruptible, and therefore, destined to never die.[19]

Secondly, as many films of the 'archaic' or 'poetic' school that discuss the artist as 'a kind of catalyst of moral principles' (Marshall 1992: 176), *Pirosmani* deals with the possibilities of artistic processes as such in a very self-reflexive way. Through intermedial operations, film as a medium is foregrounded and combined with the narrative discussion on artistic freedom. Also the question of independent and incorruptible filmmaking is raised.

Thirdly, the religious sublayer on both the narrative and poetic levels of the film language might allude to repressed elements of the Russian avant-garde tradition. Noemi Smolik asks why Larionov and his friends had such a feverish interest in presenting Pirosmanashvili's pictures in their *Target* exhibiton in the year 1913 (see Smolik 1995: 103). Her explanation of this interest goes beyond the usual conception of Pirosmanashvili as a primitivist painter, as the 'Russian Rousseau'. She connects it with the influence of iconography on his aesthetics; religious symbols played a significant role in the avant-garde's search for renewal in artistic form and expression. The most famous symbol of this search is Malevich's *Black Square* which in its first exhibition (*The Last Futurist Exhibition 0.10*) in Saint Petersburg in 1915 was presented in that corner of the room that was traditionally reserved for the icon (see Drutt 2003: 256). Smolik indicates the astonishing resemblance in perspective and the treatment of light and colour that Malevich's paintings of peasants show to Pirosmanashvili's portraits. So, the second message quite clearly alludes to the opposite world of Russian avant-garde tradition of which Pirosmanashvili again becomes a prophet. It is his unfaltering and rigid devotion to his art and the inherent resurrection that the film dramatically 'stages' which indicates a resurrection, and in the last consequence, eternal life of the artistic principles of the Russian avant-garde.

Within the film narration one further element enhances the likelihood of such an interpretation. On the one hand, the film does not concentrate on Pirosmanashvili's 'discovery' by the Russian avant-garde movement, which forms one of the central mythologemes circling around his persona, but does stay within the parameters of Georgian culture and society that determined Pirosmanasvili's work and life. On the other hand, the whole film is framed by two young artists' search for Pirosmanashvili in Tbilisi who are never clearly identified except that one of them came 'from a far away country'. All of this associates them undoubtedly with the brothers Zdanevich and Mikhail Le-Dant'yu. Later on, Pirosmanashvili is shown to celebrate the fact that his work is known even abroad and that his name would not vanish without trace. This episode of searching for the artist is the only one that is accentuated by a narrative anachronism insofar as it serves as a second introduction to the whole film. With this search on the one hand, the film is given a second motto next to the initial citation from the Bible. On the other hand, it clearly points to the hidden meanings it carries in terms of artistic freedom, as is tragically shown in *Pirosmani*. Within this context it is also worth emphasising once again that Shengelaya's father, while he was a regime director, did collaborate with Sergei Tret'yakov, one of those avant-garde artists who lost their lives during the Stalinist purges. Therefore, the reference to his father, shown in the use of theatrical devices, can be interpreted as including not only media-conscious formal experiments with film and theatre language but also a very indirect resurrection of the contribution of the historic avant-garde movement. Finally, of course, it also alludes to the early, rich and independent film tradition of Georgia.

Taking historical circumstances surrounding the making of the film into consideration, all of these interpretations do not seem to be too far-fetched. The post-Stalinist thaw had made possible a careful reappraisal of Pirosmanashvili's paintings just as it did the historic avant-garde. It had also made a self-conscious documentation of national customs possible. In short, it had given way to a certain degree of cultural independence in various ways that had been unthinkable under Stalinism. But when the film was made, the thaw atmosphere was coming to an end and censorship was tightening again. So within this broad context one might interpret *Pirosmani* as a symbol for an actual 'resurrection', maybe symbolised by the redisplay of Pirosmanashvili's paintings in the Moscow Tret'yakov Gallery. However, it might also symbolise the ongoing struggle for artistic and national independence which was still, and even more so, under threat.

One of those who had been most affected by this renewed threat was Shengelaya's colleague and friend Sergei Paradzhanov who was prohibited from working from 1973 until 1984, a time-span that included four years in prison. Having read *Pirosmani* as a salvation and resurrection myth, it seems more than a coincidence that in 1985, on the eve of *glasnost* and *perestroika*, one of the first films that Paradzhanov managed to realise was the short film *Arabeskebi Pirosmanis Temaze* (*Arabesques on the Pirosmani Theme*) that is again dedicated to Pirosmanashvili's oeuvre. In essence this also celebrates the 'resurrection' of an artist and his artistic access to filmmaking as well as the 'tableaux style' which inherently integrates other media such as painting into the art of filmmaking. It is also one artistic resurrection of the 'poetic principle' in film language and this principle is realised by a 'rhyming' of Pirosmanashvili's paintings with the film. Paradzhanov's short film, which is aesthetically very different from Shengelaya's *Pirosmani* in spite of these similarities, nonetheless opens up a whole new set of questions that remain to be discussed.

Notes

1 For a brief and appreciative description of *Arabeskebi Pirosmanis Temaze* see Rollet (2007).

2 This is a common appraisal of Sergei Paradzhanov's films. James Steffen (2001/02: 105) states that *Sayat-Nova* (*Nran guyne/The Colour of Pomegranates*) has frequently been characterised as a 'dissident' film or 'a coded expression of Armenian nationalism'. He offers a detailed reconstruction of the complicated process of the film's censorship. For the interrelationship between Soviet censorship and film production and their consequences for film making, see also Marshall (1992: 183).

3 Apart from his childhood years which he spent in the house of rich relatives who ensured a basic schooling.

4 For a reconstructed biography of Pirosmanashvili see Kuznetsov (1984) or, in a brief English version, Okroshvaridze et al. (1995).

5   Some fifty years later this caricature inspired Picasso who worked with Il'ya Zdanevich (then Ilyazd, as he called himself after his emigration to France) in a portrait of Pirosmanashvili (see Curiger 1995: 9).

6   His mother was the actress Nato Vachnadze, one of the stars of Soviet cinema in the 1920s and 1930s. His brother Eldar also had a successful career as film director.

7   See Steffen (2001/02: 108–11) for a very detailed description of the overall atmosphere regarding the concurrent production of Paradzhanov's *Sayat-Nova* (*Nran guyne*/*The Colours of Pomegranates*) which had to deal with similar problems.

8   The titles of Paradzhanov's films sometimes vary somehow (in some cases we can even find more than one English version). I will use the original titles followed by the British or US release title as indicated in the Internet Movie Database (www.imdb.com). *Tini zabutykh predkiv* (1911) is an adaptation of the Ukrainian novel of the same name (1911) by Mykhailo Kotsyubyns'ky, which introduced modern prose into Ukrainian literature (see Nebesio 1994).

9   I am grateful to Konrad Klejsa for his valuable suggestions on this list. The spelling of names follows internationally known versions.

10 Karla Oeler relies on James Steffen's unpublished doctoral thesis *A Cardiogram of the Times: Sergei Parajanov and the Politics of Nationality and Aesthetics in the Soviet Union*, Emory University 2005. In her discussion of *Sayat-Nova* (*Nran guyne*/*The Colours of Pomegranates*) she calls this dissertation 'the most comprehensive and important English-language scholarship on the director to date' (2007: 141).

11 An English summary of the essay and its subsequent discussions in Soviet criticism is given in Marshall (1992) – the essay's title rephrases the title of a seminal book of the Russian formalist Yury Tynyanov 'Arkhaisty i novatory' ('Archaists and Innovators', 1929). Russian formalism, in turn, was the point of departure for Jakobson's structuralist definition of the poetic function.

12 Several internet sources indicate that the film was banned for two years. However, I have not been able to find any reliable data on this issue, apart from the differing release dates given in the Internet Movie Database. According to this source, the film was released in the Georgian SSR in 1969 and in Moscow in 1971. The film's many Christian elements make problems with censorship highly likely. Maybe the case was similar to *Sayat-Nova* (*Nran guyne*/*The Colours of Pomegranates*), as discussed by Steffen (2001/02) in detail. This film was eventually released (after several changes demanded by the censors) but not widely distributed. This made it virtually inaccessible to a wider audience. Steffen also hints at the acceptance of religious imagery by Soviet authorities during that era, which was possible but had to be properly contextualised as part of the national heritage. It is doubtful if the mythological representation of an artist as Jesus offered by *Pirosmani* was within these limits, even though Orthodox Christianity is clearly part of Georgian national heritage. On the other hand, the re-edited version of *Sayat-Nova*, namely *Nran guyne*/*The Colours of Pomegranates*, is still full of religious imagery and symbolism which was 'out of the ordinary' (Steffen 2001/02: 135).

13 *Pirosmani* was awarded the Sutherland Trophy from the British Film Institute in 1973 and the Gold Hugo of the Chicago International Film Festival in 1974.

14 1961 is also the year that is mentioned as the film's release date in the Internet Movie Database.

15 In Zdanevich (1965: 104), there is an overview, in which the painting is listed as the very first one under number 1. The headline reads '1895–1903'. Given this first position in this overview, it is no coincidence that the film starts with this painting.

16 I will speak of Pirosmani whenever I speak about the character in the film *Pirosmani* and of Pirosmanashvili whenever I am indicating the artist Niko Pirosmanashvili as a historical persona.

17 In 1981, the Lithuanian director Eimuntas Nekrošius staged a play titled *Pirosmani, Pirosmani* at the Vilnius Youth Theatre (State Youth Theatre of the Lithuanian SSR) which transferred the religious symbolism directly to the theatre stage (see Greenwald 1988: 562). The intertextual

relations between Shengelaya's film and Nekrošius's stage version are apparent and retrospectively foreground the film's theatrical structure. This theatrical production had been shown in the USA in 1965. Arthur Miller saw the production and has been quoted to have praised it as being 'one of the best things I've ever seen in my life ... [it is] avant-garde in the best sense' (ibid.). Zdanevich mentions a first stage adaptation of a play *Pirosmani* in Tbilisi in 1961, directed by G. Nakhutsrishvili (1965: 45).

18 The Georgian feast as a topos is described in *The Georgian Feast: The Vibrant Culture as Savoury Food of the Republic of Georgia* by the cultural historian Darra Goldstein (1992), a recipe book with an introduction that received the honour of an appraising academic review (see Frierson 1994). It is illustrated, of course, by Pirosmanashvili's paintings.

19 This layer becomes even more significant when taking into consideration that firstly, Shengelaya's brother Eldar was an active supporter of the Georgian independence movement during *perestroika*, and secondly, that Shengelaya's friend Paradzhanov might have been imprisoned because he supported Georgian dissidents, as Oeler (2007) mentions referring to Steffen, even though the official reason was his homosexuality. So biographically, a certain closeness of Shengelaya to Georgian nationalism and independence ideas cannot be denied.

Bibliography

Aidan, M. (1989) 'Notes sur l'auteur de Pirosmani: Gueorgui Chenguelaïa', *Jeune Cinema*, 197, 30–2.

Amiredžibi, N. (1988) 'Les premiers chef-d'ouevre', in J. Radvanyi (ed.) *Le cinéma géorgien*, Paris: Editions du Centre Pompidou, 53–9.

Bleiman, M. (1970) 'Arkhaisty ili novatory?', *Iskusstvo kino*, 7, 55–76.

Capdenac, M. (1975) 'Pirosmani', *Ecran: Revue mensuelle de cinéma* (15 Novembre), 53–4.

Curiger, B. (ed.) (1995) *Zeichen & Wunder: Niko Pirosmani (1862–1918) und die Kunst der Gegenwart* (Signs & Wonders: Niko Pirosmani (1862–1918) and Recent Art). Ostfildern: Cantz.

Curot, F. (2000) 'Singularité et liberté: Serguei Paradjanov ou les risques du style', in F. Curot (ed.) *Styles filmiques*. Paris: Lettres modernes Minard, 221–37.

Dallet, S. (1992) 'Historical Time in Russian, Armenian, Georgian and Kirghiz Cinema', in A. Lawton, (ed.) *The Red Screen: Politics, Society, Art in Soviet Cinema*, London/New York: Routledge, 303–15.

Drutt, M. (ed.) (2003) *Kasimir Malewitsch: Suprematismus*. New York: Guggenheim Museum Publications.

Elley, D. (1974) 'Pirosmani', *Films & Filming* (September), 48.

Elsaesser, T. and M. Hagener (2007) *Filmtheorie zur Einführung*, Hamburg: Junius.

Freunde der Deutschen Kinemathek e.V. (1975) (ed.) *Filme aus Georgien* [Kinemathek 52 (February)].

Frierson, C. A. (1994) 'Review of *The Georgian Feast*', *Slavic Review*, 53, 2, 626–7.

Glaessner, V. (1974) 'Pirosmani', *Monthly Film Bulletin*, 41, 480/491, 205.

Goldstein, D. (1992) *The Georgian Feast: The Vibrant Culture and Savory of the Republic of Georgia*. New York: Harper Collins.

Gow, G. (1974) 'Unfamiliar Talents', *Films & Filming* (February), 48–50.

Greenwald, M. L. (1988) 'Pirosmani, Pirosmani', *Theatre Journal*, 40, 4, 562–64.

Horton, A. (1978-79) 'Pirosmani', *Film Quarterly*, 32, 2, 61–3.

Jakobson, R. (1958) 'Linguistics and Poetics', in R. Jakobson, *Selected Writings*, vol. 3. The Hague/Paris: de Gruyter, 18–51.

Kuznetsov, È (1984) *Pirosmani*. Leningrad: Iskusstvo.

Liehm, M. and A. J. Liehm (1977) *The Most Important Art: Eastern European Film After 1945*, Berkeley: University of California Press.

Marshall, H. (1992) 'The New Wave in Soviet Cinema', in A. Lawton (ed.) *The Red Screen: Politics, Society, Art in Soviet Cinema*. London/New York: Routledge, 175–93.

Nebesio, B. (1994) 'Shadows of Forgotten Ancestors: Storytelling in the Novel and the Film', *Literature Film Quarterly*, 22, 1, 42–9.

Oeler, K. (2006) 'A Collective Interior Monologue: Sergei Parajanov and Eisentein's Joyce-Inspired Vision of Cinema', *Modern Language Review*, 101, 472–87.

_____ (2007) 'Nrun Guyne/The Colour of Pomegranates', in B. Beumers (ed.) *The Cinema of Russia and the Former Soviet Union*. London: Wallflower Press, 139–48.

Okroshvaridze, N., I. Kuradze and E. Todua-Sheliya (1995) 'The Life and Work of Niko Pirosmani', in B. Curiger (ed.) *Zeichen & Wunder: Niko Pirosmani (1862–1918) und die Kunst der Gegenwart* (Signs & Wonders: Niko Pirosmani (1862–1918) and Recent Art). Ostfildern: Cantz, 91–6.

Paech, J. (2002) 'Intermedialität des Films', in J. Felix (ed.) *Moderne Film Theorie*. Mainz: Bender, 287–316 [English version available at http://www.uni-konstanz.de/FuF/Philo/LitWiss/MedienWiss/Texte/interm.html] (accessed on 06 July 2009).

Papazian, E. A. (2006) 'Ethnography, Fairytale, and "Perpetual Motion" in Sergei Parajanov's Ashik Kerib', *Literature Film Quarterly*, 34, 4, 303–12.

Radvanyi, J. (ed.) (1988) *Le cinéma géorgien*. Paris: Editions du Centre Pompidou.

Rakitin, J. and W. Rakitin (1988) 'Von einem Kreuz aus Rebholz, vom Duchan, vom wundersamen Niko und den Futuristen', in Berliner Festspiele GmbH (ed.) *Niko Pirosmani: Der Georgische Maler 1862–1918*, Berlin: Argon Verlag, 18–27.

Rollet, S. (2007) 'Arabesques sur le thème de Paradjanov', *Positif*, 554, 58–61.

Smolik, N. (1995) 'Niko Pirosmani – Images Outside the Accidental and the Commonplace', in B. Curiger (ed.) *Zeichen & Wunder: Niko Pirosmani (1862-1918) und die Kunst der Gegenwart* (Signs & Wonders: Niko Pirosmani (1862–1918) and Recent Art). Ostfildern: Cantz, 103–8.

Steffen, J. (2001/02) 'From *Sayat-Nova* to *The Color of Pomegranates*: notes on the production and censorship of Parajanov's film', *Armenian Review*, 47/48, 105–47.

Zdanevich, K. (1965) *Niko Pirosmanashvili*. Tbilisi: Sabchota Sakartvelo.

Zorkaya, N. M. (2005) *Istoriya sovetskogo kino*. Sankt-Peterburg: Aleteyya.

When the Story Hides the Story: The Narrative Structure of Milcho Manchevski's *Dust*

Erik Tängerstad

In August 2001 crowds at the Lido were eagerly awaiting the film that was to open the 58th Venice Film Festival. Seven years after Milcho Manchevski's renowned debut film *Before the Rain* (1994), his long-expected second feature, *Dust* (2001), was to have its world premiere. *Before the Rain* had stunned audiences in Venice, partly because of its topic, partly because of its innovative narrative format. That film, about the break up of a Macedonian village, was seen to illustrate the ongoing dissolution of Yugoslavia. But more than its theme, it was its intriguing three-part composition that shook audiences. The film's narrative followed a spiralling trajectory that defied established film conventions. Yet again, it was so smoothly edited that one could see it without having to consciously reflect on the fact that its narrative undermined the conventional notion of the cohesion of time and space. *Before the Rain* presented a narrative film format that appeared new and refreshing when showing a side of Europe that was deeply shocking and distressing. It won the Golden Lion in 1994. After that, *Before the Rain* went on a celebrated world tour, finally reaching the status of a contemporary film classic. Would Manchevski's second feature repeat the success of his first? As it turned out, no, not really. Where *Before the Rain* had astonished and impressed audiences, *Dust* only made them confused and hesitant. Many viewers were simply put off. Almost a year later, when *Dust* opened in Britain, the film reviewer of *The Guardian*, Peter Bradshaw, wrote: 'This very tiresome, overblown piece of machismo from director Milcho Manchevski made a terrible beginning to last year's Venice Film Festival, and looks no better now' (2002).[1]

Since its release in 2001, reviewers and commentators have had a hard time making sense of *Dust*'s narrative. No matter whether they liked or disliked the film, the common opinion has been that *Dust* is an ambitious film project that fails to succeed. For example, one online reviewer, the pseudonymous Dr Kuma, seems to have been at pains when trying to tell why he/she did not like the film:

> The main problem is that although the film has many great ideas it really doesn't hold together. It's like a jigsaw with the corners missing. Although you can see exactly what it's supposed to be, it never looks complete. [...] Although I didn't particularly like the film, some of it's [sic.] images really do stick to mind, especially the way that the director links the story of the modern day robbers pilgrimage to the place he has heard so much about at the end of the film. It really is very clever and visually striking. This really should merit a good review but all I'll say is that it tries too hard to please. [...] A good idea, but dust crumbles (2002).

In 2003, *Dust* had a limited US release, opening at the same time in New York and Los Angeles. The *New York Times* reviewer, Elvis Mitchell, seems to have struggled to find a positive angle:

> Mr. Manchevski demonstrates his gifts as a visual stylist and a filmmaker in command of the technical aspect of the medium. [...] [He] employed a similar splintered-storytelling approach to insinuate the plot of his ingeniously realized *Before the Rain*, in which the slivers of apparently haphazardly scattered plot all came together. (In that film the Godardian cubist style was buttressed by titles that acted as chapter headings.) *Dust* takes this ghost story approach while simultaneously trying to limn a film rife with dovetailing displays of devices like parallels and metaphor, trying to use all these elements to explicate character. [...] It is overly convenient, and such an underexplained mystery that it never makes any sense. There's enough culture clash that *Dust* doesn't need the equivalent of a Zen koan. (2003)

On the same day Kevin Thomas wrote a review for the *Los Angeles Times*:

> '*Dust* is a bust, a big bad movie of the scope, ambition and bravura that could be made only by a talented filmmaker run amok. Macedonian-born, New York-based Milcho Manchevski, whose first film was the elegiac 1994 *Before the Rain*, attempts a Middle Eastern western, a fusion suggesting the timeless universality of chronic bloodlust. It's a potent visual idea, full of darkly amusing irony but undercut by wretched excess, underdeveloped characters and a queasy mix of sentimentality and violence. [...] *Dust* is a great-looking film of vast scope, and cinematographer Barry Ackroyd brings it a rich texture and bold panache, which could also be said of David Munns' imaginative and detailed production design and Kiril Dzajkovski's score. The passion, free-spiritedness and vision that Manchevski brings to *Dust* makes his self-indulgence all the more depressing. (2003)

151

Commentators who explicitly liked the film also claimed that they could not make sense out of its narrative. For example:

> Milcho Manchevski's *Dust* is a gloriously uneven, deliriously delightful film about the emergence of the Old West mentality into contemporary times. At least, I *think* that's what it's about: it is so convoluted and choppy that it doesn't even pretend to make a lick of sense. [...] Yet these frustrations with the story make the film fascinating rather than distracting. I think this is because Manchevski seems so confident in his storytelling abilities that we trust him even when we don't understand him. There is never a dull or belabored moment here. (Griffin 2003; emphasis in original)[2]

Even film scholars analysing *Dust* claim that its narrative structure is a failure. For example, Vojislava Filipčević writes:

> Manchevski constructs a novel East-West 'encounter' and uncovers new meanings of 'in-betweenness' in the Balkan cinema through advanced visual grammar and powerful iconography of interlinked reverse exiles and crossings (in both *Dust* and *Before the Rain*), and though a hybrid genre, cinematic critique of Balkan historical narratives (albeit with several plot shortcomings, especially in *Dust*). (2004: 4)

These examples should illustrate a broad consensus on the narrative structure of *Dust*. Even though the film is recognised to be technically well made, as well as containing many interesting passages, ultimately practically every commentator claims that it does not make sense.

However, we can question this consensus. The claim made here is that *Dust* has been consciously made to challenge established film conventions and narrative theories. It should come as no surprise, therfore, that when analysing the film by using the very same conventions and theories that it is designed to challenge, the outcome will appear flawed. This film is ambitious insofar as it does not invite conventional understandings of how to see and understand feature film. Instead, it actively tries to provoke spectators to develop a new film perception, hence a new film theory. More relevant than seeing *Dust* as a conventionally-told film narrative that does not work out is to critically analyse whether Manchevski's approach to film narrative – an approach that he calls 'Cubist storytelling' – can generate a new understanding of film narrative at large. Could a film like *Dust* provoke the formation of new film conventions and new narrative theories? Could it make us see and understand feature film in a new way?

As will be demonstrated here, *Dust* can be viewed and understood as one whole, functioning narrative that does make sense – but only when using a different theoretical approach than that usually applied when seeing and understanding feature film, and only when critically revising established film conventions.

Synopsis of *Dust*

To create a point of reference for the following discussion, first a synopsis of *Dust* should be laid out. In New York, at the close of the twentieth century, a small-time thief, Edge, has to repay a debt to some gangsters, but lacks the means to do so. To get money, he breaks into a flat, but is caught by the tenant, an elderly woman. The woman, Angela, does not call the police. Instead she keeps Edge at gunpoint and promises him a gold treasure if he hears her story to its end, so that, she says, he will know where she was born and where to bury her. Then she starts telling him a story about two Oklahoma brothers at the turn of the twentieth century, Luke and Elijah. In her convoluted story these two brothers go from West to East, ending up fighting each other in war-torn Macedonia, where they try to track down a local rebel leader called 'The Teacher'. Talking about them, she does not, however, say anything about where she was born or where she wants to be buried, nor does she say anything about her gold treasure. When Angela collapses in the midst of her story, Edge represses an impulse to run away and instead takes her to hospital. Edge is in desperate need of money, and since he has reason to believe that Angela is in possession of gold, he returns to her apartment to search for it. When he does not find it he returns to the hospital to make Angela tell him where it is. She does not.

Instead she continues her story: Elijah almost kills Luke, who is saved by a pregnant peasant woman, Neda, who takes Luke to her village. There, Luke witnesses atrocities taking place during the ongoing uprising against the Ottomans. He sees, for example, how an Ottoman officer shows the villagers the decapitated head of The Teacher. When asked to save Neda and the village, Luke abandons both her and the village, although he keeps the gold coins he has been offered. As Angela's story is interrupted again, Edge goes back to her apartment once more, and eventually finds her gold. He then returns to the hospital, only to find Angela dying. Angela dies without having told him where she was born or where she wants to be buried. Edge nevertheless concludes that she was born in Macedonia and that she wanted to be buried there. He furthermore takes care of her remains for burial. In an airplane, with the urn in his lap, he retells Angela's story to a fellow passenger.

But he does not stop at the point where the story was interrupted by Angela's death. Instead he concludes it in his own way with his own words, saying that Luke eventually did go back to the village to save Neda. According to Edge, Luke dies in a shootout and Angela was The Teacher's and Neda's orphaned baby, whom Elijah adopted and brought with him back to the United States. The film ends with a scene in which Elijah, with a baby in his arms, watches the sky and sees an airplane. Possibly, it is the same airplane in which Edge sits with Angela's ashes when adding his own end to her story. If so, the film ends when the narrative of the film and the narrative of the story told within the film merge.

Challenging established narrative conventions

This synopsis, naturally, is a simplified version of the actual film, which should hint at the film's complex narrative. At first it could appear to be a conventional movie. But it only takes a second look to notice that this film departs from established narrative norms. In a mainstream film, for example, the story told by Angela should be framed within the film narrative as a whole, so that one would have a story within a story. In *Dust*, however, the concluding sequence shows the story told by Angela and the story told by the film as a whole to be appearing on the same narrative level. Suddenly the story within a story has been transformed into two distinct stories laid beside one another and placed on the same narrative level. When Elijah looks to the sky and sees the airplane, not only is our notion of a time and space cohesion short-circuited, but also conventional narrative logics rupture.

In this film, there are frequent examples of such short-circuiting of established narrative conventions. That becomes especially notable in the way photos are treated in the film. One usually thinks that feature films show reality in the same way that photographs depict their motifs. The motif of a photo is generally thought to be independent from the photo itself, leaving photographs to be more or less consciously stylised images of independently existing reality. In the same way, a film is understood 'to be about' something: it is supposed to be depicting some kind of reality (whether realistic or fantastic) beyond the actual film. After having seen a film, conventionally, we are expected to be able to tell 'what it was about', not 'what it looked like' or 'how it was made'. As film viewers, we also expect a film to tell a narrative visually. Because we are tacitly trained to think that a film is a visual narrative, we expect it to be telling us a story through visual means, not using random story fragments as prerequisites for displaying visual effects. In short, we expect the film imagery to be a means to help us reach the goal of getting and understanding the story, not the other way around. here, *Dust* challenges our expectations.

Photographs play a crucial role in the narrative of *Dust*. The story told by Angela is often illustrated by old photographs, and sometimes presented through a voice-over placed over film imagery. This would lead the uncritical viewer to believe that the photographs and the film imagery illustrate her story. But it is not as simple as that. Often photos change during the run of the film. More than that, the photographic imagery has a tendency to diverge from the story she tells, rather than to support it. The most obvious example of this unconventional use of photographs appears at the end of the film. Although Edge is shown not to have any pre-knowledge of Luke and Elijah – the film clearly shows how Angela has to point out to him who is Luke and who is Elijah when they look at her old photographs together – nevertheless, at the end of the film, Edge shows an old photograph with himself standing in between these long-dead brothers. By this means Edge is shown to be within Angela's story, not being its external audience. When actively short-circuiting different narrative levels, *Dust* goes against basic conventions, and thereby our expectations. It should come as no surprise then that bewildered viewers, who depend on these conventions when interpreting a film, find difficulty in understanding *Dust*.

The gold treasure at the centre of the film is key when understanding how its narrative works. Angela hints that she is in possession of a gold treasure. Because Edge believes that she indeed has one hidden somewhere in her apartment, he sticks with her even after she has stopped holding him at gunpoint. Angela talks about a gold treasure, too. So, in the film, a gold treasure is shown in her story, as well as in her apartment. Following established film narrative principles, the treasure she is talking about should be identical to the one she keeps hidden. Since the same coins have been used on set when shooting the scenes when the gold treasure appears in her story, as well as when the gold treasure appears in her apartment, the spectator actually sees the same coins – the same filmic devices – twice. But following the film narrative, there is no affinity between the treasure in her story and the treasure in her home. Angela tells how dying Luke, alone on a Macedonian hilltop in the early twentieth century, spread the gold coins around him. How could those very same gold coins almost a century later appear in a refrigerator door (where Angela has hidden them) in Brooklyn? The only reasonable answer is that they could not: there is no affinity between the one gold treasure and the other one. The narrative of *Dust* never even indicates that there should be such an affinity, even though the film imagery hints at the opposite. Through the usage of this narrative device – the notion of the gold treasure – *Dust* turns the idea of identity into a problem. At the same time, the film openly challenges the fundamental film norm that if a thing is shown twice in the same film, the viewer should be able to conclude that it is the same thing shown.

Dust explicitly puts forward the point that images can 'lie' in the same way as a verbal voice can. In that sense, the film challenges the basic notion of 'seeing is believing', the convention that states that a viewer should be granted the privilege of taking film imagery at face value. In *Dust*, the viewer should never take the imagery, or for that matter the narrative as such, at face value. That point is made explicit in a sequence in which Edge objects to the number of soldiers in Angela's story, an objection that leads to a negotiation about story content. The narrative is not an object that the active narrator hands over to passive audiences. The narrative, instead, is made up in the encounter when active audiences make sense of what the narrator tells. This point is explicitly brought forward in *Dust*. It is, therefore, somewhat ironic to see how reviewers and commentators, when trying to make sense out of the film, take their point of departure in the idea that films contain fixed story contents that are transmitted to passive audiences. This film is actively and explicitly taking that idea to task.

The story is never to be found in a film itself. It is, instead, to be found in the active encounter between the film and the interpreting audience: through the audio-visual information provided by the film, the audience conceives the story. If one uncritically takes the film imagery at face value, then *Dust* will hardly make sense. But if one instead critically revises the complex and contradictory relationship of film imagery and film narrative, then its logic suddenly appears. In short, *Dust* is a film that challenges well-established film conventions to such an extent that it is almost condemned to be misunderstood by audiences bound by traditional narrative standards. If the basic film convention rules that 'what you see is what you get', Manchevski has made a film in which 'what you see is not what you get'. There is no self-evident correspondence between what is shown and what is told. There is not even any self-evident correspondence between different segments of imagery within the film, as has been demonstrated through the example of the gold treasure.

Cubist storytelling

When working on *Before the Rain* Manchevski started to develop a new approach to narration. His experiments with circular and slightly fractured narrations making that film made him develop his own approach. Later, he started to call it 'Cubist storytelling'. However, he has never turned this approach into any explicit theory or working method. Instead, it has remained a catchword when he talks about his films. In an interview from 2003, for example, he both propagated his notion of Cubist storytelling and contrasted it with mainstream feature film:

> I am interested in Cubist storytelling – when the artist fractures the story and puts it back together in a more complex (and, thus, more interesting) way. More importantly, when the artist keeps shifting the emotional tone of the film, bringing a narrative film closer to the experiences of modern art. [...] Mainstream narrative cinema is all about expectations, and really low expectations, to that [sic.]. We have become used to expecting very little from the films we see, not only in terms of stories, but more importantly and less obviously in terms of the mood, the feeling we get from a film. I think we know what kind of a mood and what kind of a feeling we're going to get from a film before we go see [sic.] the film. It's from the poster, from the title, the stars, and it's become essential in our decision-making and judging processes. I believe it's really selling ourselves way too short. I like films that surprise me. I like films that surprise me especially *after* they've started. I like a film that goes one place and then takes you for a loop, then takes you somewhere else, and keeps taking you to other places both emotionally and story-wise... (Quoted in Raskin 2003; emphasis in original)

This quotation sums up two recurring themes in Manchevski's presentation of his work. He wants to connect to modern art, and he criticises mainstream feature film for its lack of artistic ambition, or even, at times, explicitly anti-artistic tendencies. The term 'Cubist storytelling' can therefore be seen as a marker that he uses when distancing his own work from other films – both mainstream movies and art film – as well as when connecting to modern art. Over the years, Manchevski has often presented himself as writer, storyteller or photographer with a deep interest in art, both classical and contemporary. In a 2002 interview made for the Macedonian journal *Golemoto Staklo* ('The Large Glass'), Manchevski gave journalist Sonja Abadzieva detailed answers on his notion of Cubist storytelling and how that notion influenced *Dust*. After having told Abadzieva that he liked art exhibitions better than film screenings, Manchevski stated that feature film could be something other than what it now is:

> The text has not been imposed by the nature of the medium, nor by the conventions of the particular medium. You see, film doesn't have to be the way we see it today: to last two hours, to have a beginning, middle and end, leading and supporting roles, three acts, a closed, defined ending, with catharsis and happy ending. But the convention is so strong and we have so clung to it – like little children – that we expect to see all of this. If the film lasts one hour, we feel as if something is missing. [...] For me *Dust* is close to cubism mostly in how it deconstructs the material when re-presenting it. But, whereas in painting cubism refers to visual material, in film, or in *Dust* at least, we have narrative material, decomposed and recomposed in time wheras [sic.] time is a category used in the artistic expression. This was not planned. I did not set off with idea [sic.] of making a cubist film. But, I did intend to play with time and structure, and after having walked three quarters of the road, I realized that *Dust* is maybe transposition of a cubist view to filmmaking. [...] [Narrative film is] supposed to be entertaining, but that does not mean it should be stupid. I tried to make *Dust* entertaining, rather than 'art film' torture; yet I didn't want to give up on the artistic ambition. A film should and can be both entertaining and artistic. (Quoted in Abadzieva 2002)

The point exemplified here is that Manchevski actively and consciously tries to break loose from established narrative film conventions by challenging those conventions from within. When doing that he wants to produce work that can be regarded as entertaining contemporary art, rather than contributing to an existing tradition of experimental film art. When making sense out of a film like *Dust*, one has to accept its challenge to produce new narrative theory with which the film is to be seen and understood. A spectator who tries to apply those existing film theories and conventions that *Dust* is designed to challenge will only be confused – and will eventually dismiss the film as a narrative failure. Yet when managing to break away from established narrative film conventions it appears as anything but a failure.

The alter ego

The lack of affinity between the gold in Angela's apartment and the gold in her story is only one of the film's numerous examples of applied Cubist storytelling. For example, the film indicates that Angela should be the biological daughter of The Teacher and Neda, and the adopted daughter of Elijah. Still, Angela does not concentrate her story on any of the people whom the film depicts as her parents. Instead, it clearly shows that Angela keeps talking about Luke. The case becomes even more remarkable since, according to Angela's story, Luke died before she was born, so there cannot have been any personal relationship between the two. Furthermore, Angela adds information about Luke's life that she cannot possess, such as Luke's thoughts and dreams.

It appears as if Angela is telling Edge a complicated saga instead of handing him the factual information he needs in order to do that which she asks (or demands) him to do. According to the way she tells her story, the manner in which Elijah comes across Luke in Macedonia is highly unlikely. It should be noted that when Elijah leaves Luke dying on the hilltop he cries out 'You never were! You never were!' Here a question becomes pertinent: what if indeed the character Luke never was? At the same time that Angela says that Luke dies, she has a heart attack and dies too. In this sense, *Dust* shows Angela to be identifying completely with the character she is telling Edge about: when she tells of his death, she dies too. Luke appears to be Angela's alter ego.

If indeed Luke is Angela's fantasy character, then her story about him should be understood as a metaphoric self-depiction of her own life. If so, nothing that Angela tells Edge has happened in the way she tells it. Nothing which we viewers see is to be taken at face value; while it – all of it! – has to be taken metaphorically. Here, Manchevski's Cubist storytelling technique of 'what you see is not what you get' should be kept in mind. Contrary to conventions stating that feature film is fiction that mimetically represents reality, *Dust* is fiction that mimetically represents another fiction – but at the same time emphasising that fiction is one of reality's basic elements: it is not possible to draw a clear line of demarcation between facts and fiction. Art is fiction, and as such not statements presenting truth *per se*. Art is but a 'lie' that enables the critical spectator to encounter truth. Or with Manchevski's own words: 'The narrative film is not CNN. By way of lying, the narrative film tells a truth, which is sometimes more relevant than facts, as opposed to CNN which tells lies through facts' (quoted in Abadzieva 2002).

In *Dust*, Angela appears to have made up the story of Luke in an attempt both to conceal her own life story and at the same time to hint at basic traits of that life story. In that sense Angela's whole approach is self-contradictory: she simultaneously hides and negates, and opens up and tells. As a compromise between these two incompatible and contradictory acts, she tells the story of Luke. According to Angela's story, Luke was a villain who betrayed everyone, including himself. Luke being Angela's alter ego, she would regard herself as a villain who throughout her life has betrayed everyone, including herself. The film shows how she is deceiving Edge. By promising him something that she apparently is not going to give him, she betrays him. She has promised him her gold, but even at the moment of her death she does not intend to hand it over to him. Instead, she is relieved when Edge tells her that he has discovered her secret; only then she can die in peace. And he, interestingly enough, is shown not to recognise that she is using him when playing a game of double standards – thereby the character Edge hinders spectators from seeing and understanding that the story Angela tells hides the story she hints at: the story hides the story.

But if Luke is Angela's alter ego, what has she done that is so awful that she cannot talk about it, even though she apparently wants to talk about it and constantly hints at it? *Dust* does not offer much of a clue. Bewildered spectators are left guessing. The only thing that seems clear is that Angela accuses herself of some kind of hideous crime. The gold treasure that she keeps hidden symbolises that terrible, covert criminal act. In this sense, the gold symbolises guilt, not wealth. Gold here is a metaphor for sorrow and restriction, not for happiness and freedom. Consequently, Angela is shown to be living in a state of guilt, not in one of wealth: she is poor, even though her gold should make her rich. Why is this? When the film ends, spectators are left uncertain. We will never know what kind of hideous crime she tries to repress, even at her moment of death. Actually, spectators will not even know whether there has even been a crime committed in the first place. The only thing that seems certain is that there is a guilt complex at play, even though it is impossible to trace the origins of that guilt complex.

The difference between history and the past

At one level *Dust* can be said 'to be about' storytelling as such, especially feature film storytelling. Arguably, however, the film makes an even more complex claim. It questions the possibility of knowing past events that never became recorded history. Ultimately, Manchevski's film is conceived on the rupture between the past and history. The past is that which has happened, and history is latter-day notions of that which has happened: latter-day notions of the past are not and cannot be identical with the past as such. How are we to deal with this complicated relationship between past and history? This question is made explicit in *Dust* when Angela, alone at night, cries out: 'Where does your voice go when you are no more?'

What happens with all those events, or actions, or human beings that once were but never became recorded, and therefore forever elude every living memory? The test case of *Dust* is the atrocities that took place during the Ilinden Uprising, a Macedonian revolt against the Ottoman Empire. Behind the Ilinden Uprising stood Macedonian nationalists who wanted to break loose from the Ottoman Empire and form a sovereign Macedonian nation state. The revolt began on the day of Saint Elijah (Ilinden) during the summer of 1903, however the Ottomans soon ruthlessly put it down. The atrocities carried out during the crushing of the uprising were notorious, even though they to a large extent only lived on in the minds and memories of the surviving perpetrators.

Many of the Turkish officers that led the campaign against the Macedonian rebels were themselves Turkish nationalists, who opposed the then-current state of the Ottoman Empire. Together with young intellectuals in the empire, these officers formed a reform movement, popularly called the Young Turks. In 1908 these Young Turks started a revolution to reform the disintegrating Ottoman Empire. Their revolution further weakened the empire and triggered the two Balkan Wars of 1912 and 1913, which in turned paved the way for the outbreak of World War I in 1914. The brutal atrocities committed during the Balkan Wars can only be described in terms of ethnic cleansings and genocides (in plural). And again, many of these atrocities never became recorded history. They passed without leaving traces (except for painful voids) or remained only in the minds and memories of the perpetrators, since their victims had been wiped out. If these past atrocities would be living on and transmitted to history, it would be in the format of unresolved guilt complexes and the question of how survivors' next generations would deal with these guilt complexes.

When actively forming the present-day Turkish nation-state during the break up of the Ottoman Empire in the wake of World War I, Turkish veterans from these Macedonian and Balkan wars were to commit the genocide of the Armenian people. Genocides that have taken place later during the twentieth century can be more or less directly linked to the atrocities committed in Macedonia during the years before the outbreak of World War I. Although the past has happened, it has only to a limited extent been represented in the format of history. And the question remains as to what extent it could really be represented in that format. This topic is explicitly brought forward by Manchevski's *Dust*. When the film is seen as a way of working out the question of how to deal with the differences between the past and history in the wake of genocide, it starts to take on great significance.

Conclusion

At the very centre of the narrative of *Dust* one finds Angela's cry in the middle of the night, 'Where does your voice go when you are no more?'. That question crystallises the problem of how to deal with our own mortality in the face of the present that is in constant flux, and the past that has never become recorded history. This problem becomes both urgent and delicate when dealing with past genocides. In order to understand this problem, one has to make a clear distinction between the past and history. However, the conventional notions that history equals the past, and that feature film mimetically can show the past through its imagery, obscure this crucial distinction. To better understand our existential conditions, we have to critically revise established narrative theories and well-known film conventions. Through his film *Dust*, Milcho Manchevski has offered a weighty contribution to this important debate. When viewers find the film flawed, it is not necessarily because its narrative fails. It could just as well be that it is the applied theories and norms used when interpreting and making sense out of the film that are flawed and insufficient. If so, *Dust* is a film that provokes us to reconsider our understanding of feature film narratives, as well as the validity of commonly applied narrative theories.

Acknowledgement

The author would like to thank Milcho Manchevski for his personal engagement in this work, for his constant support when providing background materials, as well as when answering questions during the long-drawn-out research period that preceded the writing of this chapter. The author would also like to thank Iris Kronaur, John Moore, Marina Kostova, Branko Petrovski, Zoran Petrovski and the Macedonian Museum of Contemporary Art in Skopje for invaluable help and support during the research for the chapter.

Notes

1   Other British reviewers were not as brutally dismissive as Bradshow, but for example Tom Dawson, who reviewed the film for *BBC Movies*, was not too impressed either: 'The Macedonian director Milcho Manchevski's long-awaited follow-up to *Before the Rain*, *Dust* replaces the earlier film's powerful solemnity with overblown excess. A variation on the Cain and Abel story which borrows heavily from the action scenes in Peckinpah's *The Wild Bunch*, *Dust* is explicitly concerned with the process of storytelling' (2002).
2   Daniel Griffin presents himself as a university staff member with a personal interest in film analysis, not as a professional film critic.

Bibliography

Abadzieva, S. (2002) 'Milcho Manchevski: "We Were Explaining Joseph Beuys' Performance to a Live Rabbit"', inteview with Milcho Manchevski, translated by A. Ilievska, *The Large Glass (Golemoto staklo)*, issue 14–15. On-line. Available: http://www.manchevski.com.mk/html%20en/m_writings_sonja.html (accessed on 07 September 2008).

Bradshaw, P. (2002) 'Dust' (film review). *The Guardian* (03 May). On-line. Available: http://www.guardian.co.uk/film/2002/may/03/culture.peterbradshaw4 (accessed on 07 September 2008).

Dawson, T (2002) 'Dust' (film review). *BBC Movies* (17 April). On-line. Available: http://www.bbc.co.uk/films/2002/04/17/dust_2002_review.shtml (accessed on 07 September 2008).

Dr Kuma (2002) 'Dust'. *Phase 9 Movies* On-line. Available: http://www.phase9.tv/moviereviews/dust.shtml (accessed on 07 September 2008).

Filipčević, V. (2004) 'Historical Narrative and the East-West Leitmotif in Milcho Manchevski's *Before the Rain* and *Dust*', *Film Criticism*, 29, 2, 3–33.

Griffin, D. (2003) 'Dust', *Film as Art: Daniel Griffin's Guide to Cinema*. On-line. Available: http://uashome.alaska.edu/~dfgriffin/website/dust.htm (accessed on 07 September 2008).

Mitchell, E. (2003) 'Gunfight at the Old Macedonian Corral: A Western With a Flexible Compass'. *New York Times* (22 August). On-line. Available: http://query.nytimes.com/gst/fullpage.html?res=9C00E2DD1639F931A1575BC0A9659C8B63 (accessed on 07 September 2008).

Raskin, R. (2003) 'On unhappy endings, politics and storytelling. An interview with Milcho Manchevski', *P.O.V.* No 16 (December; the interview is dated 'New York, 11 October 2003'). On-line. Available: http://pov.imv.au.dk/Issue_16/section_1/artc9A.html (accessed on 7 September 2008).

Thomas, K. (2003) "Dust" stretches to set a visually gripping but unrealistic and overtly violent gun-slinging showdown in Macedonia'. *Los Angeles Times*. On-line. Available: http://www.calendarlive.com/movies/reviews/cl-et-dust22aug22,2,2447833.story (accessed on 07 September 2008).

Refusing to Conform:
Forms of Non-narration

Primitive Gazing: Apichatpong Weerasethakul's Sensational Inaction Cinema

Matthew P. Ferrari

'…out of the mode of story time and into that of the Descriptive mode, into the *time-lessness* of painting, into a place where things shine more purely because their surfaces have been cleansed of story pressures' (Chatman 1990: 55).

'Dreams. Floating. I like free forms. Images flashing by have more weight than a coherent narrative. […] Sometimes it is beautiful to just look and not think – like when you take a journey in a foreign land' (Apichatpong, quoted in Römers 2005: 44).

The existence in Thailand of an alternative film culture to popular and Hollywood cinemas is in no small part due to the work of Apichatpong Weerasethakul. Splitting his time between short experimental and feature-length films, Apichatpong has been at the forefront of an experimental film and video culture emerging alongside mainstream industry successes in Thailand. While a Thai cinema 'revival' has occurred in both mainstream and independent arenas of production and consumption since 1997 (see Chaiworaporn and Knee 2006: 60), widespread international recognition stems largely from the festival and art-house circuit accolades of Apichatpong's feature films, most significantly, *Blissfully Yours* (2002) and *Tropical Malady* (2004).

In these, his second and third features respectively, we witness an aesthetic maturation marking a distinctive cinematic storytelling style with allusive narratives. Stories that are deceptively simple in their surface meaning as an appeal to the senses, they are mysterious and often beautiful works that demand from viewers an extraordinary form of personal engagement. These two films, as a core of

Apichatpong's corpus, share a likeness on two key levels that makes it fruitful to examine them together: first, they are both organised around a bifurcated, two-part narrative structure; and second, they both display a primitivist 'return to nature' serving as the organising basis for much of their storytelling powers.

With regard to narrative style, *Blissfully Yours* and *Tropical Malady* share with earlier modernist and avant-garde artistic texts a desire to disrupt the canonic (Western) story form of an introduction to characters and setting, the introduction of a conflict, disturbance or puzzle, followed by a goal-oriented causal chain of action or events leading to a resolution of the conflict (see Nichols 1994: 72). Instead of narrative action, Apichatpong creates an atmospheric pastiche drawn from traditional Thai folk shards, popular culture, personal memories and the vivification of dreams. In more reductive terms, these films represent an interest in joining the ancient and modern – primitive and civilised – in a transcultural aesthetic amalgam. To borrow from Mariana Torgovnik (1990), they reflect the vibrancy and narrative potential found in the creative interplay between 'savage' sensibilities and 'modern lives'.

In this chapter I shall discuss *Blissfully Yours* and *Tropical Malady* on several levels. First, on a formal level in terms of their non-narrative impulse, perhaps best characterised as a 'descriptive' cinematic textuality favouring atmospheric stasis over the conventional unfolding of a story (see Chatman 1990). This cinematic form of description emphasises the sensuality of symbolic environments and how the characters inhabit them (and similarly, how they are inhabited by their environments). In the strict sense these are narrative films, or they operate as what Seymour Chatman would call a 'narrative text-type' (1990: 6). That is, films unfold in time; the medium's specificity is such that it requires duration for its presentation from start to finish. Exceptions are filmic 'experiments' that disrupt this narrative discourse, such as video installation 'loops' in which beginning and end are not plainly evident. Painting and sculpture are non-narrative text-types in the sense that, while one's personal experience of them occurs in time, they do not 'regulate the temporal flow' (Chatman 1990: 7) of narrative like film, literature or even music. Yet while Apichatpong's films operate 'externally' under the forward-flowing discourse of narrative cinema, their 'internal' narrative *action* – the 'sequence of events that constitute the plot' – is powerfully diminished through loose plotting and character development, extended shot duration and other formal devices emphasising instead sensually extended (often 'spiritual') spatio-temporal durations (see Chatman 1990: 9). I argue that this manner of cinematic storytelling is best articulated functionally in terms of a 'descriptive' text-type – a kind of sensual or 'sensational inaction cinema'. In this sense the films embody a non-narrative textual impulse (although not to the degree of formal rupture enacted by many 'structuralist-materialist' experimental films) while still operating within a narrative discourse (see Smith 2000: 13).

Second, I attempt to historicise these forms of storytelling by considering their aesthetic relationship to other institutional cinema contexts; namely, the category of the 'art film' and its intermediate relationship between the 'avant-garde' (or experimental film) and Hollywood cinema. Situating *Blissfully Yours* and *Tropical Malady* within a legacy of art film poetics is also productive in thinking about Apichatpong's transnational cultural identity and Euro-Western aesthetic influences, and additionally, the recurrence of border motifs configured through characters and symbolic spaces.

Lastly, I suggest the films' shared storytelling impulse is rooted in a cultural reiteration of the wider humanistic and spiritual search for origins, configured in these instances as a form of 'primitive passions' (see Chow 1995). Culturally specific, Apichatpong's version of 'primitive passions' suggests a submission to the senses and a 'return to nature' as a means to the cessation of suffering associated with the oppressive and marginalising forces of society. *Blissfully Yours* and *Tropical Malady* implicate the value of traditional forms of knowledge residing in personal reintegration with nature, evoking a close affinity with certain Buddhist ideals, of dream states associated with shamanistic worldviews, and also engaging in a postmodern version of 'primitivist fantasy' (see Foster 1996: 175).

Sensational inaction: cinematic 'description'

As Seymour Chatman explains (drawing from Aristotle), 'the fundamental narrative verb is *do* [...] *action* is the fundamental narrative element' (1975: 213). If a film is not advancing a plot through character action, then what remains may be characterised as a form of cinematic 'description' (see Chatman 1990: 38–55). He takes up this question at length, approaching the very possibility of a cinematic form of 'description,' and in particular the possibility of 'explicit description' as opposed to the 'tacit description' that the cinematic image necessarily involves (1990: 38-40). That is, unlike literary narrative where plot progression may be temporarily 'suspended' or 'paused' for the sake of describing selected particularities of setting, atmosphere, character and so on, description in the cinema most often occurs tacitly, as a byproduct of plot action (1990: 38–43).

According to Chatman, then, explicit cinematic description occurs when story time is temporarily 'suspended', something intuitively contrary to the 'temporal demands of the medium' in which 'screen time moves inexorably forward'; thus, an explicit form of cinematic description requires formal narrative 'lingering,' or 'prowling' for details, either through special effects like slow motion, or through camera movements, shot duration and cutting that is unmotivated by plot progression (1990: 41–43). Explicit cinematic description then requires story time to halt, while narrative discourse (or screen time) continues. Again, as Chatman argues, 'film cannot avoid a cornucopia of visual details, some of which are inevitably "irrelevant" from the strict plot point of view' (1990: 40), but to make these details explicitly relevant requires the subordination of story time to the particularities of the image.

This notion of explicit description in cinema is especially productive for understanding how these films tell their stories. *Tropical Malady* and *Blissfully Yours* are replete with forms of narrative pause, where images are temporally unmotivated by plot action. In such a challenging auteur cinema as this, one that so adamantly resists over-determining interpretive manoeuvres, what can be more certainly posited is an aesthetic value system that favours the sensual cinematic description of quotidian social rhythms, the mysteries to be found in appreciating the primordial or mystical durations of 'wild' spaces, overall textual openness and cultural complexity over coherent storytelling and explicit narrative action.

Blissfully Yours tells the story of Min, a Burmese immigrant living illegally in Thailand, and his Thai girlfriend, Roong. The other central character, Orn, is a middle-aged woman who rents a room to Roong and helps care for Min while Roong spends her days as a factory worker painting Disney figurines. Min is a 'threshold person' – an illegal alien who does not speak Thai, is undocumented, has no position, no voice. He is liminal: 'betwixt and between the positions assigned and arrayed by law' (Turner 2004: 80). The three characters are only very loosely developed, established primarily through the subtle suggestion of loss and quiet psychic pain. Orn toils unhappily at her factory job, and Roong mourns the loss of a child, appearing to compensate for her deep sense of loss through an extra-marital affair. The first part of the film is set within the characters' work and social worlds assigned spatially to industrial Thailand, while the second part of the film is set in the border jungle with Burma, where the characters commune with nature and escape their worldly burdens.

Tropical Malady works similarly as a two-part structure, the first part 'social' in constitution, the latter part a disintegration of the social rooted in the dark, primordial dream-time of the jungle's mystical durations. The Thai-language title of *Tropical Malady*, *Sat Pralad*, translates roughly as 'strange animal' or 'monster'. Presumably the title suggests a double meaning, referring at once to the figure of the tiger-shaman in the film's latter part, and to a challenging narrative style that resists classification. *Tropical Malady* is a film of peculiar non-narrative textuality working to conjure primitivistic or mystical temporal orders in times when they are increasingly difficult to imagine, much less inhabit, and yet, perhaps for this reason acquiring greater urgency as aesthetic and representational themes in world cinema. The film demonstrates an extraordinary form of cinematic 'description' by way of its suspensions of story action, in turn affecting the significance of its culturally marked spatial and environmental sites within which the narrative discourse is enacted. *Blissfully Yours* also favours a form of narrative stasis and atmospheric 'lingering' over conventional, causal plot development. In their eschewing of classical cinematic values, offering instead an appreciation of the unknowable, of border forms and subjects, and perhaps most substantially, other phenomenological durations, the monstrous serves as a convenient metaphor for these narrative forms.

The first part of *Tropical Malady* depicts the casual development of a relationship between Keng, a soldier, and Tong, a peasant boy who works in town as an ice-cutter during the day and then returns to his parent's farm in the evening. They meet when Keng's patrol unit finds a dead body in the area of Tong's farm. They begin to spend time together and a mutual attraction is evident. Their tender intimations of attraction provide the central basis for engagement in part one, framed within a style of casual, observational accounting of Thai daily life. Their flirting is erotic, but understated and even desexualised, appearing at times as a form of animal curiosity and companionship as much as it resembles modern love.

One hour into *Tropical Malady*, having witnessed this meandering description of two men sensuously exploring each other's worlds in a largely social backdrop, the screen goes black for a cinematic eternity (fifteen seconds), and then commences a new story of a soldier hunting a tiger-shaman in the jungle. In *Tropical Malady*'s first part, forward narrative momentum yields to a simple observational view of cultural details from Thai daily life, fundamentally organised around the pleasures of lingering looks at faces, in the quotidian rhythms and sensuality of work and play, in social communion and in its other – isolation. The film's latter portion, however, gives way to a mystical exploration of one soldier's submission to, and transformation within, the 'wild' space of the jungle and its mystical forces.

In *Tropical Malady*, the demarcation of two separate but interpenetrating stories requires viewers to produce their own synthesis. They are not exactly two halves of a unified whole, as the film remains resolutely 'open' in the end, but neither are they quite sufficient on their own. The continuities and disjunctures between story parts – a dialectic of formally opposed but thematically and emotionally interrelated forces – are the basis of *Tropical Malady*'s intellectual rewards. Related to this is a formal blurring of fiction and non-fiction modes, striking a delicate balance between presenting a documentarian's sensory-oriented description of Thai rural and village cultural spectacle without quite becoming fully-fledged documentaries, and fictional premises without the films becoming wholly fictional narrative features. And yet somehow each mode would be anaemic without the other given the unique manner in which the films conflate them.

Without conventional character or plot development, the descriptive quality of their 'life worlds' – the sensual acts they participate in, and the urban and rural environmental atmospherics they relate to – are the most tangible elements. The non-narrative description of life worlds is enacted through the use of static framings, long-take cinematography, single-shot sequences, understated 'performances' by social actors (many non-professional actors) and a sound design that renders environmental ambience on an equal (and often greater) plane as character dialogue. Characters break the fourth wall by looking at the camera, and shot durations linger without any appreciable sense of character exposition or plot action. There is almost no use of eye-line match cuts that facilitate viewer identification with characters. Additionally, characters are often framed in extreme long shot, positioning them as subordinate to their environments, something that takes on greater significance in the latter, jungle episodes of both films. And because characters are so hazily drawn and plot motivations largely absent, the inhabitation of cultural atmospherics and marked environmental settings acquire a schematic significance over the course of the film. These narrative elements did not emerge in isolation, but are instead storytelling tropes traced back to a highly varied modernist legacy, though perhaps given this historical intertext these complex assemblages are more befitting the label 'postmodern'.

Art film poetics and border subjects

In historico-aesthetic terms *Tropical Malady* and *Blissfully Yours* reside somewhere at the intersection of 'avant-garde' (or 'experimental') narrative film and documentary modes of production. The 'art film' is one label, another, 'modernist,' though the latter is fraught with irresolvable debates as to whether it constitutes a historical phenomenon or merely a set of (ahistorical) aesthetic and narrative procedures (see Kovács 2007: 11–14). Either way, Apichatpong's cinema shares key features of these 'art film' categories, David Bordwell's argument that the 'art film' as a generic mode of production with its own set of storytelling conventions and accordant viewing 'procedures' points to the 'loosening' of the 'cause-effect linkage of events' as one of its key features (1999: 717). *Tropical Malady* and *Blissfully Yours* share many other 'art film' narrative conventions outlined by Bordwell, such as: an emphasis on realism, naturalism, unconventional plot 'manipulations', 'authorial expressivity', 'drifting episodic quality', 'maximum ambiguity' and so on (1999: 716–21).

Apichatpong has admitted that his formal education at the Art Institute of Chicago – which introduced him to modernist avant-garde and experimental filmmakers such as Andy Warhol, Bruce Bailie, Hollis Frampton and Marcel Duchamp – has influenced his storytelling mode. He explains that *Tropical Malady* is a 'structural film' (referring to the 1960s American experimental film movement) but 'different'; 'I always keep the classic experimental filmmakers up on a pedestal, but I am really losing touch with new developments in the field' (quoted in Römers 2005: 43). We can see the 'anti-narrative sentiment' of 'structuralist-materialist' filmmakers in both films (see Smith 2000: 13). We also witness in these non-narrative forms what Gilles Deleuze refers to as a characteristic of modernist art cinema, the use of 'pure optical and sound situations' in which images do not 'imply any imminent action' (see Kovács 2007: 42). Storytelling for Apichatpong, like so much of modernist art cinema, is rooted in the depiction of mental states, dreams, memories or what András Kovács more generally refers to as 'psychic landscape' (2007: 149). Yet despite the obvious affinities, these films are not plainly derivative of such earlier aesthetic movements, but a cosmopolitan admixture of materials drawn from Euro-Western film idioms and a rich mix of Thai culture-collecting and subjective experience.

Another important historical frame of reference for Apichatpong's films is that they reflect a consistent thematic concern with border forms and subject, such as: immigrants, women, labourers, homosexuality and human/non-human boundaries, that are so characteristic of the thematic concerns of postcolonial, diasporic and 'Third Cinema' counter-discourses. Consider again *Blissfully Yours'* central border character, Min, a Burmese immigrant. Min's deteriorating skin is itself border motif; the deterioration of his body's physical boundary is symbolic of the deleterious effects of national boundaries. His skin is a symbolic motif mirroring the human dissolution of national boundaries, and the national boundaries' dissolution of humans. In one especially poignant scene, Min is held in the river, floating on his back, peeling the flaking skin from his body. The scene is ritualistic, akin to a baptism, coding Min as a liminal entity amidst a greater rite of passage. Eyes closed, we briefly hear Min's inner monologue in voice-over, only to be overwhelmed by the jungle acoustics. The rhythmic drone of insects and other jungle sounds is the film's predominant acoustic element. The eclipse of Min's voice by the ambient sounds of the jungle indicates the importance not of exposing Min's thoughts (or 'point of view'), but instead to formally describing the interpenetrations of the internal and external, ascribed here more broadly within the dialectic of the 'social' and the 'natural'. Most important in this cinematic description is not the content of Min's thoughts but our awareness of his merging with the natural world, and most significantly, the importance of recognising fundamental primal and spiritual connections between people despite differences in national and cultural identity, endorsing an aesthetic ideal of submitting to the senses as a ritualistic means to knowledge, healing and personal transformation.

'Primitive passions' and Thai tradition in an age of globalisation

I present nature in my films to evoke how our identity depends on clothes and other means of self-representation. In the jungle, you don't have to care about such things. It's a place where your primal instincts are set free from a cage. And any reference to time is removed as well (Apichatpong, quoted in Römers 2005: 45).

Each of Apichatpong's first three feature films, *Mysterious Object at Noon* (2000), *Blissfully Yours* and *Tropical Malady* depicts forms of rural/urban tension. In the latter two, rural spaces take on the status of a sacred domain for escaping the oppressive structures of a modern social world, while in *Mysterious Object at Noon*, rural and village life worlds comprise repositories of traditional cultural knowledge. Each stages rural/urban narrative tensions that problematise the globalisation of Thai culture, and its corollary, the precarious status of traditional Thai cultural knowledge and values. On this latter point, *Mysterious Object at Noon* is more interested in the very conditions of possibility of traditional knowledge, utilising the surrealist game Exquisite Corpse to enact a collective storytelling project outside of Bangkok, evocatively teasing out the possibility of collective knowledge and participatory/ shared national-cultural narration.

Apichatpong's films, especially the two under discussion here, are largely organised around manifestations of nature sited to the rural, and the trope of a 'return to nature' that is common to many narrative traditions throughout the world, although in this case, the centering of stories on nature and the rural must necessarily be linked to a specific discourse of modernisation, rural development and a cultural 'crisis' in Thailand tied to processes of globalisation. For the filmmaker, the rural places depicted are of great personal significance. As a native of Khon Kaen in Northeast Thailand, Apichatpong has lived through the most rapid period of modernisation and cultural rupture in Thailand. Apichatpong says of these depictions, it is 'the environment I grew up in – I want to capture the transformation of that rural area' (quoted in Römers 2005: 45).

On the one hand the place of nature in these stories is impossible to separate from its larger symbolic cultural status in Thailand; on the other, we must not lose sight of how they are configured in a highly personalised way (as suggested in the quote at the outset of this chapter). In addition to Apichatpong's awareness of rural transformation in Thailand due to economic development, his stories are also very much interested in an artistic experimentation that interrogates how the 'social' and the 'natural' constitute each other, and the possibilities for communing with one spatio-temporal field at the expense of the other. Following *Blissfully Yours*, *Tropical Malady* represents a progressive deepening of this aesthetic inquiry into the possibility of a 'natural', mystical or 'primitive' order and its ability to be represented cinematically.

While these stories are highly personal, quite often explicitly depicting memories and sensations from Apichatpong's own life, they also represent the aestheticisation of tradition so characteristic of 'primitive passions' – as a distinctive 'structure of feeling' – represented in other contexts (see Chow 1995: 42). Quite crucially, far from being solely personal aesthetic explorations of authenticity rooted in 'nature', the primitivism of these films is inextricably linked to the awareness of modernisation, cultural crisis and a discourse of rural transformation in Thailand. Speaking from the context of Chinese cultural transformation and fifth generation Chinese cinema, Rey Chow explains that the 'politicizing of modern culture, too, is invested in primitivism. In fact, it is precisely when the older culture turns "aesthetic" and "primitive" in the sense of an *other* time, that the flip side of primitive passions, in the form of a concurrent desire to invent origins and primariness, asserts itself' (Chow 1995: 37). And while Apichatpong's primitive passions certainly have more bearing for a specifically Thai cultural context, this strong nature/social dialectic also exceeds such cultural specificity, as invocations of nature comprise a 'form of the past used to deconstruct the present' (Chow 1995: 40) which no doubt has resonance with the Euro-Western cinephile audience largely responsible for elevating Apichatpong's films to their current level of cultural prestige.

Nature invoked in *Blissfully Yours* and *Tropical Malady* serves as a form of the past, or what we commonly refer to as 'tradition'. In Thailand, tradition is most prominently encoded spatially through rural and village life. Craig Reynolds explains that local knowledge is central to debates in Thailand about the effects of globalisation; that what is most threatened by globalisation are 'local customs, local practices, local culture, even local knowledge' (2002: 308), which was especially heightened following the 1997 economic crisis and the beginning of an age of IMF dependency. Debates surrounding the globalisation of Thai culture took the rhetoric of an 'authentic' versus a 'synthetic' Thai culture, prompting the mobilisation of a new conception of Thai identity known as *phum panya*, translated as 'local knowledge, indigenous knowledge, native wisdom, local genius' strongly rooted in rural identity (Reynolds 2002: 329). Thus Apichatpong's primitive passions are in direct dialogue with such local conceptions of spatial and environmental significance during a moment of cultural rupture. Invocations of nature in these stories also derive from Thai Buddhism, another powerful source of relief from the anxieties associated with modernisation and the incursion of a commodity culture upon traditionally agrarian life-worlds.

Buddhism is a paradigm of resistance to the, in many instances, deleterious forces of economic globalisation, not only in Thailand but elsewhere in the world. A new age 'reformist Buddhist perspective' has emerged in opposition to the harmful effects of economic development on traditional ways of life. Donald Swearer sees this as a 'return to the fundamental verités of a simpler era believed to be embodied in an earlier historic age or represented by an idealized, mythic time of primal beginnings' (Swearer et al. 2004: 4). Where the spread of a money economy into traditionally subsistent areas has resulted in a shift away from traditional worldviews towards increasingly consumer-based subjectivities, Buddhism provides a spiritual model prescribing 'plants, trees, and the land itself' as a source of 'potential spiritual liberation' (Swearer et al. 2004: 5). The core Buddhist beliefs of understanding the source and nature of suffering, the virtue of compassion and the renunciation of material wealth, closely inform the atmospheric intermingling of characters with nature defining *Blissfully Yours* and *Tropical Malady* (in the former configured as curative rituals), enacting a religious aesthetic or, perhaps even a cultural style. We witness this most overtly in *Tropical Malady*'s latter portion where intertitle tableaux paintings of human-tiger hybrids invoke the mural paintings often found on the walls of temples, harkening back to an ancient tradition of Thai storytelling (see Stephens 2004).

Apichatpong's films grow out of an imaginary society/nature dialectic functioning as a critique of the oppressive and marginalising forces of economic development, nationalist immigration policies and repressive value systems, tending to associate liberation with the stripping of socio-cultural accretions and a return to primeval states of sensual awe, fear and sexual pleasure. Wilton Martinez describes the concept of the 'primitive' as 'both an essentialist *presence* – an "original" and "basic" form of life characterized by instinct and survival – and as a "lack" or regressive *absence*, signaled by a lack of culture, of development' (1992: 146; emphasis in original). In *Blissfully Yours* primitivism is associated with the need for marginalised border subjects to heal through a highly eroticised integration with the 'wild'. (This motif runs throughout Apichatpong's films where tensions are established between modern medicine and traditional folk healing methods, an awareness no doubt related to having parents who are doctors).

The primitivism of *Tropical Malady* is more rightly located in multiple appropriations of folktales and literature, resulting in a deeper mystical and magical-realist inflected storytelling project, or, what Chuck Stephens (2004) has aptly described as a 'Buddhist-Surrealist meditation on storytelling'. *Tropical Malady* is at least in part inspired by the jungle adventure stories of Thai novelist Noi Inthanon, but the seriousness and darkness of the film is rooted in an interest in dream-states and shamanistic and animistic-inspired folktales, all intermingled with the spectre of homo-social bonding and affection established in the film's first part. *Tropical Malady* is concerned – unlike *Blissfully Yours* – with a romantic primitivistic fantasy of ecological integration in which humans are inseparable from nature. As suggested in the film's opening intertitle: 'All of us are by nature wild beasts. Our duty as humans is to become like trainers who keep their animals in check, and even teach them to perform tasks alien to their bestiality.'

The second half of *Tropical Malady* is perhaps one of the most profound cinematic depictions in recent memory of the transformation of a modern 'social' subject into something resembling an animal state. And indeed, this principle is something fundamental to shamanism and animism. Social integration, as Alan Cambell explains, meant 'shotguns and radios, hence an umbilical cord to the outside society to get hold of lead shot and batteries' (2003: 134). As the second part of *Tropical Malady* begins, Tong enters the jungle with a shotgun, a radio and a flashlight for seeing through the darkness. By the end of his transformation these materials are meaningless. He loses one way of being by submitting to an *other*, ancient way of being. This transformation is configured as a dis-integration of communication between Keng and society. The radio transceiver Keng brings with him only transmits unintelligible voices overwhelmed by static. This same sound-design element is later heard coming from a firefly, and then again from a glowing tree like a supernatural antenna between nature and society. Towards the end, Keng finds his transceiver to be entirely dead. He is periodically seen peeling leeches from his skin, a sign of his physical merging with nature. He covers himself in mud to hide his scent and further erode his social status. The military 'camouflage' he wore upon entering the jungle – emblematic of one socio-political institution and its uses for blending in – becomes strange artifice by the end.

Lastly, it goes without saying that sexuality is a recurring form of primitive passions, something rendered quite explicitly in *Blissfully Yours* as part of a natural curative ritual. In *Tropical Malady* sexuality is at key points de-familiarised from its conventional manifestations through polymorphous perversion and human/non-human blurring by way of animal bonding motifs like licking and playfulness. Apichatpong claims that the homo-social bonding in *Tropical Malady* is not a direct reflection on his own homosexuality, but this is surely a part of his creative imaginary. Sexuality in *Tropical Malady* depicts a gradual eroding of typical cues of modern affection in order to expose something primal, deeper and unknowable in the magic that is sexual attraction.

Conclusion

Interpretive projects such as these can be hopelessly inadequate in terms of achieving an honorable translation between (audio-visual) cinematic and lexical spaces, a 'murdering to dissect' that seems especially resonant in the present case where the subjective viewing experience is its own complex work (see Stam 2000: 193). A summation seems incongruous given the complexity and openness of these films, but nevertheless. The temporal programme of *Blissfully Yours* and *Tropical Malady*, then, subverts classical standards of storytelling action and narrative completion. Instead, the films surrender to 'sensational inaction', a descriptive mode that enables the uncanny probing of 'natural' and mystical durations so contrary to the postmodern pace of life with its relentless profusion of images and demeaning of stillness. More holistically, the indeterminate narrative structures find a fit here with liminal subjects, border spaces and threshold states of consciousness. What conventional traditions of storytelling elide for the sake of order and more consolidated meanings, Apichatpong's cinema recuperates to experience, something I argue has great significance with respect to mediated conditions of sensory stimulation, knowledge production and spiritual life in contemporary times.

Rey Chow submits that 'the weakening of the plot has to do with the distrust of storytelling as a means of arriving at the truth; it is the distrust of a convention because it is too conventional' (1995: 162). This opens the way for the descriptive lingering on characters in space, a 'spatiotemporal integrity' which at times invokes a powerful realist ontology of film – a 'romantic ecologism' one associates with Andre Bazin or Siegfried Kracauer – only to be complicated by formal and thematic turns toward the magical and irrational (see Stam 2000: 78). Apichatpong's cinematic storytelling is not simply 'modernist', 'Thai' or even merely 'personal', as it is so frequently labelled. It is something *other*, the monstrous perhaps, defying unified and orderly comprehension. Or, perhaps better still, a *strange animal*.

Bibliography

Bordwell, D. (1999) 'The Art Cinema as a Mode of Film Practice', in L. Braudy and M. Cohen (eds) *Film Theory and Criticism*. New York and Oxford: Oxford University Press, 716–24.

Cambell, A. (2003) 'Submitting', in G. Harvey (ed.) *Shamanism: A Reader*. London and New York: Routledge, 123–44.

Chaiworaporn, A. and A. Knee (2006) 'Thailand: Revival in an Age of Globalisation', in A. Ciecko (ed.) *Contemporary Asian Cinema: Popular Culture in a Global Frame*. Oxford and New York: Berg, 58–70.

Chatman, S. (1975) 'The Structure of Narrative Transmission', in R. Fowler (ed.) *Style and Structure in Literature*. Oxford: Basil Blackwell, 213–57.

_____ (1990) *Coming to Terms: The Rhetoric of Narrative in Fiction and Film*. Ithaca and London: Cornell University Press, 38–55.

Chow, R. (1995) *Primitive Passions: Visuality, Sexuality, Ethnography, and Contemporary Chinese Cinema*. New York: Columbia University Press.

Ferrari, M. (2006) 'Mysterious Objects of Knowledge: An Interpretation of Three Feature Films by Apichatpong Weerasethakul in Terms of the Ethnographic Paradigm', unpublished master's thesis, Ohio University, Athens.

Foster, H. (1996) *The Return of the Real: The Avant-Garde at The End of The Century*. Cambridge: MIT Press.

Kovács, A. B. (2007) *Screening Modernism: European Art Cinema, 1950–1980*. Chicago and London: University of Chicago Press.

Martinez, W. (1992) 'Who Constructs Anthropological Knowledge?: Towards a Theory of Ethnographic Film Spectatorship', in P. Crawford and D. Turton (eds) *Film as Ethnography*. Manchester: Manchester University Press, 131–61.

Nichols, B. (1994) *Blurred Boundaries: Questions of Meaning in Contemporary Culture*. Bloomington: Indiana University Press.

Reynolds, C. (2002) 'Thai Identity in the Age of Globalization', in C. Reynolds (ed.) *National Identity and Its Defenders*. Chiang Mai: Silkworm Books, 308–38.

Römers, H. (2005) 'Creating His Own Cinematic Language: An Interview with Apichatpong Weerasethakul', *Cineaste*, 30, 4, 42–7.

Smith, M. (2000) 'Modernism and the Avant-Gardes', in J. Hill and P. Gibson (ed.) *World Cinema: Critical Approaches*. Oxford: Oxford University Press, 11–28.

Stam, R. (2000) *Film Theory*. Oxford: Blackwell.

Stephens, C. (2004) 'Tiger, Tiger, Burning Bright', *The San Francisco Bay Guardian Online*. Available: http://www.sfbg.com/39/04/art_film_weerasethakul.html (accessed on 27 October 2004).

Swearer, D., S. Premchit and P. Dokbuakaew (2004) *Sacred Mountains of Northern Thailand*. Chiang Mai: Silkworm Books.

Torgovnik, M. (1990) *Gone Primitive: Savage Intellects, Modern Lives*. Chicago and London: University of Chicago Press.

Turner, V. (2004) 'Liminality and Communitas', in H. Bial (ed.) *The Performance Studies Reader*. London and New York: Routledge, 79–87.

Ghosts in the National Machine:
The Haunting (and Taunting) Films
of Tracey Moffatt

Jennifer L. Gauthier

In June 2007, Screen Australia (formerly the Australian Film Commission) published 'Dreaming in Motion', a report celebrating the role of Aboriginal Australians in the film history of the nation. Documenting the work of Aboriginal filmmakers and community media organisations, this report re-writes the story of Australia's national cinema, which has been dominated by white Euro-Australians; special mention was made of the pioneering work of filmmaker Tracey Moffatt (Screen Australia 2007: 4). In his seminal work on Australian national cinema, Tom O'Regan testifies to her importance for a contemporary Australian national cinema wrestling to come to terms with a multicultural reality: 'For this post-national project, there is no more important figure than Aboriginal and Islander Tracey Moffatt' (1996: 326).

Born in Brisbane, Australia in 1960 to an Aboriginal mother, she was raised in the working-class suburb of Mt. Gravatt in a white household with many siblings. She graduated from the Queensland College of Art in 1982 and moved to Sydney to begin her work as a photographer. Moffatt has exhibited her photographs and videos all over the world to widespread acclaim. A pioneer in Aboriginal cinema, she started making movies before a specific Aboriginal film funding body was created.[1] Moffatt's moving picture oeuvre contains over seventeen works including documentary shorts, music videos, narrative films and art installation pieces. The focus here will be on *beDevil* (1993), her only feature-length film to date, with reference to her two short films, *Nice, Coloured Girls* (1987) and *Night Cries: A Rural Tragedy* (1990).[2]

As a contemporary Australian Aboriginal filmmaker, Moffat uses Indigenous strategies to speak back to national narratives, calling into question the official history of

Australia and of Australian national cinema. Moffatt's revisionist histories, or rather 'herstories', reflect her embodied knowledge as an Aboriginal woman. Her work takes seriously Audre Lord's question and caveat: 'What does it mean when the tools of a racist patriarchy are used to examine the fruits of that same patriarchy? [...] The master's tools will never dismantle the master's house' (1984: 13). Moffatt dismantles the master's house with her distinct brand of Indigenous counter cinema.[3] Her films reconstruct the relationship between storyteller and audience that might be lost when an oral tradition is transferred to film. Foregrounding the openness of the cinematic text, she creates films that exist only in and through the involvement of an active audience. Using an experimental aesthetic, Moffatt calls upon her audience to make meaning, to actively interpret her films and thus to connect the stories to our own lives. Her avant-garde narrative structure, sound design and *mise-en-scène* draw us into her stories, asking us to set aside our preconceived notions of what a film should be.

Aboriginal storytelling

Telling stories is a universal act that unites all human beings. We make sense of our world and our place within it by crafting narratives out of the raw material of experience. Stories help us reinvent ourselves and connect with others. In Aboriginal culture, storytelling is fundamental; 'the Australian Aboriginal worldview is rooted in a "fundamentally narrative understanding of the universe"' (Klapproth 2004: 66). Storytelling helps Indigenous people come to terms with colonisation and remember the past (see Attwood and Magowan 2001: xii). It also functions to keep the culture alive and pass on traditions; storytelling is a means to educate the young about cultural norms and values.

For Aboriginal peoples, storytelling is 'intrinsically interwoven with their understanding and conception of their physical environment' (Klapproth 2004: 69). It creates a strong link between people and places, and between past and present, celebrating an abiding connection to the land and to the ancestors who lived on the land. Aboriginal stories create a sense of landscape, community and place; for Aboriginal Australians, the land, its people and the stories they tell are intimately linked. Stories are the repository of Aboriginal culture and the medium through which an individual situates herself within that culture; storytelling constructs a powerful bond between the storyteller, the story and the audience.[4]

With the increased accessibility of film and video technology, Indigenous peoples have begun using these media to tell their stories. Scholars in various fields have vigorously debated the impact of this shift on Indigenous cultures. In his 1986 policy study on Aboriginal television for the Australian government, American researcher Eric Michaels suggests that 'mass media are logically and practically the inverse of the personal Aboriginal exchange system' (1986: 5); television and film deliver information to everyone equally, upsetting the balance and hierarchy of the Aboriginal kinship structure, exposing information that should remain secret and transmitting taboo images. His observations highlight the important cultural values that are communicated through the relationship between storyteller and audience.

Anthropologist and filmmaker David MacDougall lays out the basic dilemma: mass media might introduce Indigenous people to new values, new priorities and new ways of seeing, but they can also be used to support and strengthen aspects of their traditional culture. He writes: 'One reason for Aboriginal interest in television can be traced to the desire to control it before it controls them. But another is simply that it offers new opportunities for influence and self-expression' (1987: 54). Ultimately, MacDougall suggests that 'Aboriginal people, both individually and collectively, are turning to film, video and television as the media most likely to carry their messages to one another and into the consciousness of white Australia' (1987: 58).

Although Tracey Moffatt brought Aboriginal film to prominence, Aboriginal media production in Australia began in the mid-1980s before the introduction of AUSSAT, the first communications satellite to be launched over central Australia. Pre-empting this event, Michaels assisted the Warlpiri-speaking people of Yuendumu in creating their own community media organisation, the Warlpiri Media Association. In a parallel development, the Central Australian Aboriginal Media Association (CAAMA) started in 1980 as an FM radio station and has since grown to become a highly successful production company. In 1988, CAAMA launched Imparja, a commercial television station owned by Northern Territory and South Australian Aboriginal stakeholders.[5] At the national level, the Australian Film Commission (now Screen Australia) created an Indigenous Unit in 1993 (later renamed the Indigenous Branch) to support Aboriginal storytelling on film with various training programmes and funds. Aboriginal filmmakers working within the Indigenous Branch such as Rachel Perkins, Ivan Sen, Beck Cole and Warwick Thornton are following the path that Moffatt blazed.

Indigenous aesthetics

Moffatt's work exemplifies what Maori filmmaker Barry Barclay (2002) has called Fourth Cinema.[6] Fourth Cinema is cinema made by First Nations or Indigenous peoples and it has an Indigenous essence. This essence may only be grasped by Indigenous people, but like all cinema, Fourth Cinema works on many different levels. Barclay contrasts this essence, or inner logic of the film, with the 'accidents' – the surface features, or elements of *mise-en-scène* that fill the screen. Fourth Cinema films take a unique point of view, turning First Cinema on its head. Barclay uses the Hollywood film *The Mutiny on the Bounty* (Lewis Milestone, 1962) to illustrate this idea. In the initial conquest scene, Captain Bligh orders his men to go ashore and have sex with the native women. The camera sits on the deck of the ship and films the approach of the white men from the invader's perspective. Barclay asks:

> What happens when the camera is shifted from the deck onto the shore? The camera, cut loose from First Cinema constraints and in the hands of the natives, does not work anything like as well away from the ship's deck (as the ship men see it), because allowing the camera to operate ashore under God knows whose direction would defeat the purposes of those in control of First Cinema, whose more or less exclusive intention has been, over one hundred years of cinema, to show actions and relationships within Western societies and Western ideological landscapes. Furthermore, the First Cinema enterprise is likely to be greatly deflated if there is a camera ashore, a camera outside First Cinema, a camera with a life of its own, watching. (2002: 14)

Fourth Cinema re-envisions the act of colonisation from an Indigenous point of view, upsetting the traditional hierarchy of the gaze. This power shift makes an important political statement and infuses Fourth Cinema with radical potential.[7]

The notion of Indigenous media as a form of political activism is championed by Faye Ginsburg. She sees Indigenous media as 'part of broader movements for cultural autonomy and self-determination that exist in complex tension with the structures of national governments, international politics, and the global circulation of communications technology' (1993: 558). In contrast to mainstream films, made simply for entertainment purposes, Indigenous films participate in a process of identity construction or re-negotiation; they 'mediate culture' as Ginsburg explains (1991: 104). These activist texts interrogate the national imaginary and construct 'an inclusive if uneasy vision of the nation that, at least televisually, is beginning to take account of its Aboriginal citizens' (1993: 561). Ginsburg sums up the radical potential of Indigenous media when she states that 'indigenous people are using screen media not to mask, but to recuperate their own collective histories and stories – some of them traumatic – that have been erased in the national narratives of the dominant culture and are in danger of being forgotten within local worlds as well' (2002: 40). In proclaiming Aboriginal peoples' continued existence, Aboriginal media texts challenge narrow conceptions of the national imaginary, national identity and national cinema.

Working as an Aboriginal filmmaker in contemporary Australia, Tracey Moffatt creates what Laura Marks has called 'intercultural cinema', characterised by experimental films that attempt to 'represent the experience of living between two or more cultural regimes of knowledge or living as a minority in the still majority white Euro-American West' (2000: 1). In this specific brand of postcolonial cinema, filmmakers work to reconstitute their history, performing 'acts of excavation' (2000: 26). According to Marks, intercultural cinema is 'constituted around a particular crisis: the directly political discrepancy between official history and "private memory"' (2000: 60). Moreover, this type of cinema calls for participatory spectatorship, assuming 'the interestedness, engagement and intelligence of its audience' (2000: 19).

In her efforts to speak back to national history and re-negotiate indigeneity, Moffatt adapts the 'master's tools' for her own use. She is an example of what Leela

Gandhi calls, 'mimic men' (or more correctly, 'mimic women'), whose 'generic mis-appropriations constantly transgress the received and orthodox boundaries' (1998: 150). Gandhi suggests that 'the paradigmatic moment of anti-colonial counter-text-uality is seen to begin with the first indecorous mixing of Western genres with local content' (ibid.). As Homi Bhabha notes, mimicry calls forth hybridity, 'at once a mode of appropriation and of resistance' (1990: 120). Moffatt appropriates the narrative film as a mode of telling stories about Aboriginal life and culture, but she cracks open this traditionally closed form to invite audience reflection and participation. She imports Hollywood's most powerful export into a local context, stretching its boundaries and re-writing its definition.

Nice, Coloured Girls

As Marks observes, formal experimentation is integral to intercultural cinema, as it challenges the notion that cinema can represent reality. Moffatt's experimen-tal aesthetic foregrounds the very complexity of representation in all of its forms. Her stories and storytelling techniques are characterised by hybridity, attesting to her position as an Aboriginal woman living in contemporary Australia. In her early short films, *Nice, Coloured Girls* and *Night Cries: A Rural Tragedy*, Moffatt introduces viewers to her unique style of storytelling and her politically charged themes. These films lay the groundwork for *beDevil* with their overt references to national history, national cinema and the lingering effects of institutional racism.

Moffatt's first narrative short, *Nice, Coloured Girls* re-writes the colonial history of Australia from an Aboriginal woman's perspective. It follows three Aboriginal women as they venture out into the King's Cross, Sydney nightlife, pick up a white man and exploit him for dinner and drinks. The film's experimental style calls attention to the constructed nature of history and narrative; it openly juxtaposes reality and artifice. Karen Jennings notes that the film is structured around a number of binary opposi-tions, including past/present, fact/fiction, nice girls/nasty girls, predator/prey and exploiter/exploited (1993: 70), but Moffatt sets up these oppositions only to call attention to their fabrication. Her film actively challenges the rigidity of the binaries, preferring to celebrate moments of blending, blurring and in-betweenness.

The film's *mise-en-scène* and narrative structure challenge traditional Hollywood conventions. Moffatt tells her story through a combination of staged dramatic sequences and non-diegetic inserts. The dramatic sequences are played out both in actual locations and on sets; the constant shifting back and forth calls attention to the cinema's false reality. Borrowing a trope of early ethnographic films, she presents the women's dialogue in titles at the bottom of the screen. This strategy takes away their voices, highlighting the Aboriginal disempowerment wrought by colonialism and anthropology. However, Moffatt restores their power through the actions that they take and by giving them control of the gaze, or in Barry Barclay's words, by put-ting the camera on the shore. Much of the film is shot from their point of view; they look back at the white man as he attempts to objectify them. E. Ann Kaplan notes that this strategy is revolutionary, as it constructs a 'complete reversal of the gaze. This is not just a resisting look: it puts the project of gazing squarely in the position of the aboriginal female protagonists' (1997: 295).

Throughout the film, a female Aboriginal elder confronts the audience with her gaze and laughter; this is her reaction to the 'official history' contained in the journal entries of the white sailors that act as the film's voiceover. Moffatt also challenges white authority as the elder destroys a painting of the harbour that is similar to one contained in the journals of Lt. William Bradley, one of the men present at first contact.[8] The wall on which the drawing is hung is violently knocked down so that it collapses backward. This segment depicts the literal dismantling of colonial history; Moffatt has torn down the master's house.

Juxtaposing stylised stage sets and constructed tableaux with location shots of the city, Moffatt sets up a dialectic between truth and fiction. But her fictions are obvious; they do not pretend to be real. Instead, she challenges what we have taken to be real, not only the 'official' history of conquest as related by white sailors, but also the anthropological accounts captured in ethnographic films by white filmmakers. The film offers 'herstory' as an antidote to history. Placing Aboriginal women at the centre of the narrative, taking their point of view and speaking back to white men's accounts of Australia's founding and original inhabitants, Moffatt's film is decidedly feminist. Moreover, her aesthetic strategy foregrounds the artifice of cinema and the labour involved in meaning construction. With its multilayered text structured by false dichotomies, *Nice, Coloured Girls* confounds simple interpretation, and in so doing, reminds us that when it comes to colonialism, nothing is ever that simple.

Night Cries: A Rural Tragedy

Moffat's second short film embraces a more explicitly avant-garde aesthetic. Drawing upon her own personal experiences, and again, firmly rooted in Australian history, the film features a middle-aged Aboriginal woman who is caring for her elderly white mother in a remote part of the bush. Set against a painted backdrop that evokes the work of Aboriginal landscape painter Albert Namatjira, Moffatt's beautifully-crafted tableaux and evocative soundtrack create a moving portrait of loss and alienation. Although not an overt reference to the Stolen Generations, *Night Cries* wrestles with the residue of strained familial relations.[9] Even now, Aboriginal children have higher rates for entering the child protection system and are more likely to be taken away from their families (see Australian Human Rights Commission 2006). The film ushers in a return of the repressed in national history.

As in parts of *Nice, Coloured Girls*, the setting in *Night Cries* is highly stylised; it reads as a stage set upon which the characters act out the national trauma for all to see. Marcia Langton, an anthropologist who plays the daughter, suggests that Moffatt inverts colonial history to 'play out the worst fantasies of those who took

Aboriginal children from their natural parents to assimilate and "civilize" them' (quoted in Kaplan 2005: 131). Moffatt has suggested that the film speaks back to Charles Chauvel's *Jedda* (1955), the first Aboriginal-themed Australian feature film. Directed by a white Australian, it tells the story of an Aboriginal girl brought up in a white family caught between two cultures: 'I took two of the film's characters, Jedda, the black woman, and her white mother, and aged them as if thirty years had past [sic]. In the original film, Jedda is thrown off a cliff and killed. I wanted to resurrect her, and place the two of them back in the homestead situation, living out their days' (quoted in Murray 1990: 22).

Revisiting this classic text of Australian national cinema, Moffatt re-writes it from an Aboriginal perspective, but Moffatt mixes the history of national cinema with her own personal history: 'As I developed the script, the film became less about them and more about me and my white foster mother. I was raised by an older white woman and the script became quite a personal story. The little girl who appears in some of the flashback sequences looks a lot like me. That was quite intentional' (quoted in Murray 1990: 22). The blending of her individual experience with the nation's history blurs the boundaries between the personal and the political.

Moffatt also blurs the boundaries between national cultures, blending American and Aboriginal popular culture. The film opens with an epigraph from the Hollywood film, *Picnic* (Joshua Logan, 1955), adapted from William Inge's play: 'Look at that sunset Howard! ... It's like the daytime didn't want to end ... like it was gonna put up a big scrap and maybe set the world on fire to keep the night time from creepin' on.' The quote calls attention to the fabricated sunset in the backdrop, frozen in a liminal moment between day and night. Moreover, the fake landscape belies the romanticised vision of the bush as seen in classic Australian films.

Footage of Jimmy Little performing his hit, 'Royal Telephone' frames the story. Little, born in 1937, was the best-known Aboriginal performer of the 1960s, recognised for his gospel and popular songs and later, his low-key brand of activism. His motto: 'walk softly softly and speak softly softly' was criticised by some who embraced a more radical type of activism (see Australian Screen 2009). Little's performance helps to establish the subtext for the film and evoke the lingering effects of colonialism in Australia. He is filmed against a black background, clad in a gray suit, playing the guitar; he is an icon of Aboriginal success, but also of Aboriginal fetishisation. When he broke into the music business in the 1960s, he was a novelty, and perhaps seen as not-threatening because he sang gospel music. Questions that his presence raises about racism and Aboriginal participation in society simmer below the surface of the film.

Jarring cuts coded as memories disrupt the narrative. While these memories are at first tender, they become more disturbing and threaten to overtake the main narrative. A recurring scene features a little girl and two little boys playing on the rocks at the edge of the ocean, while their mother stands by. The mother swings the little girl back and forth in her arms, then later the boys begin to throw clumps of seaweed at the girl until she is covered and crying. Coated in the dark and shiny strands the little girl screams for her mother, who is gazing out at the sea, oblivious to her daughter's plight. After a repeated shot of the little girl crying, we see the mother cradling her in a towel.

This sequence is overlaid with an eerie soundscape made up of static, feedback and the screams of both humans and birds. While at first the images evoke positive memories, this nostalgia is belied by the unsettling sound and the repeated shots of the little girl in distress. The entire sequence plays out just out of reach; we do not know exactly what is happening, but it is definitely a traumatic event. Kaplan notes that the structure of *Night Cries* mimics the structure of trauma as the daughter's memories intrude on the present without full explanation (2005: 131).

Sound plays a crucial role in establishing the mood of the film. Moffatt and her sound designer, Deborah Petrovich create an innovative and powerful soundscape that envelops the viewer. The blast of a train whistle blurring into screams opens the film, while the sounds of everyday life punctuate the silence between mother and daughter. In the last shot of the film, the daughter lies next to her dead mother, while the sobs of a baby shatter the silence. To close the film, 'Royal Telephone' fades in and we see Jimmy Little singing again. This time, his upbeat manner is belied by the film's content, causing the spectator to reflect on the irony in Little's message.

The importance placed upon the soundtrack in *Night Cries* upsets the traditional visual/aural hierarchy in mainstream cinema. The fact that the soundtrack contains no dialogue further thwarts viewers. This aesthetic choice suggests the ineffable quality of the emotions and memories that the film evokes, both Moffatt's and the nation's. As Laura Marks suggests, 'a political cinema is characterized by gaps and silences, the sites of emergence from these smug sedimented discourses [the official discourse of invisibility, extinction and racism]' (2000: 56). Moffatt's avant-garde strategy challenges not only Hollywood hegemony but also an Australian cinema that has often fashioned itself on Hollywood. She creates an alternative national cinema through her evocation of repressed racial politics, her references to Aboriginal cultural icons and her experimental aesthetic.

beDevil

Moffatt expands upon these themes in her only feature-length film to date, *beDevil*. Made for $2.5 million with funding from the Australian Film Finance Corporation, it is comprised of three short films based on ghost stories that were told to Moffatt by members of her family, both white and black (see Conomos and Caputo 1993: 28). Moffatt has described the film this way: '"bedevil" is a very playful, old-fashioned word no one really uses any more. It means "to haunt and taunt". The style of the film is teasing. You're following characters who are haunted by something, and I suggest perhaps we're all a little haunted in a way, and we probably don't ever come to terms with it' (quoted in Summerhayes 2004: 14). Cynthia Baron notes that 'Moffatt's films establish connections between personal ghost stories and national nightmares' (2002: 159). As in her earlier films, Moffat seeks to come to terms with the colonial past and its lasting impact on the present (and the future) and to work through the trauma that has marked Aboriginal peoples' lives. The impossibility of this effort is represented by the experimental style of the film; its gaps, fissures and unexplained sequences defy full understanding.

Much of the film is highly stylised, making use of elaborate stage sets, vivid lighting schemes and a richly layered soundtrack. Moffatt has noted that she was influenced by Japanese filmmakers Yasujiro Ozu and Masaki Kobayashi: 'The sound is really half the movie in their case and it's half of the movie in *beDevil*' (Conomos and Caputo 1993: 28). Her visual images reference Australian painters Russell Drysdale and Geoffrey Smart; she was also influenced by the film *Walkabout* (Nicholas Roeg, 1971), specifically its movement through varied landscapes (see Conomos and Caputo 1993: 28–30). The horror element of the film she attributes to her admiration for William Friedkin's *The Exorcist* (1973) and her opening credits seem to pay homage to Hitchcock (see Conomos and Caputo 1993: 31). The film moves back and forth through space, time and genre; we never know what is going to happen next. Moffatt privileges this unpredictability in her narratives: 'never let the audience know what is coming next,' she has said (quoted in Conomos and Caputo 1993: 30). *beDevil*'s creepy atmosphere, ominous music and suspenseful plot echo classic Hollywood horror movies, but it is the horrifying trauma lurking beneath these 'surface accidents' that gives the film its distinct power.

Throughout *beDevil*, ghosts represent the residue of the past in the present. In the first story, 'Mr. Chuck', the ghost of an American soldier lurks below the waters of a swamp. When a white architect arrives to build a movie theatre over the swamp, strange things begin to happen. The Aboriginal children who play in the area are wary of the dark bubbling mud; one of them, Rick, falls into the swamp twice. To depict his tale, Moffatt borrows liberally from the horror film genre; scary music and quick cuts heighten the suspense and finally a muddy face emerges from the roiling pit. Attentive viewers have been prepared for this scene by subliminal images that Moffat inserts throughout the story: a man's face covered with sand appears twice, superimposed over the main action. Even more ominous is the image of the architect's face twisted into a menacing grin, his tongue flicking out. The second story,' Choo Choo Choo Choo', is about a family who is visited by several different spirits: a ghost train, the ghost of a little blind girl who was killed on the tracks, coloured lights in the sky (the elders call them 'min min lights') and a small doll totem which appears randomly on the set. The family home, situated next to the train tracks, may be haunted also; the characters hear whispers and strange sounds and a mysterious figure emerges from around one corner of the porch. The last story, 'Lovin' the Spin I'm In', features Beba and Minnie, two ghosts of an Islander couple who lived in an apartment building owned by Dmitri. Dmitri is trying to get his tenants to move out so he can sell the building to a developer, but the ghosts ultimately disrupt his plans.

Moffatt's ghostly apparitions haunt the viewer as they haunt the characters, representing memories of the past that linger in the present.

As in her previous films, Moffatt structures *beDevil* through a series of layered dichotomies. Her *mise-en-scène* distinguishes the past and present with past events played out on an obviously fake stage set, and actions in the present filmed on location. This strategy calls attention to the constructed nature of history and memory, as Alessandra Senzani (2007) notes. Moffatt also uses stage sets to suggest that nature has been worked over by culture, and that the Australian landscape idealised in so many films is a myth; it no longer exists. Her set design highlights the irony of a national cinema's focus on a landscape that was in fact, stolen.

The swamp in 'Mr. Chuck' is evoked through a painted backdrop. Neither fully of the land nor the sea, the swamp is a liminal space, accessed through Rick's memory. It is a menacing place with a deep gold sky and black water; the camera slowly circles above this site of trauma and taboo. In contrast to this stage set are location shots from which the story is narrated in the present. The ghost story is told through mock interviews with two narrators, Rick, the Aboriginal child who grew up near the swamp and Shelley, a white woman from Bribie Island where the swamp is located. While the interviews carry the weight of documentary truth, Moffatt undermines the authority of any one story by alternating the two opposing narratives. Rick says: 'I hated that place ... that island,' while Shelley muses, 'I've always loved this place, our island home.' Here Moffatt casts a critical eye on the idea of a singular official discourse of history, privileging polyphony instead. The camerawork supports these conflicting descriptions of the island: the swamp's artificial, dank and claustrophobic feeling is countered by sweeping sunlit pans of Bribie Island. The island (in the present) is captured by helicopter shots of its myriad leisure activities, including boating, golfing, bike riding and sunbathing. While this footage is more obviously 'real', Moffat calls attention to the way it too is constructed as if for a tourism commercial.

The doubling of the narrators evokes the binary opposition Aboriginal/white. Rick tells his story from a jail cell, while Shelley sits in a large, canal-side home. In the past, Rick and his sisters are contrasted with the lily-white, blond twins of the architect who is designing the movie theatre. The Aboriginal children roam about in nature, while the twins ride shiny red bicycles, or play with toy guns in holsters. In a particularly poignant moment, the white children point their toy guns at Rick and his sisters. The white father is doting, petting the twins and feeding them treats, while Rick's 'uncles' growl at the children and beat them behind closed doors. Moffatt depicts this abuse in a characteristically artistic, but obtuse manner: the white twins stand outside Rick's shack, listening to incomprehensible screams, until a rivulet of blood flows beneath the door.

Moffatt ultimately subverts the racial binary through her *mise-en-scène*. Shelley stands behind a large window looking out onto the world, just as Rick is imprisoned behind the glass wall of his cell. As Catherine Summerhayes suggests, this strategy asks the viewer to reconsider the opposition between imprisonment and liberty

(2004: 19). Through Shelley, Moffatt suggests that white Australians are also impris-oned by the nation's history of racial violence, but she also emphasises that Aboriginal people were the direct victims of this violence. Rick's fate underscores the stark dif-ferences in incarceration rates for Aboriginal and white people in Australia.[10]

'Choo Choo' uses the same *mise-en-scène* strategy to represent the past and the present. The family's home in the past is situated in a painted backdrop with stylised ant hills and dirt mounds; it is a darker, more sinister version of the one in *Night Cries*. The present is captured in documentary-style footage on location in a town. 'Choo Choo's' ghost story also has dual narrators of differing ethnicities: Ruby, an Aboriginal woman who grew up in a house by the railroad tracks, and Bob Malley, an Asian-Australian who runs a curiosity museum.

Ruby tells us about the haunting of her family's home as she and her netball team prepare a meal of *haute bush cuisine*. We are introduced to the rowdy group of women as they ride in the bed of a pick-up truck, blasting country music. The song being played, 'Ghan to Alice', celebrates the train route from Adelaide to Alice Springs, and it is sung by Auriel Andrews, who plays Ruby. This is a particularly striking example of Moffatt's doubling strategies, as Andrews is present as a character in the film and also through her voice coming from the boombox. Evoking the trauma of a lost home, the lyrics of the song talk about being called 'back home again', but Ruby's home is in shambles, as we see in the background. She seems not to be traumatised by this fact; she and her friends talk to the camera as they cook and serve up such Aboriginal delicacies as roasted pig, yabbies (freshwater prawns) with Hollandaise sauce and fresh-caught snake. This sequence is filmed as a television cooking show, a further blurring of genres. In another instance of doubling, the younger Ruby (a character based on Moffatt's mother) is played by Tracey Moffatt herself, a kind of inside joke, which, as Summerhayes notes, calls to mind the self-representational practices of artists Cindy Sherman and Frida Kahlo (2004: 17).

'Lovin the Spin I'm In' takes place in a completely artificial urban environment; nature has been totally expunged. City streets are evoked by storefronts and direc-tional traffic markings on the ground; the buildings are obviously set pieces. Because all of 'Lovin the Spin I'm In' takes place on sets, the past and the present are distin-guished primarily through the tint of the image. The past is rendered in red, as if washed in blood, while the present is all cold grays and blues. Both of these con-trast with the more distant past, when Beba and Minnie first met. These sequences are sunny and golden, the colours of nostalgia and happiness. As the camera moves through a grassy field like a person running, we hear sounds of carefree laughter. These scenes suggest past freedom as compared with present imprisonment. Their story remains a mystery however, as Moffatt never clearly explains these wordless sequences. Beba's mother, Emelda, refuses to leave the apartment building and the only other remaining tenant is a Frida Kahlo-lookalike, who recites Kahlo's roman-tic battles with Diego Rivera in her apartment. Kahlo's presence calls to mind the many ways that she blurred boundaries in her life and art. Moffatt's homage to Kahlo evokes the notion of split subjectivity, evoking Aboriginals' situation in contemporary Australia.

Moffatt's preoccupation with land is to be expected, but her way of dealing with landscape is inventive and evocative. Her use of constructed sets and overt allusions to development underscore the trauma of loss and alienation that her characters experience. If Aboriginal stories map a landscape that describes an individual's relationship with the world, then Moffatt's films chronicle what happens when this landscape is destroyed.

In 'Mr. Chuck' the American army is stationed on Bribie Island during World War II, and Mr. Chuck's body permanently occupies the swamp. Moreover, white Australian developers build a movie theatre over the swamp and American war films are imported for exhibition. 'The Oasis', as the theatre is called, suggests a peaceful respite from the tensions of daily life. However, the theatre signifies the ongoing occupation of the land by an outside presence, first the American military, and then Hollywood. The theatre serves as a precursor to the vast commercial development that characterises Bribie Island in the present. These modern 'improvements' represent the working over of nature by culture through the act of colonisation.

Modernity and commercial development are signified in 'Choo Choo' by the train. A real train brings Ruby's family their supplies; the tracks are carved through the landscape like an open wound. The ghost train that haunts them suggests the inescapable influence of the white man's technology. Trains are a symbol of movement and technological progress, but also an actual cause of Aboriginal displacement. 'Lovin' the Spin I'm In' references development most overtly, as Dmitri plans to build a casino-resort where the apartment building stands. Wrapped around the ghost story of Beba and Minnie is Dmitri's battle to get his tenants out, in particular the last holdouts, Emelda and Frida. Moffatt rewrites the story of Aboriginals being evicted from their land in modern multicultural terms: Dmitri's investors are an Asian man and an Italian man and he himself is a Greek immigrant. In Dmitri's embrace of capitalism the old must be removed to make way for the new and as Tom O'Regan describes: 'The Islanders become the ghosts in the (capitalist) machine' (1996: 330).

Just as the ghosts frustrate Dmitri's attempt to develop his land, Moffatt's ghosts disrupt the dichotomies that structure *beDevil*. They are both dead and living, figures of the past and the present; they occupy that in-between place of the sacred and the taboo (Lévi-Strauss 1968). Ghosts defy rational explanation, just as *beDevil* eludes full understanding. Much about the characters and their actions remains unknown, frustrating our desire for mastery over the narrative. Moffatt does not fully explain any of the hauntings in *beDevil*, forcing us to come to our own conclusions.

Conclusion

Moffatt's stories require the active participation of the audience. Her multilayered images and soundscapes demand prolonged attention; as Cynthia Baron observes, 'the *mise-en-scène* elements, sound-image combinations, and sequence-to-sequence relationships are so dense with meaning that they invite, require, and reward the kind of contemplation often reserved for one's leisurely, studied encounters with art gallery exhibitions' (2002: 153). Tom O'Regan suggests that 'rather than pre-empting our speculative interpretation, interrelatedness and the invitation to "intersubjective dialogue" are foregrounded, so she can enlist us to project and assign meaning to her films' (1996: 327). However, even an active stance may not lead to full understanding, as Moffatt's films refuse simple explanations and resist plenitude. This strategy is intentional; as Laura Marks notes: 'When postcolonial filmmakers make difficult, hard-to-read works, they are not simply trying to frustrate the viewer, but to acknowledge the fact that the most important things that happened are invisible and unvisualizable' (2000: 57).

Viewers may be aware that their grasp of Moffatt's films is limited or imperfect. As a white American film scholar, I can interpret Moffatt's work within its postcolonial context, but there will always be something more that cannot be explained. The 'essence' of Indigenous cinema is the residue of the trauma that Indigenous peoples have survived. Moffatt re-establishes the bond between storyteller and audience, not through traditional character identification as in Hollywood cinema, but through the search for meaning. As the active spectator works to fill in the gaps, she re-activates the trauma. This is where Moffatt's work is most transformative: it revises the history of the nation and the history of national cinema. Through her unique brand of Indigenous counter cinema, Moffatt reveals the ghosts of the past that haunt the present.

Notes

1   Her films have been supported by the Australian Film Commission, the Women's Film Fund, the Australian Film Finance Corporation, the Australian Film, Television and Radio School and the Department of Aboriginal Affairs.
2   *Night Cries: A Rural Tragedy* and *beDevil* were both shown at the Cannes Film Festival.
3   The notion of counter cinema originated with feminist film theorists of the 1970s, such as Clare Johnston, Laura Mulvey and Annette Kuhn. They saw cinema as both a political tool and a form of entertainment and sought to challenge Hollywood's patriarchal cinematic codes with strategies of openness, fragmentation, displacement and discontinuity. They also borrowed the concept of 'making strange,' from Bertolt Brecht, highlighting filmmaking strategies that would construct a new relationship between the spectator and the film. See Kuhn 1990, Johnston 2000a and 2000b and Mulvey 2000.
4   The sum of these stories is what makes up the Aboriginal concept that non-Indigenous peoples have come to call 'The Dreamtime' or 'The Dreaming'. See Stanner (1956).
5   CAAMA produces a wide variety of film and television projects of all genres, supporting the efforts of Aboriginal peoples to tell their stories to both a local and a global audience. Most recently, CAAMA co-produced Warwick Thornton's debut feature film, *Samson and Delilah*, which won the 2009 Camera d'Or at the Cannes Film Festival. See Screen Australia (2007) and Ginsburg (1991

and 2002).

6   See Willemen (1993). Barclay made the world's first Indigenous feature film, *Ngati* in 1987.

7   For additional information see Barclay (1990).

8   Bob Hodge and Vijay Mishra discuss this drawing entitled, 'First Encounter with the Native Women at Port Jackson', noting that it provides important clues as to Bradley's coding of the event: 'it acknowledges that this was an erotic as well as a strategic encounter' (1990: 36).

9   This chapter in Australia's history is just being acknowledged. The Stolen Generations refers to as many as 100,000 Indigenous children who were forcibly removed from their homes and put in residential schools run by the government or churches. The 1997 report, 'Bringing Them Home' revealed the extent of these racist policies and their lasting impact on the children (now adults). On 13 February 2008, Prime Minister Kevin Rudd issued an apology to the Aboriginal peoples of Australia (see European Network for Indigenous Australian Rights 2009).

10 According to the Australian Human Rights Commission (2006), Aboriginal people made up 22% of the total prison population in 2005 and were nineteen times more likely to be in prison than a non-Aboriginal person.

Bibliography

Attwood, B. and F. Magowan (2001) 'Introduction', in B. Attwood and F. Magowan (eds.) *Telling Stories: Indigenous History and Meaning in Australia and New Zealand*. Crows Nest, NSW: Allen & Unwin, xi–xvii.

Australian Human Rights Commission (2006) 'A Statistical Overview of Aboriginal and Torres Strait Islander Peoples in Australia'. On-line. Available: http://www.hreoc.gov.au/Social_Justice/statistics/index.html (accessed on 20 November 2009).

Australian Screen (2009), 'Education Notes for *Jimmy Little's Gentle Journey*'. On-line. Available: http://www.aso.gov/au/titles/doucmentaries/jimmy-littles-gentle-journey/clip3 (accessed on 19 November 2009).

Barclay, B. (1990) *Our Own Image*. Auckland: Longman Paul.

_____ (2002) 'Fourth Cinema'. Lecture for the Auckland University Film and Media Studies Department, Auckland, NZ.

_____ (2003) 'Exploring Fourth Cinema'. Lecture for the National Endowment for the Humanities Summer Institute, Hawaii.

Baron, C. (2002) 'Films by Tracey Moffatt: Reclaiming First Australians' Rights, Celebrating Women's Rites', *Women's Studies Quarterly*, 1–2, 151–77.

Bhabha, H. (1990) *The Location of Culture*. London: Routledge.

Conomos, J. and R. Caputo (1993) 'Bedevil', *Cinema Papers*, 93, 26–32.

European Network for Indigenous Australian Rights (2009) *The Stolen Generations*. On-line. Available: http://www.eniar.org/stolengenerations.html (accessed on 15 August 2009).

Gandhi, L. (1998) *Post-Colonial Theory: A Critical Introduction*. New York: Columbia University Press.

Ginsburg, F. (1991) 'Indigenous Media: Faustian Contract or Global Village?', *Cultural Anthropology*, 6, 1, 92–112.

_____ (1993) 'Aboriginal Media and the Australian Imaginary', *Public Culture*, 5, 557–8.

_____ (2002) 'Screen Memories: Resignifying the Traditional in Indigenous Media', in F. Ginsburg, L. Abu-Lughod and B. Larkin (eds) *Media Worlds: Anthropology on New Terrain*. Berkeley: University of California Press, 39–57.

Hodge B. and V. Mishra (1990) *Dark Side of the Dream: Australian Literature and the Postcolonial Mind*. North Sydney, NSW: Allen & Unwin.

Jennings, K. (1993) *Sites of Difference: Cinematic Representations of Aboriginality and Gender*. South Melbourne: Australian Institute Research and Information Centre.

Johnston, C. (2000a) 'Women's Cinema as Counter-Cinema', in E. A. Kaplan (ed.) *Feminism & Film*. London: Oxford University Press, 22–33.

_____ (2000b) 'Dorothy Arzner: Critical Strategies', in E. A. Kaplan *Feminism & Film*. London: Oxford University Press, 139–48.

Kaplan, E. A. (1997) *Looking for the Other: Feminism, Film and the Imperial Gaze* London: Routledge.

_____ (2005) *Trauma Culture: The Politics of Terror and Loss in Media and Literature* New Brunswick, NJ: Rutgers University Press.

Klapproth, D. (2004) *Narratives of Social Practice: Anglo-Western and Australian Aboriginal Oral Traditions*. Berlin: Monton de Gruyter.

Kuhn, A. (1990) 'Textual Politics', in P. Erens (ed.) *Issues in Feminist Film Criticism*. Bloomington: Indian University Press, 250–67.

Lévi-Strauss, C. (1968) *Structural Anthropology*. New York: Basic Books.

Lord, A. (1984) *Sister Outsider*. Berkeley: Ten Speed Press.

MacDougall, D. (1987) 'Media Friend or Media Foe?', *Visual Anthropology*, 1, 1, 54–8.

Marks, L. (2000) *The Skin of the Film: Intercultural Cinema, Embodiment, and the Senses*. Durham and London: Duke University Press.

Michaels, E. (1986) *The Aboriginal Invention of Television in Central Australia*. Canberra: Australian Institute of Aboriginal Studies.

Mulvey, L. (2000) 'Visual Pleasure and Narrative Cinema', in E. A. Kaplan (ed.) *Feminism & Film*. London: Oxford University Press, 34–47.

Murray, S. (1990) 'Tracey Moffatt', *Cinema Papers*, 79, 19–22.

Naficy, H. (2001) *An Accented Cinema: Exilic and Diasporic Filmmaking*. Princeton: Princeton University Press.

O'Regan, T. (1996) *Australian National Cinema*. London: Routledge.

Screen Australia (2007) *Dreaming in Motion*. On-line. Available: http://www.screenaustralia.gov.au/documents/SA_publications/DreaminginMotion.pdf (accessed on 10 July 2009).

Senzani, A. (2007) 'Dreaming Back: Tracey Moffatt's Bedeviling Films', *Post Script – Essays in Film and the Humanities*, 27, 1, 50–71. On-line. Available: http://gateway.proquest.com/openurl?url_ver=Z39.882004&res_dat=xri:iipa&rft_dat=xri:iipa:article:citation:iipa00467739 (accessed on 13 August 2008).

Stanner, W. E. H. (1956) 'The Dreaming', in T. A. G. Hungerford (ed.) *Australian Signposts: An Anthology*. Melbourne: F.W. Cheshire, 51–65.

Summerhayes, C. (2004) 'Haunting Secrets: Tracey Moffatt's *beDevil*', *Film Quarterly*, 58, 1, 14–24.

Willemen, P. (1993) *Looks and Frictions: Essays in Cultural Studies and Film Theory*. London: British Film Institute.

The Reluctance to Narrate: Elia Suleiman's *Chronicle of a Disappearance* and *Divine Intervention*

Linda Mokdad

The first two instalments of Elia Suleiman's trilogy on the Palestinian-Israeli conflict, *Chronicle of a Disappearance* (1996) and *Divine Intervention* (2002), have helped cement the director's singular status in the history of sporadic Palestinian film production.[1] While Palestinian cinema has been animated by an overriding desire to narrate from its inception, Suleiman stands out for his lack of commitment to narrative filmmaking. The efforts of contemporary Palestinian filmmakers to assert the existence of a homeland that official Israeli history denies have produced strategies that appeal to urgency, pathos and proximity – all of which have become familiar constituents in visualising the Palestinian narrative of suffering and dispossession. And yet the films of Suleiman, which mobilise techniques and conventions associated with deferral, detachment and distance, are clearly engaged with an entirely different set of aesthetic values. Suleiman's departure from the norms established by Palestinian cinema, and the ensuing confusion this has created around the categorisation of his work, provide a useful entry point into the examination of his films. However, unlike the vast majority of criticism that minimises the relationship Suleiman's work has with other Palestinian films, I want to suggest that foregrounding this interaction not only helps illuminate the workings of Palestinian cinema at large. In other words, both *Chronicle of a Disappearance* and *Divine Intervention*, in their dialectic interplay with the broader values and tendencies of Palestinian cinema, intervene to raise important and timely questions regarding the conventions and structures that have come to regulate the construction of Palestinian film narratives.

Contemporary Palestinian cinema

Suleiman's foray into filmmaking in the 1990s is part of a larger wave of Palestinian film production that first emerged in the 1980s. Scholars of Palestinian and Arab cinemas have used various designations for this body of films, including 'the fourth period' (see Gertz and Khleifi 2008), 'new realism' (Shafik 1998) and 'new Middle-Eastern cinema' (Levy 2005), all of which loosely overlap to suggest that contemporary Palestinian films rewrite and challenge the older dogma of revolutionary Palestinian filmmaking by putting forward more personal and nuanced narratives of the Palestinian-Israeli conflict.[2] The 'intercultural' (Marks 2000), 'accented' (Naficy 2001) or 'structurally exilic' (Naficy 2006) qualities critics have attributed to Palestinian cinema speak to the status of many Palestinian filmmakers who live in one form of exile or another and who are often trained abroad. In the absence of an economic and industrial infrastructure these filmmakers have most commonly relied on external financing, namely European, American and, to a lesser extent, Israeli sources of funding (see Asfour 2000; Gertz and Khleifi 2008: 34). The conditions produced by such economic exigencies have played a pivotal role in shaping (and perhaps more pessimistically, in regulating) contemporary Palestinian cinema. In unfavourable terms, this financing has often come with certain restrictions and demands, such as the insistence on using foreign rather than local production crews. In a more positive light, this external economic support has expanded film production, while providing Palestinian filmmakers with the capital required to make fiction feature films.[3]

Importantly, this source of funding has also increased the visibility of Palestinian films around the world, where they are mostly viewed at film festivals. Given the challenges to distribution and exhibition one would expect to find in occupied Palestine, these films are, in fact, much more likely to be seen by a foreign rather than a local audience. Here I would disagree with Nurith Gertz and George Khleifi's claim that the intended 'target audience' of these contemporary films was initially 'in the West Bank, the Gaza Strip, and Israel' (2008: 36). Rather, I would suggest that the goal of contemporary Palestinian cinema (not only because it has been met with Arab and Israeli forms of censorship) has always been to reach an external audience. If, as Edward Said has claimed, Palestinian cinema needs to be understood in relation to either the way 'Palestinians stand against invisibility', or the way they 'stand against ... a visual identity associated with terrorism and violence' (2006: 3), it seems Palestinian filmmakers would have far more to gain by targeting a global rather than a local audience. This is a critical point because both the desire to appeal to humanitarian concerns and to address the international community figure profoundly in the shaping of Palestinian film narratives, and the manner in which they make recourse to pathos. It might be said that Palestinian narratives are about the act or gesture of narrating itself.

Despite the fact that Suleiman has probably benefited more than any other

Palestinian filmmaker from these external sources of funding, the aforementioned aesthetic affects and conventional practices are absent in Suleiman's work, suggesting that his films fit rather awkwardly under the umbrella of contemporary Palestinian cinema. Attempting to situate Suleiman within the boundaries of Palestinian cinema also yields its share of other problems. For one thing, Suleiman himself has taken every opportunity to distance his films from other examples of Palestinian cinema, as reflected in his claim: 'My tastes don't have much to do with mainstream Palestinian or Arab cinema' (quoted in Porton 2005: 27). Palestinian film critics have often reinforced Suleiman's alienation by either misunderstanding his use of irony, or by viewing it as an indulgent and insensitive response to so dire a situation (see Bourlond 2000). *Divine Intervention*'s poor reception among certain Palestinian groups, who criticised the film for accepting funding from the Israeli Fund for Quality Films and who subjected Suleiman to accusations of disloyalty, also testifies to the director's somewhat fragile footing in relation to more conventional Palestinian filmmakers (see Erickson 2003).

However, there is something equally unsatisfying about the pervasive tendency to limit the understanding of Suleiman's work, and his appropriation of modernist techniques and affects (distantiation, absurd humour, stasis and minimalism) to certain traditions of art cinema. The regularity with which Suleiman is compared to Western auteurs such as Jacques Tati, Robert Bresson, Jim Jarmusch and Jean-Luc Godard (see, for example, Gabriel 2002; Erickson 2003; Rich 2003; Chaudhuri 2005; Porton 2005; Bresheeth 2007) not only perpetuates an all too familiar trend of defining or elevating 'Third World' filmmakers by associating them with filmmakers from the United States or Europe, this well-intentioned but patronising gesture also bypasses the work involved in understanding Suleiman's specific approach to the conflict. Instead, it risks contributing to nondescript or universalised readings of his work – readings that frame or locate the angst and violence of his films in the human condition. This is not to say that Suleiman's films do not have a global appeal. The accessibility of his films, his relative financial freedom, wider-reaching distribution (he is, for instance, one of the few Palestinian filmmakers to receive commercial distribution in the USA), and critical success (*Chronicle of a Disappearance* and *Divine Intervention* were nominated for a number of awards, with the latter winning the Jury Prize at the Cannes Film Festival), support claims in favour of Suleiman's universalism.[4] But his films appear to be compromised when their form is emphasised at the expense of content, just as they are when critics attempt to neatly group them with other Palestinian films that approach the conflict using profoundly different means. Rather, we should question why Suleiman adopts strategies affiliated with art cinema to approach the specificities of the Palestinian-Israeli conflict. Doing so insists on acknowledging the interplay between Suleiman and other Palestinian film narratives. Before addressing how this intertextuality shapes *Chronicle of a Disappearance* and *Divine Intervention*, it might be useful to anchor Palestinian films in a broader political context that allows us to disentangle them from the much broader conservatism we attach to the relationship between nation and narrative.[5]

Edward Said's well-known essay 'Permission to Narrate' was written as a critical response to the massacres of Sabra and Shatila in 1982 which left over 2,000 Palestinians and Lebanese dead during the Israeli invasion of Lebanon. Explaining that the absence of a Palestinian narrative was in part what allowed this perpetration of violence by the Lebanese Christian Phalangists under the watchful eyes of the Israeli military to be tolerated (and even, sanctioned), Said emphatically called for the 'acceptance of a narrative entailing a homeland' – a narrative he argued had been denied to the Palestinians on a variety of levels (2000: 253; originally published in 1984). Said gleaned various conventions and strategies from a number of already existing narratives (mostly contributed by people situated outside the conflict), and advocated that they be used by Palestinians themselves – conventions and strategies that resonate with the way Palestinian films and videos (beginning to appear during this same period) continue to be made today – the emphasis on a 'beginning and an end', the need for a 'record' or 'evidence' and the appeal to 'active sympathy' (ibid.).

Written over twenty years later, Said's preface to a collection of essays on Palestinian cinema, edited by Hamid Dabashi and entitled *Dreams of a Nation: On Palestinian Cinema* (2006), again champions these strategies, while specifically attending to the role of cinema in constructing Palestinian narratives. My purpose in pointing to the primacy of narrative in Palestinian cinema is to argue that Suleiman challenges Palestinian films that privilege causality and express an investment in representation and explanation. A closer examination of his films reveals a number of substantial departures from the methods of Palestinian narrative encapsulated by Said's essays.

Silences, distances and interventions

Suleiman's early video *Homage by Assassination* (1993) prefigures the characteristics, thematic preoccupations and stylistic flourishes that are more fully realised in the feature films *Chronicle of a Disappearance* and *Divine Intervention*, including the difficulties and failures of communication and representation, the materialisation of Suleiman's onscreen persona E. S. and so forth. While his first video *Introduction to the End of an Argument*, (1990; co-directed with Jayce Salloum), a collage of images and (mis)representations of Arabs circulated by Hollywood films, is most unlike his later films, it still manages to touch on ideas that will preoccupy Suleiman throughout his career. Laura Marks has claimed that the film 'laments the impossibility of speaking as an Arab, particularly a Palestinian, when one is already so utterly spoken for in Western contexts' (2000: 58). I would suggest that Suleiman's feature films go even further than this by blurring the line between the 'impossibility of speaking as a Palestinian' and the *refusal* to speak as a Palestinian. While this may first appear to be a negligible distinction, it calls for a dramatic shift from studying Suleiman's films for symptoms or signs of passivity, to approaching them as reflections of agency and activity.

Chronicle of a Disappearance and *Divine Intervention* map out similar narrative trajectories: in the former, Suleiman's alter ego E. S. has returned home to visit his family after years of voluntary exile in New York, and in the latter he has again come back home to visit his ailing father who will die by the end of the film. Both films offer snapshots of private and public space in Nazareth and Jerusalem that remain largely isolated from each other, connected more by the logic of Suleiman's formal techniques than by any narrative cohesion. With the exception of fantasy revenge sequences that mark the endings of the films, both *Chronicle of a Disappearance* and *Divine Intervention* alternate between glimpses of Suleiman's parents and neighbours, caught in the minutiae of everyday life, and oblique and humorous references to Israeli occupation and oppression (the absence of Palestinian comedies testifies to Suleiman's singularity in this regard). Largely episodic, both films are framed by endless repetitions of actions, many of which are never fully explained to us. All of these elements – Suleiman's use of humour, his interest in the mundane, the confusion that results from a lack of narrative clarity – involve a rejection of the norms audiences have come to expect in the visualisation of the Palestinian-Israeli conflict.

But it is perhaps how his narratives approach language that most distinguishes *Chronicle of a Disappearance* and *Divine Intervention* from other Palestinian films. Hamid Dabashi attributes an emphasis on orality to Palestinian documentary (2006: 12), an emphasis I would argue extends to Palestinian feature films made during this period. As part of their propensity for historical reconstruction, Palestinian documentary and fiction films often employ language in the service of providing testimony, evidence and memory. Often these forms of expression are inflected with a kind of pathos that encourages what Said has called 'active sympathy'. Michel Khleifi's *Fertile Memory* (1980) and *Wedding in Galilee* (1987) both appeal to language in this regard: the former is constructed from divergent but equally expressive narratives in which two women recount for us the difficulties of life under occupation, while the latter film's action is motivated by a passionate speech the *mukhtar*, or village leader, gives in order to convince an Israeli military governor to break curfew for his son's wedding. The documentaries of Mai Masri also provide a space for narratives that privilege the voices of women and children and that appeal to the role of language as a form of emotional connection and personal expression. In *Children of Shatila* (1998), children are asked to narrate their tragic and moving histories, while being given the opportunity to record themselves with the video camera. *Frontiers of Fears and Dreams* (2001) centres on the heartrending meetings of two young Palestinian girls, first through email and letters, and finally in person at the Lebanese/Israeli border dividing them. The film's inclusion of national folk songs and Palestinian history establishes a connection between the girls, while furnishing a useful backdrop of information for its audience. *Frontiers of Fears and Dreams*, like a number of other Palestinian films, belongs to the 'epistolary mode' Hamid Naficy attributes to exilic filmmaking in general and Palestinian cinema in particular, or what he defines as 'the use of the letter's formal properties to create meaning' (2006: 94). What he argues 'becomes an important strategy for self-expression and self-narrativization' (2006: 95) is yet another way in which narratives (spoken or written) play a decisive role in Palestinian films.[6]

Suleiman, on the other hand, establishes a remarkably ironic tension in his films regarding the role of orality. While his films promise to serve as chronicles – both of the films' titles suggest as much (*Divine Intervention* also goes by the title *A Chronicle of Love and Pain*) – the 'narrator' or Suleiman's avatar E. S. never speaks in either film. The narrative of *Chronicle of a Disappearance* teasingly takes on the structure of a diary format made up of a string of entries E. S. types on his computer keyboard. However, the computer functions as a barrier that hinders his attempts at expression, and diminishes the possibility of any close or personal interaction with his character. Neither the underwhelming and repetitious entries (which simply read 'The Day After'), nor the majority of images that capture action *in media res*, provide any sense of narrative elucidation or progress. E. S.'s undeviating deadpan or expressionless reactions to any occurrence (including the invasion of his home by Israeli soldiers) do little to encourage spectatorial identification or sympathy. The films set in motion a play between the expectation of narration or speech and its ensuing absence – one that contributes to the tension the film establishes with its alternation (and at times, conflation) of the catastrophic and the mundane. However, more important than Suleiman's choosing to remain silent is the way he upsets our expectations regarding what I would suggest have become somewhat typical (and perhaps, even, stereotypical?) forms of Palestinian narrativisation.

Although many critics have focused on the films' silence, there are a number of scenes built around acts of speech, and more specifically, various forms of oral narration that directly address the audience. These scenes call attention to themselves particularly because of the films' overall backdrop of silence, and yet they punctuate the films' refusal to provide explanation or clarification. E. S.'s father's vitriolic and indiscriminate tirades against his neighbours, or the sadistic Israeli soldier who uses his voice to humiliate Palestinians at a checkpoint in *Divine Intervention*, testify to the frustration, violence and failure of language. Likewise does the comical diversion offered by a neighbour who irrepressibly and compulsively inserts the number 'six' into every sentence he utters. The bout of logorrhea experienced by E. S.'s mother in *Chronicle of a Disappearance*, during which she provides a long-winded history of an impossible-to-follow family feud, ultimately tells us nothing and leads us nowhere. But there is perhaps no better example of Suleiman's desire to divest in language than our introduction to a Palestinian writer who directly addresses the audience and promises that he is going to tell us a 'good' story. Instead, he tells the same, uneventful and cryptic tale passed down to him by his grandfather – a story that his grandfather obsessively returned to throughout his life.

These episodes might be read as allegories of the long and convoluted history of

Palestinian-Israeli relations. They might also be interpreted as Suleiman's commentary on the failure of communication, or the impossibility of representing trauma. The obscurity, circularity and endless repetitions that shape these references to language, and express the symptoms of a compulsive melancholia, certainly seem to provide the possibility for such readings. But again, is Suleiman not doing something more here than suggesting the inadequacy of narrative to represent trauma? Does not such an assessment of his work, in fact, come dangerously close to *prescribing* the experience of exile or trauma to Suleiman's films based on critical consensus that characterises most Palestinian cinema in these terms? It appears far more useful to *describe* how his films comment on what have become certain requirements and demands of Palestinian film narrative.[7] Suleiman's subversion of narrative expectations – his critique of overused strategies and conventions – is lost if we merely cull his films for symptoms of trauma and loss, even if his films unsurprisingly express them.

Suleiman explicitly addresses how the style and form of his films are overlooked in favour of thematising and essentialising the Palestinian experience. A commonly cited scene from *Chronicle of a Disappearance* foregrounds the audience's participation in this formulation. When E. S. is asked to explain the 'cinematic language' of his films to an audience gathered at a conference, his microphone fails to work, despite persistent attempts to fix the problem. Obstacles largely present themselves by way of the audience, who seem uninterested and distracted by the persistent ringing of cellular phones and crying babies. In its figuration of a diegetic audience, *Chronicle of a Disappearance* is also nudging us, the film's audience, to consider our role as witnesses to the visualisation of Palestinian suffering and dispossession. Gertz and Khleifi are touching on an important point with their observation that 'there remains a doubt as to whether the speaker is, indeed, mute or perhaps it is the audience who are deaf' (2008: 177). I would modify this question by asking if Suleiman's films are criticising a kind of generic discourse of victimisation that audiences have come to expect, or which serves to reinforce their expectations. Suleiman may be suggesting that little room has been provided for his 'cinematic language', which is frequently lost to the exigencies of the conflict and supplanted by a language of overused and imposing symbols. But by refusing to fulfill the expectations of a narrative marked by pathos and suffering and by refusing to appeal to an audience that has grown more familiar with and perhaps insensitive to the codification of Palestinian dispossession, Suleiman is pointing out our complicity as spectators.

Palestinian cinema has contributed much-needed images of life under an ongoing and brutal Israeli occupation, but these images have come with a price. In a certain sense, Palestinian cinema remains challenged by the weight of ethnography – the idea that 'they' have to explain themselves to 'us'. It seems that in serving to both assert their existence and provide narratives that counter their associations with violence, i.e. terrorism, they have risked speaking from a place that is delimited to victimhood. But is it not a twisted logic that has Palestinians bearing the responsibility or burden of explanation? In this regard, Dabashi has claimed that 'perhaps the singular achievement of Elia Suleiman as a filmmaker is the dropping of a virtual, white, male European as the principal interlocutor of the Palestinian predicament – the presumption that unless "he" is convinced, the Palestinian dispossession has not happened' (2006: 159). In other words, Suleiman refuses to translate the conflict for Western audiences – he speaks neither from a place that asserts Palestinian identity, nor from a defensive position that works to disavow negative representation.

Instead, Suleiman adopts art cinema conventions to trouble the relationship between visuality and knowledge, a relationship that many Palestinian narratives are highly invested in maintaining, given efforts to overcome a kind of invisibility. Suleiman's films are replete with visual gags that serve to undermine the truth of the image, and just as commonly, his films limit access to the visual, not only by obscuring it but also by denying the audience a body or perspective with which to identify. In both films, the *mise-en-scène* is infused with a sense of concealment. Faces are often obscured by darkness, blocked from view or partially positioned outside of the frame. In fact, Suleiman's films are always calling attention to the limits of our vision with his uncomfortable configurations of on-screen space or by placing the spectator in disadvantageous viewing positions. Suleiman, for instance, never allows for the possibility of proximity with his subjects. With the exception of an extreme close-up of the face of E. S.'s father that marks the opening of *Chronicle of a Disappearance* (and what I would argue is another moment where Suleiman sets up expectations he will not deliver on), his characters are most often captured in long shots. Another example involves *Divine Intervention*'s depiction of the checkpoint, an important trope in Palestinian cinema and a ubiquitous marker of daily oppression. Eschewing the immediacy, proximity or urgency that often characterises the tense and climatic scenes featuring checkpoints or roadblocks in Palestinian narrative and documentary films, Suleiman represents lengthy checkpoint scenes through a series of extreme long shots. The audience's distance from the action excludes it from any kind of intimacy with the violence that is suggested onscreen and reinforces the audience's status as outsiders, unable to access the suffering of the Palestinians which remains an unknowable quantity.

The question of accessibility raised by both *Chronicle of a Disappearance* and *Divine Intervention* often returns us to the images, devices and strategies that have come to inform a great number of narratives made by Palestinian filmmakers. Contrary to the deployment of history (generational, national or one defined by trauma) in Palestinian films, both *Chronicle of a Disappearance* and *Divine Intervention* evacuate causality or historical markers of violence on a variety of registers. For instance, there are no specific references to the *intifada*, the occupation of Gaza or the West Bank or other specifics of the conflict. In lieu of historical explanation, time instead is demarcated by the quotidian, expressed as events that are trapped in a repetitive cycle in which days are barely discernible from one another. Both films evacuate the violence we have come to associate with the Palestinian-Israeli conflict, emptying out the meaning of symbols and tropes that have become affiliated with the turmoil of the region. Suleiman instead uses our own expectations regarding the violence of the conflict against us by endlessly delivering a new image or perspective that dismantles our understanding of the one preceding it. Is this not what gives profundity to his visual gags, which as Lina Khatib has noted, 'challenge the audience's expectations of both Palestinian and Israeli actions, thereby commenting on our own prejudices towards both sides' (2006: 130). In this way, the films continually work to subtract, postpone or deflate the meaning of images.

A case in point is the 'Holy Land Souvenir Shop' in *Chronicle of a Disappearance*, where the religious tumult of the Middle East is denied its traditional meaning. Instead of the typical associations conjured by the contentious birthplace of Christianity, Judaism and Islam, we are provided with images of E. S.'s cousin filling vials with tap water to be fraudulently sold as holy water. No one ever visits the shop and nothing ever happens there. Suleiman also seems to liken our viewing of the Palestinian-Israeli conflict to a kind of tourism, in which violent images of the conflict contribute to a spectacle that has become increasingly and too easily digested. This analogy is supported further by a shot of a spinning rack that features, among other humorous postcards, one that reads, 'Patrolling the Borders', and which bears an image of armed Israeli soldiers standing near a security fence. This is not to argue that Suleiman avoids engaging with the violence of the conflict. There are numerous scenes that document Israeli oppression such as the darkly comical scene of the blindfolded Palestinian prisoner forced by an Israeli soldier to give directions to a tourist, or Suleiman's utter lack of a response to his house being invaded by Israeli soldiers, in *Chronicle of a Disappearance*. However, Suleiman's humourous and absurd depictions emphasise the normalisation of Israeli violence against the Palestinians and its absorption into the fabric of everyday life. These depictions also enable Suleiman to comment on the region's violence without providing a sensationalised portrait of it.

Causality is also absent from the episodic and disjointed formal structure that shapes Suleiman's narratives. In this regard as well, there is no attempt made on Suleiman's part to situate the spectator. The omission of establishing shots in the films, and the abundance of shots featuring strangely framed, often de-centred views of buildings, stairs and other forms of architecture, can be understood as reflecting a kind of dislocation we again might attribute to the exilic status of Palestinians. However, these visual tactics might also be understood as a refusal to provide information or explanation. Events are captured *in media res* and many elements in the plot do not add up to a story, but rather lend themselves to erasure or disconnection. The role of arbitrariness is central to Suleiman's films for a number of reasons. It is used as a gesture against the insistence to infuse every image with meaning that can only be traced back to the conditions of identity provided by the conflict, and by implication, most Palestinian film narratives. This idea is well articulated by a minor character in *Chronicle of a Disappearance* who exclaims: 'Here everything is political, nothing innocent. Anything you say or do will be interpreted.' The tendency to thematise and interpret even Suleiman's arbitrariness as somehow reflecting the violence of Palestinian life under occupation, seems only to point to the difficulty of escaping these kinds of readings.

Conclusion

Suleiman's stylistic and narrative techniques – the use of repetition, arbitrariness and humour, the minimalism that limits action and emphasises physical and emotional detachment, and the insistence on withholding personal, sentimental and causal information – challenge what audiences have come to expect from Palestinian films.[8] Suleiman appropriates and recycles the iconography and symbolism deployed by a majority of Palestinian film narratives, with the purpose of recontextualising and deconstructing them. Ultimately, he uses style to undermine the importance of narrative – for example the endless and unexplained repetition of (near identical) events, many captured in mid-action, which challenge causality, or his use of long shots to visualise tropes (such as the checkpoint) or characters, eschewing the immediacy, proximity and pathos-inflected representation more commonly deployed by Palestinian narratives. Of course in doing so, Suleiman cannot help but remain somewhat indebted to the workings of Palestinian cinema, but his alternative use of this iconography, if not his dismantling of it altogether, disrupts the assumptions that have gone into both its creation and reception.

While Suleiman's work raises important questions regarding such assumptions, unfortunately the effectiveness of such questions seems diminished in light of how his films have been read. When the approach to Suleiman's films is limited to questions of style, or his appropriation of traditions and structures affiliated with art cinema, the way his films interact with other Palestinian film narratives is sacrificed, thereby minimising the forcefulness of his commentary. An emphasis on his formal techniques alone also risks replacing some of Suleiman's very pointed arguments and ideas regarding the representation of the Palestinian-Israeli conflict with universal and nondescript assessments of his films (even if his appropriation of modernist techniques and his refusal to situate the audience is, ironically, what accounts for his popularity on the film festival circuit). Conversely, the tendency to read Suleiman's films as reflections of the conditions associated with Palestinian identity also appears to ignore their purpose. This approach ignores how Suleiman's use of style disrupts both the conventions and reception of Palestinian films. His films do not simply offer *other* representations of the Palestinian-Israeli conflict – they question the overused tendency to thematise Palestinian cinema at the cost of ignoring style, or rather, they challenge the understanding of style as merely another reflection of Palestinian trauma, melancholia and exile. Unfortunately, this has often translated into a kind of failure or impossibility to represent the crisis of the Palestinians. While this impossibility is implicit in and true of any attempt to represent trauma, Suleiman's films seem less concerned with the impossibility of representation and motivated more by the refusal to represent or to contribute to a trajectory that in some ways seems predetermined.

Despite the many challenges and obstacles thrown its way, Palestinian cinema has provided deeply moving accounts of the Palestinian-Israeli conflict – ones that give voice to many who continue to suffer the injustices of second-class citizenry in Israel, or who continue to struggle under Israel's occupation of the West Bank. We might question, as some critics have done, whether Suleiman's distance is too indulgent, his style too extravagant to address so catastrophic a situation, but that would only deflect the question Suleiman is asking the audience of Palestinian films to consider. Rather than suggest his own passivity or detachment, both *Chronicle of a Disappearance* and *Divine Intervention* interrogate our roles as spectators, ones who have become accustomed to trajectories that provide explanations but that are met with such little action. Suleiman's films seem to reflect the gaze of Western viewers back at themselves, asking them to consider their role as passive observers. While sympathy might affirm or reinforce the spectator's sense of justice, we might also ask whom this sympathy is servicing if it does not motivate action. In lieu of confining Palestinian films to readings that underscore a sense of paralysis or futility, Suleiman's work asks us to consider how our own expectations and biases have confined Palestinian film narratives to a self-fulfilling melancholia.

Notes

1 Suleiman's *The Time that Remains* (2009) premiered at the Cannes Film Festival to positive reviews. Spanning the creation of Israel in 1948 to the present day, the film is the final instalment of Suleiman's trilogy.

2 In *Palestinian Cinema: Landscape, Trauma, and Memory* (2008), Nurith Gertz and George Khleifi divide the history of Palestinian filmmaking into four distinctive periods. However, the first two periods are marked by very few films still extant; the construction of their history has relied on the compilation of anecdote and testimony. The third period (1968–82), what has also been referred to as Palestinian revolutionary cinema, galvanised around the defeat of the Arabs in the 1967 war against Israel. More than sixty Palestinian films were made during this period, almost all of them documentaries affiliated with and funded by resistance movements such as the PLO, the PFLP and the DFLP. The audiences for these films consisted mostly of Palestinians. Regretfully, these films are said to have been stored in an archive, but are now also mostly lost. The most common consensus seems to be that they could not have survived their storage conditions.

3 That said, the number of Palestinian documentaries continue to outnumber Palestinian feature films.

4 Suleiman was not eligible for the Foreign Language Academy Award category because Palestine is not acknowledged as a nation by the UN, despite, as many critics have pointed out, the fact that Hong Kong and Taiwan (also not considered nations by the UN) are eligible for nomination. However, in 2006, Hany Abu-Assad's film *Paradise Now* (2005) was nominated for an Academy Award as a submission from the 'Palestinian territories'.

5 As Ella Shohat succinctly declares, 'hegemonic Europe may clearly have begun to deplete

its strategic repertoire of stories, but Third World peoples, First World diasporic communities, women, and gays/lesbians have only begun to tell, and deconstruct, theirs' (2006: 70). On a similar note, Edward Said's essay 'Permission to Narrate', written shortly after the emergence of post-revolutionary Palestinian cinema, makes important distinctions between Israeli nationalism and Palestinian nationalism: 'The major difference is that Zionism was a hothouse flower grown from European nationalism, anti-Semitism, and colonialism, while Palestinian nationalism, derived from the great wave of Arab and Islamic anticolonial sentiment, has since 1967, though tinged with retrogressive religious sentiment, been located within the mainstream of secular post-imperialist thought. Even more important, Zionism is essentially a dispossessing movement so far as non-Jews are concerned. Palestinians since 1967 have generally been inclusive, trying (satisfactorily or not) to deal with the problem created by the presence of more than one national community in historical Palestine' (2000: 248–9).

6   Naficy notes, for example, the role of language in Mona Hatoum's *Measures of Distance* (1988) that encompasses a number of epistolary strategies, among them Hatoum *reading* aloud the letters her mother has sent her from Lebanon (2006: 98). Naficy also discusses the presence of this mode in a number of other Palestinian films such as Jean Chamoun and Mai Masri's documentary *Wild Flowers: Women of South Lebanon* (1986) and Suleiman's very own *Homage to Assassination*, which he explains 'despite Suleiman's refusal, silence and loneliness within the film's diegesis […] is an impassioned epistle from Suleiman to the world' (ibid). I disagree with Naficy in the latter instance, which I discuss in more detail in terms of Suleiman's feature films and which I understand less as a predicament of his exilic status and more as a refusal to 'represent'.

7   Suleiman has lived abroad in places such as New York and Paris, and this fact has been used as a way to explain the distance he espouses in his films, which stands in for both his physical distance and self-imposed exile. His distance is also said to reflect that he is not from the West Bank or Gaza, but the much more comfortable space of Nazareth.

8   Both *Chronicle of a Disappearance* and *Divine Intervention* bear resemblance to what David Bordwell has called parametric narration, defined as 'style centered' or 'poetic' narration (1985: 274–5). It also accords nicely with Suleiman's own discussion of his films in terms of 'poetic images', or what he has described as a democratisation of the image, and one that allows for a multiplicity of readings. My purpose in suggesting his narratives are parametric is to further highlight Suleiman's emphasis on style – one that raises important questions regarding the status of Palestinian narratives today.

Bibliography

Asfour, N. (2000) 'The Politics of Arab Cinema: Middle Eastern Filmmakers Face up to their Reality', *Cineaste*, 26, 1, 46–8.

Bordwell, D. (1985) *Narration in the Fiction Film*. Madison: University of Wisconsin Press.

Bourlond, A. (2000) 'A Cinema of Nowhere: An Interview with Elia Suleiman', *Journal of Palestine Studies*, 29, 2, 95–101.

Bresheeth, H. (2007) '*Segell Ikhtifa / Chronicle of a Disappearance*,' in G. Dönmez-Colin (ed.) *The Cinema of North Africa and the Middle East*. London: Wallflower Press, 169–79.

Chaudhuri, S. (2005) *Contemporary World Cinema*. Edinburgh: Edinburgh University Press.

Dabashi, H. (ed.) (2006) *Dreams of a Nation: On Palestinian Cinema*. London and New York: Verso.

Erickson, S. (2003) 'A Breakdown of Communication: Elia Suleiman Talks About *Divine Intervention*', *Indiewire*. On-line. Available: http://www.indiewire.com/article/a_breakdown_of_communication_elia_suleiman_talks_about_divine_intervention/ (accessed on 15 January 2009).

Gabriel, J. (2002) 'Chronicles of Dark Humor', *Al Jadid*, Fall, 8, 41.

Gertz, N. and G. Khleifi (2008) *Palestinian Cinema: Landscape, Trauma, and Memory*. Bloomington: Indiana University Press.

Khatib, L. (2006) *Filming the Modern Middle East: Politics in the Cinemas of Hollywood and the Arab World*. London and New York: I.B. Tauris.

Levy, E. (2005) 'Border Crossings: The New Middle Eastern Cinema', *Chronicle of Higher Education*. On-line. Available: http://chronicle.com/article/Border-Crossings-the-New/33479/ (accessed on 25 November 2009).

Marks, L. (2000) *The Skin of the Film: Intercultural Cinema, Embodiment, and the Senses*. Durham and London: Duke University Press.

Naficy, H. (2001) *An Accented Cinema: Exilic and Diasporic Filmmaking*. Princeton: Princeton University Press.

_____ (2006) 'Palestinian Exilic Cinema and Film Letters', in H. Dabashi (ed.) *Dreams of a Nation: On Palestinian Cinema*. London and New York: Verso, 90–104.

Porton, R. (2005) 'Notes from the Palestinian Diaspora: An Interview with Elia Suleiman', *Cineaste*, 28, 3, 24–7.

Rich, R. (2003) 'Divine Comedy', *The Guardian*, 26 March.

Said, E. (2000) 'Permission to Narrate', in M. Bayoumi and A. Rubin (eds) *The Edward Said Reader*. New York: Vintage Books, 243–66.

_____ (2006) 'Preface', in H. Dabashi (ed.) *Dreams of a Nation: On Palestinian Cinema*. London and New York: Verso, 1–5.

Shafik, V. (1998) *Arab Cinema: History and Cultural Identity*. Cairo: The American University in Cairo Press.

Shohat, E. (2006) 'The Cinema of Displacement: Gender, Nation, and Diaspora', in H. Dabashi (ed.) *Dreams of a Nation: On Palestinian Cinema*. London and New York: Verso, 70–89.

Index